Self-Publishing

2nd Edition

by Jason R. Rich

for dummies®
A Wiley Brand

Self-Publishing For Dummies®, 2nd Edition

Published by: **John Wiley & Sons, Inc.**, 111 River Street, Hoboken, NJ 07030-5774, www.wiley.com

Copyright © 2023 by John Wiley & Sons, Inc., Hoboken, New Jersey

Published simultaneously in Canada

For general information on our other products and services, please contact our Customer Care Department within the U.S. at 877-762-2974, outside the U.S. at 317-572-3993, or fax 317-572-4002. For technical support, please visit https://hub.wiley.com/community/support/dummies.

Wiley publishes in a variety of print and electronic formats and by print-on-demand. Some material included with standard print versions of this book may not be included in e-books or in print-on-demand. If this book refers to media such as a CD or DVD that is not included in the version you purchased, you may download this material at http://booksupport.wiley.com. For more information about Wiley products, visit www.wiley.com.

Library of Congress Control Number: 2023942042

ISBN 978-1-394-20127-3 (pbk); ISBN 978-1-394-20129-7 (ePub); ISBN 978-1-394-20128-0 (ePDF)

Printed and bound by CPI Group (UK) Ltd, Croydon, CR0 4YY

C9781394201273_100823

Contents at a Glance

Table of Contents

Introduction

Y ou may have personal and/or professional reasons why you want to get published. Perhaps you hope to supplement your income or generate an entire income as a writer. Maybe you have important information to convey or a compelling story to tell.

If you want to become an author who has a published book as a result of working with a major publishing house, you have a challenge in front of you because of the highly competitive nature of the book-publishing business.

Would-be authors also have a way to see their work professionally published in book or e-book form, and then distribute it to the general public, through *self-publishing.* New technologies — such as print-on-demand (POD) to create printed books — eliminate the need to print thousands of copies of a book at one time, enabling you to print as few as copy instead. The cost of self-publishing a book has also dropped dramatically in the past few years. Now, virtually anyone can access (and afford) the means to publish a book. Never before has the opportunity to publish a professional quality book or e-book been within reach of any aspiring author.

REMEMBER

People all over the world want information, to gain new skills, to enrich their lives with new knowledge, or to enjoy an escape into the imaginary world that a really good story can create. So, if you have expertise that other people can benefit from or an amazing story to tell, self-publishing may give you the perfect route to take.

This all-new edition of *Self-Publishing For Dummies* helps you take your idea for a book, develop the idea into content to fill a full-length manuscript, and then have it published in print and/or e-book format. This book describes the incredible opportunity self-publishing offers to aspiring writers and authors, business leaders, entrepreneurs, consultants, and anyone else who has a great idea for a book.

About This Book

Self-publishing puts you in total charge of your publishing project. A successful publishing venture requires effectively dealing with each step in the publishing process. Without proper knowledge and experience, you can easily make costly mistakes. The information in this book helps you avoid the most common mistakes made by authors and self-publishers, and helps you properly cater your book to its intended readers. This book also lends a hand when it comes to gathering a highly skilled publishing team for your venture. By hiring freelance experts to help you with editing, design, layout, and marketing, your book can more effectively compete with all the other books currently available for sale.

Most importantly, this book shows you how to obtain traditional and online distribution for your book and properly market it to generate sales. By using marketing, public relations, and advertising strategies — along with the power and capabilities of the Internet — you can transform your book into a successful publishing venture.

REMEMBER

Keep in mind that this book isn't a "how to write a book" book or an "improve your writing skills" book. Developing the writing skills and the necessary expertise on the topic you plan to write about is your responsibility. If you need to brush up on your writing skills, I recommend that you sign up for writing classes or workshops.

Each chapter focuses on one important aspect of the self-publishing process, so you can jump around to quickly obtain the specific information that you're looking for.

I also use a few conventions to help guide you through this book:

>> *Italic* words point out defined terms or emphasize words.

>> **Boldface** text indicates keywords in bulleted lists and the action part of numbered steps.

>> Hyperlinked text highlights website addresses.

And because you need to complete many steps to ensure that you make your publishing venture a successful one, this book's six parts group topics and subdivide them into chapters covering information that directly relates to those topics:

>> **Part 1: Do It Yourself: Getting Started with Self-Publishing** introduces you to self-publishing, explains what it is, and clarifies how you can use it to publish your book. This part also helps you gather all the tools that you need

to write and publish your book, while providing you with basic information about developing and fine-tuning your manuscript.

>> **Part 2: Pulling Together the Details: Administration and Design** discusses the work that you need to do after you finish writing your manuscript but before you can print it (or publish it as an e-book) and sell it.

>> **Part 3: Start the Presses! Examining Printing Choices** outlines the handful of options that you have for publishing and printing your books. You can determine which option to choose by considering a number of factors: your budget, your ultimate goals for the book, your distribution plan, and your audience.

>> **Part 4: Making Your Book a Bestseller: Distribution Methods** explains that you can't simply write and publish a book to make it successful. This part focuses on book distribution methods and how to best use each one. You can also find out how to handle your own warehousing, order fulfillment, and shipping, if you need to deal with these tasks based on the distribution method that you choose.

>> **Part 5: Creating a Buzz: Publicity and Marketing** explores the options for letting readers know that your book exists. Developing a comprehensive advertising, marketing, and public relations campaign — and then properly implementing it — requires financial and time investment, plus a tremendous amount of creativity, planning, and initiative.

>> **Part 6: The Part of Tens** offers you ten common self-publishing mistakes to avoid, ten e-book publishing mistakes to avoid, and ways to establish your expertise and credibility as an author.

Foolish Assumptions

Before writing this book, I made a few assumptions. I know, making assumptions isn't always the best idea, but in developing the content for this book, I had to start somewhere. Here are my assumptions about you:

>> **You have basic writing skills and a great idea for a book.** This new edition of *Self-Publishing For Dummies* helps you evaluate your idea in terms of its profitability, suitability, and marketability.

>> **You already have information to convey to your readers,** whether you have a good story, or valuable and informative content. Sure, this book helps you fine-tune your approach when it comes to communicating your content to your readers, but you need to decide what information to include within your book, based on your book's target audience.

>> **You have content ready to publish or have already tried other publishing methods.** Perhaps you wrote your book's manuscript and want to bypass the traditional publishing process and do it yourself. Or perhaps you already approached major publishers to sell your book without success, and now you want to give self-publishing a whirl. If you already wrote your manuscript, this book explains how to develop it, publish it, market it, and make it available to its intended audience.

Icons Used in This Book

The icons used throughout this book help you quickly pinpoint important information, focus your attention on information that's worth remembering, and draw attention to things you should watch out for and avoid while you work on your publishing project.

REMEMBER

This icon appears when I convey information worth remembering. Sounds simple enough, right?

TIP

You see this icon whenever I provide advice or tips. The information listed with this icon can help save you time and money, or help you improve your overall productivity and chances of success.

WARNING

Watch out for this icon. It accompanies information such as common mistakes people make, misconceptions that need clarification, or potential pitfalls to avoid during the publishing process.

Beyond the Book

Within each chapter of *Self-Publishing For Dummies, 2nd Edition,* you can find information about many useful resources and companies that provide products or services for self-published authors. Keep in mind that the companies listed within this book provide only a sampling of what you can find out there. Feel free to shop around and research other companies or services before deciding which one you want to work with. Also note that pricing for various self-publishing-related services vary greatly, so shop around to get the best deal based on your project's unique needs.

Where to Go from Here

For an overview of what self-publishing is all about and to determine the best way to get started, Chapter 1 definitely gives you the best place to begin reading. Of course, the Table of Contents and Index can help you find specific topics. And don't forget to check out the online Cheat Sheet for other related self-publishing information. Go to www.dummies.com and type "Self-Publishing For Dummies Cheat Sheet" in the search bar.

Never before has the opportunity to publish a professional-looking book or e-book been available to so many people at such an affordable price. After you write your manuscript, by following the advice offered in this book, you can become a published author in a matter of weeks (or months) and begin selling your book. If you have something important, relevant, or entertaining to say, self-publishing gives you a viable option for sharing your message, story, or knowledge with the public.

1

Do It Yourself: Getting Started with Self-Publishing

Chapter **1**

Welcome to Self-Publishing!

Whether you know it or not, just about everyone has a unique story to tell, experiences to share, knowledge to disseminate, or a creative imagination that allows them to brainstorm incredible stories. Because you've started reading this book, you're likely one of these people. If you've ever dreamed of having a book published with your name prominently displayed on the cover, you're in luck! For more people than ever before, self-publishing has become a viable way to get your book published and accessible to a potentially vast audience.

Most book publishing companies aren't willing to work with first-time authors who have little or no professional writing experience, but this situation is no longer a roadblock for getting your book published. Again, thanks to new digital publishing technologies, just about anyone who has good writing skills and a great idea for content can have a book professionally published and made available to the general public in print, digital, and/or audio formats. This process is called *self-publishing.*

This chapter provides an overview of what being a self-published author involves. The rest of this book takes you step-by-step through the entire self-publishing process. Use this second edition of *Self-Publishing for Dummies* to find out what you must know so that you can put your knowledge and ideas into writing and publish your own book.

Figuring Out Whether Self-Publishing Works for You

Self-publishing offers many awesome benefits. It allows ordinary people — business leaders, celebrities, entrepreneurs, educators, students, retired people, or stay-at-home parents (that is, just about anyone) — to become a published author for a relatively low financial investment. What's required, however, is a tremendous amount of time, creativity, and discipline to write, edit, design, publish, promote, distribute, and sell your book (if you want to be successful — and who doesn't want to be successful?).

When you get hired as an author by a major publishing house, your job is simply to write the book's manuscript and perhaps gather some or all the artwork that's included within that book. For this work, you're typically paid an advance and a royalty on book sales. Various experts working for the publisher handle all the other steps (and there are many of them) in the publishing process. Keep in mind, the author is expected to participate in the marketing process when working with a traditional book publisher.

Self-publishing is different. As the author, you're still responsible for writing your book's manuscript, but you're also responsible for every other aspect of the book publishing process. The good news is that if you have a great idea for a book or knowledge that you want to share, but you're not already a skilled writer, you can find many professional ghostwriters to help you transform your thoughts, knowledge, experiences, or ideas into a professionally written and polished manuscript.

For other parts of the process, you can also find skilled editors, graphic designers, illustrators, publishing consultants, and book marketing specialists to provide any skills you're currently lacking. And you can hire these pros on a freelance basis to help out. In other words, you don't have to handle all the steps involved with self-publishing by yourself. Even when you hire a wide range of freelancers and companies to handle major steps in the publishing process, you're ultimately the decision maker and the person in charge of the entire project — from start to finish. *Note:* The more you hire and rely on other people, the more expensive the self-publishing process becomes.

Self-publishing has two major benefits:

>> **Control:** You get 100 percent creative control over every aspect of the book's content, layout, design, format, pricing, distribution, advertising, and marketing.

>> **Profits:** Instead of just getting an advance plus a royalty on sales, you get to keep most of the profits generated by the sale of the book.

We explore these two benefits (and many more) in the following sections.

Chapter 2 talks specifically about why you should consider self-publishing, and you can discover the benefits of the process. It also reveals how just about any type of content — fiction or nonfiction — can be self-published and transformed into an e-book, paperback, or hardcover. You can also find out what specific skills you need to become a self-published author.

Don't get too excited just yet! Although self-publishing does offer an amazing opportunity for just about anyone to have their book professionally published, compared to having your book published by a major publishing company, self-publishing has a few drawbacks, as well. I also go over these drawbacks in Chapter 2.

Gathering the Right Publishing Tools

Before you sit down to write a potential bestseller, gather the proper writing and publishing tools. (Chapter 4 focuses on the equipment and tools that you need to successfully write a book.) Some pre-writing tasks that you need to accomplish include

>> **Creating a comfortable writing environment:** Pay attention to your writing location and the furnishings you use, but also focus on the lighting and temperature where you will be writing.

>> **Identifying and minimizing distractions when you're writing:** Get rid of that TV or messaging app that pulls your mind away from writing, and find ways to adjust your work habits that allow you to stay focused.

>> **Putting together the perfect writer's toolbox:** Make sure that you have everything you need, not just a good word processor.

What you need in your writer's toolbox varies, based on what format(s) you ultimately want your book to take. For example, beyond just a word processing program, you need specialized software to format and publish e-books; and you have to have separate applications to design the look and feel, and prepare your manuscript for printing in the form of a traditional hardcover or paperback book. Which applications you use depends on several factors, including whether you want to print the content within your book in black and white or in full color, for example.

REMEMBER

As an author, you need certain tools to make the writing process easier and maximize your productivity:

>> You can use a Windows PC or Mac desktop or laptop computer that's equipped with a powerful word processing program (such as Microsoft Word or Google Docs) and that has access to the internet and a printer.

>> Some people opt to do their writing by using a tablet (such as an Apple iPad, Samsung Galaxy Tab, or Microsoft Surface Pro) that has an external keyboard attached. However, for most writers, this is a secondary writing tool.

>> Of course, you can also plan to write the first draft of your book freehand by using a pad and pen. (If you go this route, expect to wind up with a very tired hand!) You can find applications that automatically transform your handwriting into editable text on your computer or tablet, so you have options.

Putting Together a Winning Manuscript

The beauty of self-publishing is that you can transform almost any type of content into a professionally published book. Depending on the type of book you're writing, a full-length manuscript may be anywhere from 50,000 to 100,000 words (or longer). A compilation of poems or short stories, a photobook, or a cookbook that contains recipes follow different formats altogether. Meanwhile, a kids' book is typically less than 500 words, but a book that contains chapters can be as long as 20,000 words, while a book targeted to a middle school or young adult audience can be between 50,000 and 80,000 words. Be sure that you understand your audience and the book-length and format they're accustomed to reading.

REMEMBER

Coming up with the perfect book idea — something that's unique or that offers a new twist on something that's been written about before — is an important step in the book writing and publishing process. Equally important, you need to research your information and make sure that you have enough interesting and informative content to fill an entire book. You then need to properly organize the information so that the reader can make sense of and make use of it.

Starting with an outline and an audience

TIP

The trick to writing a successful book involves first brainstorming and carefully outlining exactly what you plan to write, and then clearly defining your book's audience. Make sure that the content within your book (and later all the marketing for it) targets that specific audience. I explain how to determine your target audience in Chapter 3. Not only do you need to define who will potentially want to read your book, but you also must then make your published book accessible to this audience and market it so that the right people find out about its existence.

Most authors begin the writing process by creating a detailed outline for their book's manuscript before they start researching, writing, and adding visual elements such as photos and illustrations. Chapter 5 focuses on how to prepare an outline, research the content for your book, and decide what elements you want to incorporate into your manuscript.

REMEMBER

Everything within your book must be completely original, unless you have written permission to include someone else's copyrighted materials within your book. Plagiarism is something you want to avoid as a writer. Meanwhile, developing your own voice as a writer is something that you want to establish early on when your writing career is taking off. In Chapter 5, I focus a bit on AI tools for writers and why you should *not* rely on them to create your manuscript.

Fine-tuning your manuscript

The manuscript editing process requires several steps. An excellent strategy has you begin by editing your own work, and then hiring a professional editor to fine-tune the manuscript. In Chapter 6, find out what a professional editor does and how to hire someone who's highly skilled. Editing requires a very different skillset than writing, and people train for many years to master how to edit well.

Keep in mind that software and online-based tools can do a pretty good job helping you fine-tune your manuscript, as well as correct grammar and spelling errors. But *none* of these tools is a replacement for hiring a professional editor to review your manuscript before the layout and design process, and then again before it goes to press.

Prepping the manuscript for publishing

REMEMBER

In the publishing world, the document that you create, containing your written work and supplemental materials that will eventually be published into a book, is referred to as a *manuscript.* After you edit the manuscript and format, lay out, and design the pages to look like pages within a traditional book, the finished document is referred to as *galleys.* This galley content gets printed as a traditional softcover or hardcover book, or formatted as an e-book.

An *e-book* is a published book that's distributed in a digital format such as epub, PDF, or a platform-specific format. Readers can access it by using a dedicated e-reader (such as an Amazon Kindle or a Barnes & Noble Nook), on a computer screen, or on the screen of a mobile device (including a smartphone or tablet). The pages of an e-book look exactly like the pages of a traditionally printed book, but among other things, the reader can choose the typeface and font size for the text displayed.

Dealing with Administration and Design

Depending on what your goals are for the book, some self-published authors establish their own small publishing company (a formal business entity), especially if they plan to directly sell and distribute their own printed books. Discover, in Chapter 7, why you may benefit from forming a company.

Taking care of the administrative details

Even without establishing your own publishing company, you need to complete some administrative tasks before your self-published book goes to press or is released in any digital format. For example, based on how you plan to distribute and sell your book, you likely need to acquire a unique International Standard Book Number (ISBN), a Library of Congress Control Number, and a copyright. Chapter 8 outlines how to accomplish many of these tasks. (However, in some cases, if you hire a printer that specializes in working with self-published authors, the printer often handles most or all these tasks for you — but for a fee. See Part 3 for more info on print and digital publishing choices.)

TIP

Many companies offer comprehensive publishing solutions for self-published authors, including print-on-demand (POD) and small-print-run printers. These companies can handle some or all of the necessary administrative tasks on your behalf. Using one of these comprehensive publishing solutions can help first-time authors because the service makes the whole process easier and saves you considerable time. However, depending on which service you hire and what tasks you expect it to handle, you'll need to pay for their work upfront and out of pocket — which is a financial investment on your part that could be anywhere from several hundred to several thousand dollars. You can read more about short-run printers and POD companies in Chapter 12 and Chapter 13, respectively.

Crafting a book design

In addition to the many administrative tasks that you (or someone on your behalf) must complete before a book gets published, you need to lay out and design the manuscript, as well as create the book's front and back covers. These tasks apply to both traditionally printed books and e-books. However, you can more easily and quickly complete the process for e-books than for what will ultimately be a traditionally printed softcover or hardcover book. You can handle these steps yourself, using desktop publishing and graphic design software (see Chapters 9 and 10 for details about tools used for page layout and cover design), or you can hire a professional graphic designer to do this design work for you. Chapter 9 focuses on how to design and lay out the interior of your book, using desktop publishing software running on a Windows PC or Mac. Chapter 10 provides information regarding how you need to create the most impressive and high-impact front and back cover possible.

TIP

You've probably heard that saying, "You can't judge a book by its cover." Well, when it comes to self-publishing, the appearance of your book's cover and a well-written book description both play a huge role in whether readers are likely to purchase your book. Hiring an experienced book cover designer is one of the expenses you should splurge on during the publishing process.

Checking Out Your Printing Options

Printed books come in all shapes and sizes, and you have options when it comes to printing your book. Based on which printing method you choose, going with an industry standard trim size will keep your costs down. A printed book's *trim size* refers to the dimensions of the book (it's width and height). Page count determines its thickness. The most common trim sizes for standard books are: 5 × 8 inches, 5.5 × 8.5 inches, or 6 × 9 inches.

Here are the major self-publishing print options:

>> **Traditional printing:** Using offset printing technology to publish a large quantity of books at one time. Major publishing houses use this process, and it offers many advantages (but also a few drawbacks) for self-published authors. Unless you know, with 100 percent certainty, that you can sell hundreds or thousands of printed copies of your book, don't pursue this printing method as a self-published author.

>> **E-book publishing:** The least expensive way to publish and distribute a book. Because using a dedicated e-reader, a computer, or a tablet has become a very common way for readers to acquire and read books, it makes sense to have your book available in popular e-book formats. I cover how to create, publish, and distribute e-books in Chapter 11.

TIP

If you want (or need) to keep your initial financial investment low and know that your target audience tends to like e-books, strongly consider pursuing e-book publishing exclusively. When you use specialized software (such as Vellum), you can create and publish e-books more quickly, easily, and affordably than you can print books. In fact, you may be able to publish an e-book entirely by yourself.

>> **Short run printing:** Have a relatively small number of books printed in one batch. In fact, you can initially order just a few dozen or a few hundred copies of the book. You have to pay a higher printing cost per book than you do with a traditional printing option, but the financial risk is much lower if your book doesn't wind up selling as well as you expect. You can find out more about this printing option in Chapter 12.

Consider this option if you plan to sell your book directly to readers in-person or online, but you don't want to commit to a large print run that you need to pay for upfront and then need to warehouse until you can sell the copies.

>> **Print-on-demand (POD):** The most viable option for many self-published authors who want to create and sell printed copies of their book. Despite having a few small drawbacks, POD requires a relatively low initial financial investment and requires the author to maintain little or no inventory. With POD, individual copies of your book are printed one at a time when they're ordered. Each copy is then shipped directly to the buyer by the POD printer. See Chapter 13 for details.

REMEMBER

Before choosing which printing and publishing option is right for you, consider your goals, your distribution plan, and your budget for the book. (Keep in mind that marketing, advertising, and promotions for your book — both online and in the real-world — also require a separate, but typically significant, investment.)

No matter which printing and publishing option you choose, plan to develop a good rapport with the company that you work with. If you plan to pursue only e-book sales for your book, the publishing process is somewhat easier because you'll team up with Amazon, Barnes & Noble, Apple Books, and other e-book distribution services to handle the sale and distribution of the digital edition of your book.

Delving into Distribution

As a self-published author, one of the biggest challenges (besides writing the book) is getting it into the hands of readers. You can sell your book in many ways; the trick is to find distribution methods that work best for your book and allow you to achieve your sales goals.

Distributing a printed book

For printed books, here are some common distribution methods:

>> **Online booksellers:** In Chapter 15, you can find out about distribution options through online booksellers, such as Amazon (www.amazon.com), Barnes & Noble (www.bn.com), and Apple Books (www.apple.com/apple-books), which for many self-published authors is the most viable and inexpensive way of making a book available to the public.

>> **Retail distribution:** Chapter 16 focuses on traditional distribution through brick-and-mortar retail bookstores and other specialty retailers. Unfortunately, retail is the most difficult distribution method for self-published authors to utilize.

WARNING

When you try to distribute your book through major retailers, you compete head-on with major publishing companies that are supported by teams of professional salespeople who have well-established connections with key buyers at the various retailers. You can be at a huge disadvantage in this situation, but as you can see in Chapter 15, your book can find its way onto the shelves of major bookstores and mass-market retailers if you have the budget and can overcome the challenges that small publishers face when trying to set up this distribution method.

>> **Direct online sales:** These days, creating an e-commerce–oriented website for your book is an extremely viable option for self-published authors. With such a website, you can take orders, process online payments, and then ship out the books directly to customers. Assuming that you can keep your printing costs down, direct online sales can easily become one of the most profitable sales options for you.

REMEMBER

If you plan to sell your own book to distributors, wholesalers, retailers, booksellers, or individual consumers, you need to deal with warehousing, order fulfillment, and shipping. Chapter 16 provides an overview of what's required when it comes to distributing printed copies of your book.

Distributing an e-book

As an author, if your budget is tight and you want to focus exclusively on e-book distribution and sales, the e-book route can provide you with an incredibly lucrative opportunity. However, to be successful, you need to make your e-book available in several popular digital formats so that it's compatible with Kindle and Nook e-readers, Windows and Mac-based computers, as well as iOS and Android-based mobile devices. Not only do you need to publish your e-book in multiple formats, but you also need to create a publisher account with major e-book sellers because those sellers will ultimately distribute and sell your book for you. These online-based sellers include

>> Amazon (www.amazon.com)

>> Barnes & Noble (www.bn.com)

>> Apple Books (www.apple.com/apple-books)

>> Kobo (www.kobo.com)

The benefit to working with these established e-book sellers is that they handle the order processing, payment collection, and digital distribution of your book in a way that's copy protected (so the buyer can't make unlimited copies of the digital e-book file to give out to all their friends, for example). In exchange, as the author, you pay the e-book distribution service a sales commission up to 30 percent of the e-book's cover price. However, you can sell and distribute e-books yourself by using more complicated methods — through your own website or through social media, for example. Check out Chapter 11 to explore all of these options.

Getting Noticed: Publicity and Marketing

Your book won't sell, no matter how good it is, unless you develop a comprehensive, effective, and well-timed marketing, publicity, and advertising campaign to reach and convince your intended audience to purchase the book. This kind of campaign requires an upfront financial investment on your part — above and beyond what you spend to get the book published.

TIP

When composing your book's description and any promotional content that'll be used online, be sure to make the text SEO-friendly, which will make it easier for people to find via search engines and various search tools. This is covered in greater detail within Parts 4 and 5.

WARNING

Reality check: Very seldom does a first-time author have readers breaking down their door to get copies of their book. Often, for a self-published book to achieve sales success, you need to target it to a clearly defined niche audience that you determine has an interest in whatever you plan to write about. Ultimately, you'll want to market and promote your book to a niche audience that you determine how to reach with your sales efforts.

Looking for free publicity opportunities

You can find ways to generate free publicity in all forms of media. Radio, television, newspapers, magazines, newsletters, social media, blogs, podcasts, and vlogs provide one of the most powerful and cost-effective ways for self-publishers to generate awareness about their book. If handled correctly, you can transform public awareness directly into book sales.

In Chapter 18, you can find out how to develop the publicity materials that you need to promote your book properly; I cover items such as the press release, author bio, author photo, and the media pitch letter. Chapter 19 focuses on how to use these materials to generate media reviews, articles, and features about your book. The easiest way to get your publicity materials out there, without having to hire a public relations firm or marketing agency, involves initially focusing on obtaining publicity online through podcasts, vlogs, blogs, YouTube channels, and social media influencers who cater to your book's target audience.

TIP

As a self-published author, you need to have reviews written about your book in mainstream media and podcasts, as well as on websites and in blogs. Equally important, you need to generate positive reviews and ratings from your readers that ultimately get published on online book retailers' websites. A reader who has never heard of you as an author is much more likely to purchase and read your book if they see hundreds or thousands (if possible) of positive ratings and reviews.

Paying for advertising

You can educate potential readers about your book through paid advertising, which enables you to deliver your exact marketing message to a highly targeted audience, through specific media outlets. To get started, the most cost-effective means of advertising involves going online, using search engines, such as Google and Yahoo!, as well as popular social media platforms (including Facebook, Twitter, Instagram, and TikTok). Chapter 20 covers how to create effective ads to promote and sell your book — both online and using traditional media outlets.

Offering related products and services

Whether your book sells for $9.95 or $29.95, your profit potential is ultimately limited because the book itself is a low-priced item compared to most other products that have higher profit margins. As a self-published author, you can add to your profits in a variety of ways:

>> Use the recognition and credibility that you receive as a published author to repackage your book's content into other, higher-priced items, such as videos and audiobooks.

>> Hold lectures and host seminars or training programs related to your book's topic.

Check out how to generate additional revenue streams from the content of your book in Chapter 21.

Making the book itself a marketing tool

Some business leaders and consultants, for example, use their self-published book as a sales and marketing tool for the products or services that they offer. They give away the book to prospective new customers or clients to demonstrate the author's knowledge and competence, and to encourage new business. In this case, the author doesn't plan for the book to earn revenue on its own. Instead, it's a marketing expense that will potentially generate profitable new business.

Surveying a Brief Self-Publishing Task List and Timeline

Self-publishing your book isn't a fast and easy project. Plan on investing considerable time into each step of the process, especially when it comes to writing the manuscript. Don't take shortcuts!

Unfortunately, you just can't determine how long it will take you to sit down and write the full-length manuscript for your book until you begin writing and understand more about your personal work habits as a writer. For some people, the researching and writing process takes just weeks. For others, it takes months or even years. After you complete your manuscript, you can more accurately calculate a production timeline for your book, based on the printing and publishing decisions that you make.

After you finish your manuscript, with proper planning, you can potentially have a book professionally published in as little as two to three months. In 60 to 90 days, you could be a published author. Table 1-1 shows a rough list of tasks that you need to handle after you finish writing the manuscript and tells you where this book covers the task related details. Use the table as a guide for detailing the timeline for your self-publishing project.

TABLE 1-1   ## Post-Writing Tasks and Timeline

Task*	What It Involves	Expected Timeframe	Chapter or Part with Details
Establish your publishing company	Set up your business as a legal entity and give your publishing company a name.	1 week	Chapter 7
Edit the manuscript	Hire an editor and review edits	1-4 weeks	Chapter 6
Choose a self-publishing option: e-book or print	Hire a printer and distributor; get quotes and evaluate services; determine a format and design for the options that you choose	2-4 weeks	Part 3
Design and lay out the book	Complete on your own or hire help per chosen publishing method(s)	1 week	Chapter 9
Apply for an ISBN, barcode, and copyright	Handle depending on the publishing process and the company	A few hours	Chapter 8
Set the cover price for your book	Based on the book's format, length, publishing method(s), and so on	A few hours	Chapter 8
Create your book's front and back covers	Hire a graphic designer (even for e-books)	1 week	Chapter 10
Plan and implement a comprehensive promotional campaign	Outline marketing, public relations, and advertising efforts	Ongoing after plan creation	Part 5
Develop an online presence	Create an e-commerce website and social media accounts to promote and sell your book	Ongoing after creation	Chapter 17
Set a publication date	Decide the exact date your book will be available for sale. This will typically be dictated based on the distribution method(s) you choose.	Varies	Chapter 8

(continued)

TABLE 1-1 *(continued)*

Task*	What It Involves	Expected Timeframe	Chapter or Part with Details
Begin preselling your book	Put together and send out press materials, promote the book to potential distributors, line up booksellers to sell the book, take out ads, and so on	Ongoing after a few weeks of setup	Part 5
Have your book listed (and sold) through online booksellers	Engage with Amazon and Barnes & Noble, for example	Several days	Chapter 14
Publish and ship the book	To consumers, booksellers, retailers, and distributors, as appropriate	Varies	Part 4
Continue promoting and marketing your book while you take orders	In-person book signings or author appearances; social media activity	Ongoing	Part 5

*Some of the tasks in the table can occur simultaneously.

While you develop your timeline, allocate ample time for each step of the publishing process so that you wind up with the best possible finished product. For example, a professional editor may take several weeks to edit your manuscript. It can then take a professional graphic designer at least a week or two (potentially longer) to create a professional front and back cover, and they'll need additional time to do the layout and design work for your book's interior.

TIP

When you read each chapter of this book, consider how long each step of the process may take you, based on your unique lifestyle, responsibilities, available budget, and personal situation. Make sure that the timeline and deadlines you set for yourself are realistic, using the timeline estimates that you can find in each chapter. Stay focused on your goals and deadlines, and work hard to achieve them.

WARNING

Don't set and announce a publication date for your book until you accomplish all of the necessary tasks to have the book printed and you get a reliable timeline from your printer (or e-book publisher and distributors) about printing/publishing your book. Expect delays to happen at various steps along the way and build some wiggle room for these delays into your overall timeline. For example, your editor or graphic designer could get sick, your printer may have mechanical issues with their press, or your e-book distributors may be delayed when it comes to adding books to their respective databases because of an influx of new submissions.

IN THIS CHAPTER

» Considering self-publishing as an option for your book

» Looking at the benefits and potential drawbacks

» Surveying the skills that self-published authors need

» Becoming a full-time self-published writer — or not

Chapter **2**

Understanding the Pros and Cons of Self-Publishing

So, you've decided to write a book. You have a great idea for content, you know your topic, and you've pinpointed your target audience. Or perhaps you've already written a manuscript that you believe has the potential to become a bestseller. Now, you need to make a big decision. Are you going to approach major publishing houses in hopes of getting them to publish, distribute, and market your book, or do you plan to self-publish? As a quick reality check, it's extremely difficult to get even a small publishing company, much less a larger one, to publish a book from a first-time author. If you opt to go this route, you typically need to first establish a relationship with a reputable and well-established literary agent. Book publishers seldom accept unsolicited book proposals directly from authors.

On the plus side, thanks to a variety of technological advancements in book printing and distribution (as well as e-books and their design and digital publishing processes), self-publishing has become an extremely viable and cost-effective option to almost anyone. This chapter explores the pros and cons of self-publishing and helps you decide whether publishing your own book — in a printed or digital format — is the right approach for you.

Why Should You Even Consider Self-Publishing?

You may not be able to pursue a traditional route for getting your book published by a major publishing company, especially in today's publishing marketplace. However, don't let that fact deter you from pursuing your goal of getting your book written, published, and distributed. Self-publishing offers you — the author — a variety of benefits and significantly greater creative control over your project. Check out the additional reasons why you should consider self-publishing:

>> **Competition in the traditional book publishing industry has become extremely fierce.** Tens of thousands of books are published every year and distributed through major retail stores, but only a small fraction of those books actually become bestsellers and earn a significant profit for the publishers and authors.

>> **Getting the attention of a major publishing house is almost impossible these days.** Even if a writer creates a well-written proposal and is represented by a reputable literary agent, the chances of publication are still very slim.

Unfortunately, many potential bestsellers get passed over by the publishing houses, either because a proposal was one of thousands received that didn't get the proper attention or because the publisher didn't have the resources to take the gamble involved with publishing a book by an unknown and unproven author.

>> **You have 100-percent control over your publishing project.** This control includes what content goes in your book and how it gets promoted, distributed, and sold. You don't have to answer to editors, a publisher, a publishing company's sales or marketing department, or anyone else when developing, printing, and distributing your book. Ultimately, you also own the copywrite for your book and can potentially earn more revenue from its sale.

>> **You can set your own schedule.** Decide when you want to write, edit, publish, market, and sell your own book. You can fast-track the project and make it available to the public within a few short weeks or months, or you can take your time and handle each step of the publishing process at your leisure. You aren't tied to deadlines imposed by a major publishing house.

REMEMBER

Is self-publishing right for you? Maybe you need a checklist of sorts to see whether you fall under the criteria for becoming a self-published author. Self-publishing your book may be the ideal solution for you, if at least some of the following criteria apply:

>> You're a first-time author looking to publish, market, and distribute your own book because you can't get the attention of a major publisher.

>> You're a business professional or expert in your field and want to use a published book as a marketing tool to enhance your professional credibility and reputation.

>> You're an established author who wants 100-percent creative control over your next book project, and you want to make more money per copy sold than you would working with a major publisher.

>> You want to put information in book form, such as your autobiography or family genealogy, and distribute it to a small group of friends and family.

>> You represent a company that needs to develop book-length publications or manuals in-house.

>> You work with a group or association and need to create a fundraising item, such as a cookbook or yearbook, that you plan to sell to raise money and/or distribute to members.

>> You're a creative and imaginative person with the idea for a fictional story that can entertain readers and take them into a world you create that's filled with compelling characters and a captivating plot.

>> You own the rights to republish a currently out-of-print book that you believe still has a viable market.

>> You're an entrepreneur looking to establish and run your own publishing venture and operate it as a full-time or part-time business.

WARNING

Before making the decision to pursue self-publishing, make sure you review the potential drawbacks, which are outlined in the section "What Are Self-Publishing's Drawbacks?" later in this chapter. For the author, self-publishing requires a much greater time commitment (above and beyond just writing the book's manuscript), a lot more work, and a financial investment.

What Are the Benefits of Self-Publishing?

Some of the biggest benefits of self-publishing include

>> Having the ability to publish any type of content.

>> Maintaining total control over your entire project, including all creative aspects related to the manuscript, cover design, and marketing of your book.

>> Saving time. You can self-publish a book significantly faster than working with a major publishing house.

>> Earning significantly higher income per copy of your book sold.

>> Keeping money in your pocket. You don't have to hire a literary agent (and pay them a commission) to help you market and sell your book idea.

After many up-and-coming writers discover the challenges and drawbacks of working with a major publishing company, many opt to self-publish their own work. This opportunity becomes even more viable if you have an already-established following or potential audience for your book comprised of social media followers, your customers/clients, your students, or members of an association to which you belong.

TIP

After you decide that self-publishing is the right direction to go for your book project, you need to determine the most cost-effective and viable printing and publishing option, based on your needs, goals, and budget. Part 3 of this book focuses on actually printing and publishing your manuscript by using short-run printing methods, print-on-demand (POD) technology, and e-book publishing.

Self-publishing any type of content

No matter what type of book you're looking to write and get published, chances are that self-publishing is your answer. Thanks to the U.S. Constitution and its Amendments, the United States has freedom of speech and freedom of the press. If you're writing about a topic that may be considered too controversial or edgy for a major publishing house, through self-publishing, you have total control over the content of your book.

Even if your book's subject matter or content isn't at all controversial, its target audience may be too narrow for a major publishing house to consider it sales worthy. However, if you know exactly how to market your book to your intended (niche) audience, self-publishing your book can become a profitable endeavor. For example, social media advertising and marketing is a powerful way to reach a niche audience when it comes to promoting your newly published book. (Check out Part 5 for the full scoop on publicity and marketing.)

Through self-publishing, you can publish any type of content. The possibilities are truly endless. Here are some of the common topics or genres that authors have self-published successfully:

>> Autobiographies or biographies

>> Children's books (fiction or nonfiction)

>> Collections of artwork, drawings, or paintings

>> Collections of poems or essays

>> Cookbooks or collections of recipes

>> How-to books

>> Reference books or textbooks

>> Self-help or personal development books

>> Training manuals or guidebooks

>> Works of fiction, such as a full-length novel or collection of short stories in any genre (horror, sci-fi, romance, comedy, young adult, adventure, erotica, and so on)

REMEMBER

Self-publishing gives virtually anyone the ability to become a published author so that they can share ideas, knowledge, experience, or creativity in a variety of formats. You can then distribute these books through almost any type of distribution channel — including bookstores, retail stores, mail order, an ecommerce website, or social media, for example. (See Part 4 for more about book distribution.) And not only does self-publishing allow you to publish any type of content, but it also allows you to cost-effectively publish any number of copies of your book. With POD technology, you can print as few as one copy of your book at a time (although other printing options may be more economical, based on your objectives). More about POD is discussed in Chapter 13.

Maintaining control over the entire process

When you publish your own book, you wear both the author and the publisher hats. You're ultimately responsible for handling *all* of the work that a major publishing house typically handles on behalf of authors, including

>> Writing the manuscript (or hiring a ghostwriter)

>> Editing and proofreading the manuscript

>> Creating page layouts and design

- » Crafting a front and back cover
- » Getting your book traditionally printed and/or published as an e-book
- » Distributing your book
- » Managing marketing, advertising, and promotion

What, you're not an expert in all these areas? Well, you're in luck. For every step involved with self-publishing that I cover in this book, you can find professional help available if and when you need it.

Authors who work with a major publishing house must give up a lot of creative control over their book project. It's the author's job to write the manuscript. The publisher typically handles everything else, often without consulting the author on creative decisions. Authors who have their book published by a major publishing house don't typically get a say on cover design or about how their book ultimately gets marketed or promoted, for example. But they are expected to help market and promote their books (often at their own expense).

REMEMBER

By self-publishing your book, you're the boss. You can hire freelancers and consultants to help you edit, design, publish, distribute, and market your book, but ultimately, you're responsible for making all the creative and business decisions. So, if you're emotionally close to your book and don't want anyone taking away your ability to make creative decisions, self-publishing offers you a great opportunity to get your book into the hands of readers on your terms.

WARNING

Taking total control of your entire book project requires you to make a wide range of business decisions that impact the sales success and profitability of your book. You're responsible for the financial investment needed to print, distribute, advertise, market, and promote your book. See the section "What Are Self-Publishing's Drawbacks?" later in this chapter, to see some of the downsides of self-publishing.

Getting your book into the hands of readers quickly

Bringing a book to print yourself can happen significantly faster than if you were working with a major publisher. This rapid release is particularly true when it comes to publishing e-books. By self-publishing your book, you have the flexibility to set your own schedule and deadlines, without having to cater to the needs or demands of a major publishing company. You can base your schedule and deadlines on your life's other personal and professional demands.

When you work with a major publisher, bringing your book to print can take up to two years. Using many self-publishing techniques, such as POD or e-book publishing (see Part 3 for options), the process (after the manuscript is fully written) can take just a few weeks.

Achieving your career-related goals

Some people write books because they want to pursue writing as a career. (Check out the section "Can Self-Publishing Be a Full-Time Gig?" later in this chapter, for more about this career option.) Others, however, use their written work to promote other aspects of their established career.

Boosting your established career

After you become a published author, if your content is well produced, you instantly get a boost in credibility as an expert on whatever topic you wrote about. People respect authors and the knowledge that they share. Therefore, being a published author can help you to

>> Land a new job in your area of expertise.

>> Earn a raise or promotion with your current employer.

>> Launch or expand your own business and earn the respect of customers.

>> Become a consultant or freelancer in your area of expertise.

>> Earn extra money lecturing or teaching seminars/workshops related to your book's topic.

>> Be the media's go-to person whenever a news story breaks about your topic.

>> Pursue writing as a full-time career, assuming you're able to sell enough books or write enough articles for mainstream publications and websites so that you can earn a living.

Using your self-publication as a marketing tool

A published book that has your name on the cover can also help you pursue other professional goals. After your book publishes, you can use it as a powerful marketing tool for yourself and/or your company. The book can serve as a resume or business card for promoting yourself as an expert in your field.

Depending on how you utilize your book as a marketing tool, the profits you generate from actual book sales can be insignificant compared to the boost in income from generating new business. Potential clients and customers can find you as a result of reading your book or being exposed to publicity about your book. For example:

>> **A real estate agent** might write a book about how to purchase a new home and then use it as a marketing tool to help establish their credibility and attract new clients.

>> **A college professor** writes a book about the subject they teach, and then makes the book a reading requirement for their students.

>> **A public speaker** who lectures about a specific topic at corporate gatherings, conventions, or other events as a part- or full-time career can write a book and then sell it directly to attendees.

TIP

Many self-published authors use their book as a promotional or marketing tool and give away free copies of their book to potential and existing clients. Wouldn't you consider giving away a book that costs between $5 and $10 per copy if you could generate hundreds or thousands of dollars in new revenue? Meanwhile, after you create an e-book, giving it away as a promotional tool costs you practically nothing because you don't have any printing or shipping costs.

Earning more royalties

Major publishers typically pay authors a recoupable advance, plus a predetermined royalty on book sales as compensation. Writers who self-publish their books, however, must cover all their project's development, printing, distribution, and marketing costs out-of-pocket. The profit potential, however, can be significantly greater.

Instead of receiving a 25-cent, 50-cent, or even a dollar royalty for each copy of your book sold, a self-published author can earn 35 to 70 percent of the book's cover price, and sometimes even more. So, if your book sells for $15 per copy and you sell just 1,000 copies, the profit is between $6,000 and $9,000.

Conversely, if you're an author whose book is published by a major publishing house, you may earn only a 25-cent royalty per book. If that book sells only 1,000 copies, your earnings are a mere $250. When your book makes its initial sales, you potentially have to repay your outstanding advance to the publisher. (If the book doesn't sell, however, the advance usually doesn't need to be repaid.) Even after you pay off your advance from the publisher through book sales, your literary agent continues to take between 15 and 20 percent of your earnings as their commission for as long as the book continues to be sold. (See the following section for more about agents.)

REMEMBER

With self-publishing, you don't have to wait three to six months to receive royalty checks from the publisher. Authors who have their book published by a major publishing house often have to wait for the money they've earned, but self-published authors tend to be paid a lot faster, especially on copies of the book they sell themselves directly to customers, including through online sales via a website or through social media. Self-published authors also aren't subject to a withholding of royalties as a reserve against returns for up to six additional months.

TIP

As a self-publisher, you stand to earn more money per copy of your book sold. But it's also considerably harder — but not impossible — for self-publishers to get distribution in major bookstores. So you need to develop innovative ways to market and sell your book, both in the real world and online. Part 5 helps you kickstart your public relations, marketing, and advertising efforts.

Saving money without a literary agent

A literary agent is compensated by the author and typically receives a commission of between 15 to 20 percent of the author's revenues. As a self-published author, you don't need to work with a literary agent, which saves you money.

The job of a literary agent involves helping an author sell their book idea to a publisher, negotiate publishing contracts, and ensure that the author receives timely royalty payments from the publishing house. Not having proper representation by a literary agent keeps many authors from being noticed by major publishers.

What Are Self-Publishing's Drawbacks?

Although you can find many reasons for wanting to self-publish your book (which you can read about in the section "What Are the Benefits of Self-Publishing?" earlier in this chapter), a few drawbacks exist when committing yourself to this type of publishing venture. These cons include large time and cost considerations, distribution challenges, and finding professionals to help you produce the best book possible. The following sections take a look at some of the challenges that you might face.

Recognizing the time and costs involved

Having total control of the publishing process can be a double-edged sword. From a creative standpoint, it can be liberating. Practically speaking, the time and financial commitment may be too much for you:

>> **Time:** Although all authors have to invest the time and energy to actually write the manuscript for their book (unless they hire a ghostwriter), self-published authors also have to invest the time needed to edit, layout and design, print, market, advertise, promote, sell, and distribute their book. Each of these steps is vitally important in the success of a book, and each requires a time commitment on your part. If you're willing to write a self-published book, but you're not prepared to invest the time necessary to promote and sell it, nobody will know that your book exists. Your sales may be minimal. The more time and energy that you invest in marketing, advertising, promotions, and sales, the better your chances are of selling large quantities of books and generating high profits.

>> **Financial:** From a financial standpoint, all the costs associated with the publishing process become your responsibility as a self-published author. Depending on the approach you take, this expense can be anywhere from a few hundred dollars to thousands of dollars. The goal, however, is to invest money in marketing and advertising that generates higher sales for your book and results in higher profits. If all goes well, the investment you make will offer a much higher return on your overall self-publishing investment.

REMEMBER

After you make the decision to self-publish, you must develop a plan to handle each major task or responsibility as both the author and the publisher. If you have the time, resources, and finances to handle all aspects of the self-publishing process, you're in excellent shape. However, if you're not equipped to handle each task, and you don't have the financial resources to hire experienced professionals to assist you (and save some of your own time), your potential for achieving success can diminish dramatically. See the section "Hiring all the help you want and need," later in this chapter, for more information on hiring help.

TIP

Some of the popular turnkey self-publishing solutions, especially those that offer print-on-demand (POD) services (described in Chapter 13), can help you organize your publishing process. These services handle

>> Basic interior layout and design, and cover design

>> ISBN number registration

>> Hiring a professional editor to review your manuscript

In Chapter 7, you also see many of the business-related expenses needed in your budget while you set up your publishing company and begin making plans to write, publish, promote, distribute, and sell your book. Having your own company can have significant tax advantages, ultimately save you a lot of money, and give you and your book additional credibility.

Encountering specific distribution snags

If you compare a self-published book with a trade paperback book published by a major publishing house, the self-published book has a lot of similarities with any other book you'd see displayed on a bookstore's shelf (if you, the self-publisher, follow my advice to create a professional-looking book). In fact, you'd probably have a difficult time differentiating between the two products if you saw them side-by-side. Both a self-published book and a book published by a major publishing house follow the same basic format, including overall layout and design, and front and back cover design, as well as how the book's title, price, barcode, and other information is conveyed. The publishing materials used, such as the type of cover and internal paper stock options, are also similar between self-published and trade paperback books.

The big difference between a self-published book and a book published by a major publishing house is the resources available for distribution, marketing, advertising, and promotion. The major publishers have fully-staffed departments and experienced people handling all of these tasks. They also have established distribution with the major bookstores. As a self-publisher, you may not have these resources at your disposal.

TIP

As a self-published author, you can have your book listed on Amazon.com, on Barnes & Noble's website, and on Apple Books, for example. So you can sell your printed books or e-books online through established sellers. Chapter 15 explains how to work with these online distributors.

WARNING

Realistically, getting traditional bookstore distribution for a self-published book, especially a book from a first-time author, is extremely difficult and often almost impossible. Major bookstores have buyers that deal primarily with the major publishing houses. Unless you work with a distributor or sales representative with experience getting books into mainstream distribution, don't count on bookstore or mass-market retail distribution for your book.

Although you could sell your book through independent bookstores and specialty retailers, the sales, distribution, and marketing plan for your book should include alternate distribution options. These more viable options include online sales and direct selling. Part 4 of this book focuses on how to distribute your self-published book effectively.

REMEMBER

Make sure that your distribution expectations are realistic. You'll likely have trouble obtaining national or international bookstore distribution for your self-published book. Some of the most successful self-published authors, however, have a pre-existing way to reach their target audience. Plan on grassroots marketing to sell your book. This marketing plan might include

» Targeting existing customers or clients by using direct mail or e-mail

» Taking advantage of a public relations (PR) campaign

» Online marketing and sales

» Selling books directly to your students, clients/customers, or members of a specific association or group

Hiring all the help you want and need

To maximize your success in creating, publishing, distributing, and selling your own book, seriously consider hiring experienced professionals in the book publishing industry to help you.

Although the publisher or printing company you use to self-publish your book may offer a variety of services to help you (see Part 3 for details on printing services), consider hiring the following types of freelance professionals to handle various aspects of the self-publishing process:

» **Ghostwriter:** Helps you actually write your manuscript (see Chapter 5).

» **Photographer, illustrator, artist, or graphic designer:** Creates and incorporates graphics and other visual elements within your book (see Chapter 9).

» **Editor:** Proofreads your manuscript and final page layouts (see Chapter 6). Depending on your deal with the editor that you hire, they may edit only your book's raw manuscript. You may also need to hire a separate proofreader to review the final page layouts of your book. Handle this negotiation when you hire an editor.

» **Graphic designer:** Assists with your book's internal page layout and design, as well as the front and back cover design (see Chapters 9 and 10).

» **Sales representative:** Obtains distribution of your book through retail stores and distributors (see Chapter 16).

» **Website designer:** Creates a website and social media content for promoting and directly selling your book online (see Chapter 17).

>> **Public relations, advertising, and marketing consultant:** Creates, launches, and manages all aspects of publicity, advertising, and marketing (see Chapters 18, 19, and 20).

TIP

Determine your needs and budget before negotiating with any type of freelancer. Most freelance professionals expect to be paid on a per-project basis, or they may bill by the hour. Make sure that you hire people who have experience doing whatever it is you need them to do. Also, review resumes and portfolios of work, as appropriate, and ask for references from satisfied clients before hiring people for your team.

REMEMBER

Keep in mind, with the help of this book, you can handle most, if not all, of the tasks associated with self-publishing yourself. Taking on these tasks can save you money and allow you to get familiar with all aspects of the publishing business. Ultimately, you need to decide how involved you want to get with the process, keeping in mind that none of the major steps can be skipped if you want your book to be successful.

Do You Have the Skills that All Self-Published Authors Need?

The following sections help you determine whether you have what it takes to become a successful self-published author or if you should focus first on fine-tuning your core skills.

Being willing to work hard

Writing the manuscript for your book can be a time-consuming project. After the manuscript is complete, the business-related aspects of the work really begin. Before embarking on a self-publishing project, ask yourself, "Am I really willing to work hard and dedicate the time and energy needed to do this project right?" Are you prepared to master new skills and focus your energies where they're needed on each aspect of the book-publishing process?

REMEMBER

Each person and each project is totally different. No one can predict what type of time commitment you'll have to make when writing your book. Everyone writes at a different speed and is willing to invest a different amount of time in each step of the process. So don't compare yourself to other authors. Without procrastinating, use your time wisely to finish your book to the best of *your* ability.

Writing to your audience

You've probably decided to write a book because you have knowledge, experience, or an idea that you want to share with others. Like composing music, or creating a sculpture or painting, writing is an art form. As an expert in your field, you need to be able to communicate your thoughts and ideas clearly by using the written word.

REMEMBER

No matter what type of book you're writing, you absolutely must thoroughly understand the book's intended audience (see Chapter 3 for more about targeting certain readers). And a good author knows how to write *to* that audience. The information in your book must cater specifically to the target audience. Keep in mind, the vocabulary, sentence structure, and use of grammar and punctuation can make your book easy or difficult to understand.

For example, how you go about writing a children's book targeted to 6-year-olds, a sci-fi or romance novel, or a how-to book for college-educated professionals differs greatly. The vocabulary you use should be easy for the intended reader to understand, but you never want to insult the reader's intelligence, either.

TIP

To polish your writing skills, participate in a few writing classes. Writing classes and workshops are offered at many community colleges, through local adult education programs, and through professional writers' and authors' associations. You can also find countless Facebook groups in which up-and-coming writers regularly meet and interact online. Here are just a few:

>> **Independent Authors** has more than 25,000 members (www.facebook.com/groups/6068439569).

>> **Indie Authors International** has more than 33,000 members (www.facebook.com/groups/160213917377540).

>> **New Writers and Authors** has more than 94,000 members (www.facebook.com/groups/newwritersandauthors).

And all Facebook groups are free to join if you have a free Facebook account of your own.

REMEMBER

It's your responsibility, as the writer, to create a manuscript that's well-researched and written, and that appeals to your intended audience. If you hire an editor (see Chapter 6 about hiring an editor), the editor fine-tunes your manuscript and corrects any errors; they don't rewrite your manuscript completely to make it adhere to basic rules of English style and punctuation. Never rely on your editor to take a poorly written manuscript and transform it into what could become a bestseller (that would potentially be the job of a ghostwriter, as noted in the section "Hiring all the help you want and need," earlier in the chapter).

Injecting creativity and personality into your work

Having a great idea for a book is one thing, but being able to write a manuscript that's fun, engaging to read, informative, and well-written is something else altogether. If you're writing a how-to book, for example, what will set your book apart from the countless other how-to titles out there published by the major publishing houses, independent publishers, and other self-published authors? What will make people want to read your book? After they decide to read it, what about your book will keep their attention?

REMEMBER

Make sure that you develop your own voice as a writer. Discover how to incorporate not just your knowledge and experience, but your personality, into your writing in order to make it more appealing to readers. For some writers, creativity comes naturally. They have a gift that makes them good storytellers and excellent written communicators. Others need to work on developing their creative skills and incorporating imagination into their writing. Check out the following ways to inspire your creativity:

>> Take writing classes. You can find these at adult education programs and local community colleges. Or, participate in an in-person writer's workshop.

>> Join a professional writer's association.

>> Read magazines that cater to writers, such as *The Writer* (www.writermag.com) or *Writer's Digest* (www.writersdigest.com). And join a Facebook special interest group that caters to writers and authors (see the preceding section).

>> Check the reference section of any bookstore for books on how to write fiction, nonfiction, children's books, poetry, or other types of literature.

Becoming a good writer takes practice; you acquire that skill over time. Therefore, be prepared to write several drafts of your manuscript and have it undergo significant editing before it's ready for publication. If you're not sure whether you've managed to inject your own voice into your work, seek out constructive criticism from professional editors or other people you trust who understand the publishing industry.

REMEMBER

A bestselling book (by traditional standards) must appeal to the masses — not just a niche audience. The way you convey information still needs to cater to readers and be easy to understand. And if you're writing a novel or work of fiction, creativity is even more crucial. For example, your plot and characters need to capture the reader's imagination and take them on a journey. Keep in mind that a niche-oriented book can also have extremely strong sales potential *over the long term*. Your book may not make it onto a bestseller list, but it could sell a ton of copies.

Honing your organizational skills

From the time you start working on your manuscript through the launch of your published book, taking a well-organized and deadline-oriented approach to each and every task associated with the publishing project helps keep you on track and within your budget.

TIP

This process has many steps and involves countless details, none of which can be allowed to fall through the cracks. If you get distracted easily or have trouble dealing with time management, check out these tips to help you get back on track:

>> Keep detailed to-do lists of what you need to accomplish.

>> Set realistic deadlines for yourself.

>> Stay focused on the big picture.

>> Micromanage the entire book-publishing process, so none of the seemingly less important tasks fall through the cracks.

>> Use specialized software (such as Scrivener or LivingWriter) that can help authors manage their manuscript preparation, brainstorming, and overall writing process. You can also turn to online-based tools, for example, Novlr and Plotter.

>> Use project planning software (such as Monday, Airtable, or Trello) to help manage the overall publishing process.

REMEMBER

Don't allow yourself to become overwhelmed. The divide-and-conquer strategy works in almost every situation that you might encounter when handling the major tasks involved in self-publishing your book. When trying to complete a large task under a tight deadline, divide up that task into smaller, more manageable tasks. For example, instead of focusing on writing an entire 100,000-word manuscript, focus on completing each 5,000- to 8,000-word chapter. By focusing on and completing one chapter at a time, before you know it, your book is done.

Can Self-Publishing Be a Full-Time Gig?

If you're interested in pursuing writing (and self-publishing) as a career, consider starting out part-time, perhaps as a hobby. Write your first book or get a handful of articles published in magazines or online. Determine what area of writing you want to specialize in and begin fine-tuning your writing skills and your voice as a writer. Build up your experience, but don't give up your day job until you've established yourself as a writer with enough earning potential to support yourself.

Especially in today's economy, being a full-time freelance writer, without the consistency of a weekly or biweekly paycheck, is extremely challenging.

Affirming the traits and skills you need

REMEMBER

Being a professional, full-time, published writer can be a fun and rewarding occupation, but it's definitely not for everyone. Just because you've written one book-length manuscript doesn't mean that you have what it takes to quit your day job and become a full-time professional writer and self-publisher. Becoming a full-time writer means spending countless hours each day sitting in front of a computer typing, researching, and having minimal interaction with others. After all, for most people, writing isn't a team activity. If you're not writing, you're not being productive. If you're not being productive, you're not earning a living.

A full-time writer must demonstrate the following traits in order to earn a living:

>> Discipline and hard-work ethic

>> Deadline-orientation

>> Focus and organization

>> Extreme creativity

In addition, a professional writer needs the following abilities:

>> Strong multitasking skills

>> Excellent time-management

>> Aptitude for working alone (unmanaged) and enjoying it

And a full-time writer must be able to

>> Cater to a specific audience with their writing.

>> Sell their work.

>> Have the financial resources to market and promote themself and their book(s).

If you find writing enjoyable and rewarding, consider writing additional books, as well as contributing articles to magazines and websites. You can provide these contributions on a freelance basis and still hold down a full-time job (in order to earn a living). And, depending on how well your book sells, you might find that you can actually earn a full-time living as a writer by supplementing book sales with paid author appearances, lecturing, and freelance article writing.

If your goal is to become a full-time, self-publish author, plan on writing and publishing multiple books — not just a single title.

Watching out for authoring pitfalls

Although you can find many bestselling authors out there, you can also find many, many more writers and authors who don't achieve success for a wide variety of reasons. If you don't have the skills discussed in the section "Do You Have the Skills that All Self-Published Authors Need?" earlier in this chapter, you may not be ready to become a full-time, self-published author. Here are a few reasons why many authors fail to achieve success:

>> **They lack knowledge about their book's topic.** If you don't have the knowledge and experience that you need to be an expert on the topic you're writing about, you need to do your research before you actually begin writing.

>> **They can't cope with writer's block.** At one time or another, all writers are faced with staring at a blank computer screen and not being able to decide what to write or how to best put their ideas into words. That lack of ideas is called *writer's block*. The easiest thing to do is walk away and give up — but if you want to battle writer's block, ensure that you're chock-full of ideas that you want to write about and have plenty of research done and available. Invest the time to fully develop and outline your ideas before sitting down to write.

>> **They fail to hire freelancers to handle specialized tasks.** Too many self-published books look obviously amateurish because the authors/ publishers decide that they can handle all aspects of the book-publishing process on their own. For example:

- They design the book's covers themselves, even when they have no graphic design experience whatsoever. They end up with an unattractive cover and interior book design that doesn't appeal to the book's intended audience.

- They fail to hire an editor/proofreader, which can make a book difficult to read and make you, the author, look foolish and amateurish.

>> **They don't develop good marketing and promotional skills.** The ability to self-promote is one of the most important skills that a writer should possess, especially if you plan to self-publish your work. If you don't properly promote your work, people won't even know it exists, and they'll never read it. Part 5 of this book is full of helpful information on promoting your writing.

Chapter **3**

Determining Who You're Writing for and Why

Before you start writing your book's manuscript, you need to understand your overall objective. Why are you writing the book? Why are you the best person to write the book? Why will your book matter to the reader? What will set your book apart from all the other books that cover the same subject matter? And who is your book's *target audience* (meaning who specifically will want to read it or benefit from reading it)?

As an author, anytime you sit down to write for an intended audience, envision those people in your mind. Pretend you're holding a conversation with your readers. Constantly focus on methods that you can use to communicate with your audience in a manner that fosters understanding and keeps their interest and attention — whether you're writing fiction or non-fiction. While you develop the outline for your book, consider what you want readers to know and exactly how you can present the ideas in a way that's relevant.

This chapter focuses on defining and getting to know your book's target audience. You can find out how to address the wants and needs of your reader as they relate to every aspect of your book's creation, publishing, marketing, and sales. Decisions about everything relating to your book, including its main title, cover design, the font(s) used, the page layout, and the book content — what you say and how you say it — should all reflect the niche group you believe to be the target audience. And after you determine who will be reading your book, you apply this knowledge numerous times throughout the self-publishing process.

Defining Your Target Audience

You have many ways to define your *primary* audience (also known as your *target audience*) — in other words, the people who will want to purchase and read your book. Create, in one sentence, a clear description of your book's target audience. (You can find tips of putting that sentence together in the section "Identifying audience characteristics," later in this chapter.)

Although publishers often design mass-market books to appeal to an extremely broad audience, as a self-published author, leave that broad audience to the mainstream publishers. As a small publishing operation, you'll likely have much better success by targeting a narrower, clearly defined audience. Also, when promoting and advertising your book, you can plan to reach a niche audience (especially online) much more easily and with less expense than going for a broad audience. Selling to a broad and not-so-clearly defined audience is more difficult.

REMEMBER

You need to define your audience after fleshing out and developing the idea for your book, but before you start writing it. Then, make your writing and your promotional efforts target that well-defined niche audience. Avoid trying to sell your book to a mass-market or extremely generalized audience.

WARNING

If you don't understand who your audience is, you could easily write and publish a book that nobody has an interest in reading, or that you don't have the time, money, and resources to properly promote. Likewise, even if you have what you believe to be an incredibly awesome and original book idea, if you don't understand how to promote and advertise it to the right audience, sales suffer.

Identifying and appealing to your audience

Who do you see as being the primary audience for your book? The better you can define and get to know the traits of the people in your target audience, the easier it becomes to write a book that those people can relate to. And especially if you're on a tight budget, a clear definition of your audience helps you target effective means for marketing and promoting your book. For example, if you opt to use paid social media advertising and/or paid search engine marketing (topics covered in Chapter 20), you can have a much easier time effectively using your limited ad budget to reach a clearly defined niche audience.

Detecting audience characteristics

How you describe your intended readers can be based on a variety of criteria, such as their

Personal Characteristics	Lifestyle	Socioeconomic Situation
Age	Affiliation with a group	Income/wealth
Gender identity	Hobbies/interests	Geographic location
Personal values	Personal habits	Level of education
Religious affiliation	Relationship status	Occupation
Sexual orientation		

You get the idea. Carefully consider your audience's characteristics (as you see them) and add in anything else that helps you identify the people you want to reach.

TIP

Define your book's niche target audience as clearly and succinctly as possible. For example, you might determine your book will appeal primarily to single females, between the ages of 18 and 35, who live in a major city, have a college degree, earn at least $45,000 per year, and enjoy cooking and travel. Maybe they also own their own car, are active on Instagram and TikTok, and follow the latest trends in fashion and makeup.

Building your book to match your audience's characteristics

After you truly understand who the target audience is for your book, you can make much more intelligent choices about your book's construction. That is, you can match the following book components to your audience:

>> **Title:** Choose a catchy and attention-grabbing title for your book that the reader can relate to.

>> **Appearance:** Decide on the appearance, color scheme, and overall design of the book's cover.

You also need to make sure your book properly targets your readers'

>> **Knowledge:** Understand the reading level, intelligence, and level of pre-existing knowledge that your readers possess (as it relates to your book's topic). As an author, always use appropriate vocabulary when writing your manuscript.

>> **Preferences:** Cater to your readers' wants, needs, and interests throughout the book.

- **>> Expectations:** Make sure your book meets or exceeds the expectations of the readers.

- **>> Questions:** Figure out what problems your book can help the readers solve, questions that your book will answer, information that your book will convey, and the way(s) that your book will ultimately benefit the people reading it.

And keep your readers in front of mind when getting your book out to them:

- **>> Methods:** Determine how you'll market, advertise, and promote the book in creative ways that quickly create a demand for your book in the most cost-effective ways possible.

- **>> Message:** Make sure your book and related marketing efforts don't accidentally insult your audience or cause them to negatively misconstrue information.

Although Mark Twain once said something to the extent that writers should write what they know, you'll face countless times as a writer when you need to step outside of your core base of knowledge. During these times, you absolutely must understand your audience and what they want to get from reading your book so that you can do the necessary research to gather or create the right content and present it in the most appropriate way possible. While you research the topic(s) that you plan to write about, invest an equal amount of time and effort toward getting to know your target audience. As you can read about later in this chapter (see the section "Engaging with people in your target audience"), you have many ways to become acquainted with your audience online and in the real world.

REMEMBER

Especially if you're writing any type of how-to or instructional book, never assume that your readers have the same level of knowledge or passion for a subject matter that you, the author, do. Clearly define key terms and explain core concepts in a way that makes your book easy to understand, relatable, and appealing to your intended readers.

Setting the groundwork for an audience-centered book

TIP

When you figure out who specifically you're writing your book for, get to know your audience so that you can address their wants and needs. Every aspect of your book should appeal to this audience. Then, when it comes to marketing and selling your book, you also need to tailor these efforts specifically to your target audience.

Before you proceed any further with writing the book, make sure you can answer the questions in Table 3-1 with just one sentence for each.

TABLE 3-1   **Prewriting Questions to Answer**

The Questions	Write Your Answers Here
What will your book be about?	
In what ways will your non-fiction book bring benefit to the reader? (Will it entertain, educate, solve a problem, help the reader overcome a challenge, teach a new skill, or convey specialized knowledge?)	
If the book is fictional and designed to entertain readers, what will make it unique?	
In what ways will your book help the reader improve their personal, professional, or financial life?	
Who will want to read your book and why?	
In your opinion, who else *should* want to read your book and why?	
What will readers expect from you as the author (your writing style) and your book (in terms of its content)?	
Specifically, who is the target audience for your book?	

Determining who else will want to read your book

What secondary audience will your book appeal to? For example, would your book make a good gift for a parent or grandparent to give to a child? Is the book suitable to give as a gift to a spouse, friend, or coworker? After carefully and clearly defining your book's core audience, spend an equal amount of time defining a secondary and tertiary audience for your book. You also want to market to these groups later when you want to expand book sales.

Pondering your secondary and tertiary audiences

Table 3-2 contains three examples of book concepts, their target audience, and a potential secondary audience.

Table 3-2 also gives you possible results of determining your book's secondary readers, and these questions illustrate some of the thought processes involved:

>> **Who might want to share your book?** In addition to considering that a child is a member of your target audience, think about who else might buy your book so that they can read it to a child or give it to a child as a gift.

TABLE 3-2 ## Identifying Other Readers for Your Book

Concept	Primary Audience	Possible Secondary Readers
A children's book	Children in a specific age group	Parents, grandparents, older siblings, teachers, therapists, and others who work with children
A cookbook inspired by Italian food recipes that passed down from your great-grandmother	People who regularly prepare meals for their family and who also come from an Italian heritage	Anyone who has a passion for cooking, who enjoys finding out about cuisine from different parts of the world, or who wants to pass down food-related family traditions
A romance novel about a woman who meets and falls in love with the man of her dreams	Women who are huge fans of romance novels (typically, women in their early 40s who have a college degree)	Those between the ages of 11 and 18 just discovering the genre; also, the 18 percent of regular romance novel readers who are men

>> **How is your book's content best presented?** For example, most people who use cookbooks prefer printed, full-color books, so you use this information when developing your publishing plan.

>> **What publishing format is best for your concept?** When you're deciding what formats to publish your romance novel in, by performing a few minutes' worth of added research, you can find out that, these days, e-books make up 60 percent of all romance book sales.

REMEMBER

A *tertiary audience* for a book consists of people in an established or defined group that might take an interest in your book based on its subject matter. This more peripheral audience could still help you generate book sales. For example, a tertiary audience may come from special interest groups, religious groups, people who work in a specific industry, or members of a specific association.

Gathering intel and targeting potential readers

To help you more clearly define and understand your book's potential audiences, visit a bookstore in person or online, and research what books already exist that are similar to yours in terms of topic, focus, approach and/or content. Pay attention to specific phrases or keywords used to describe a book; this plays a huge role in search engine optimization (SEO) and how easy it is for people to find your book. Also, focus on

>> **How the publishers are marketing and promoting those books, and how they define each book's respective audience:** Although the marketing and audience may seem obvious after reading a book's title and description, you can certainly get an even clearer idea if you read a few of the reader reviews published about the book and determine who wrote each review. Keep in

mind, based on a book's description and cover design, for example, you may need to extrapolate who the intended audience for the book is, but this *should* be very obvious.

>> **What book format(s) your target audience prefers reading:** For example, although younger people have grown up reading e-books and likely own a dedicated e-reader or tablet, someone over the age of 55 or 60 probably doesn't feel comfortable reading books in a digital format. That said, the older people who do use e-readers typically like the ability to adjust the typeface and point size of what they're reading.

Although you never want to exactly copy what your competition is doing to avoid plagiarism or copyright infringement issues, you can certainly use the information that you acquire for inspiration.

As a reader, whether you purchase a book from a bookstore or shop online for books, the stores (real or virtual) typically sort and display their books by category or genre, making it easy for a potential reader to find exactly what they're looking for. As an author and publisher, it's your job to properly categorize your book, which you can most easily do by first understanding what your book is about and who it will appeal to.

TIP

To help you properly define your book's category, head over to the Book Industry Study Group's Complete BISAC Subject Headings List page (www.bisg.org/complete-bisac-subject-headings-list). This page contains a list of subject headings (categories and sub-categories) that the book publishing industry uses (BISAC stands for Book Industry Standards And Communications).

Choose a category that most closely relates to the topic of your book and its content. Ultimately, when creating listings for your book through online-based booksellers, choosing the most appropriate categories can help people find your book by using that bookseller's search tool or when they're browsing based on a specific subject.

TIP

After you define your book's target audiences, use this information when planning every aspect of your book and how it will be promoted:

>> Try working something about the audience into your book's title.

>> Incorporate wording that identifies your audience in the book's description.

>> For marketing purposes, use the reader-related information that you glean when compiling a list of keywords or phrases that best describe your book.

Researching Your Target Audience

Now that you understand who you're writing for and trying to sell books to, get to know your audience through research and first-hand interactions. Figure out ways to interact with members of your target audience on social media, online, and in-person — especially if you yourself aren't a member of that demographic.

TIP

While you're writing your book and preparing your sales and marketing materials, including developing a website specifically for the book, consult with multiple people whom you consider to be your target audience. Ask them to read a draft of your manuscript and review your other materials to ensure that they find it all appealing and relatable. If you don't have people in your life — such as relatives, friends, or coworkers — who fit into your book's target audience, seek out people online or people who attend activities/events that attract people from the audience that you're trying to reach.

Even if you consider yourself to be a part of your book's target audience, still reach out to other people who are also in that group and whom you trust to provide you with honest feedback. Chances are, your mom will always say your book is wonderful (even if it's not), so seek out honest opinions from people who are less blinded by their love for you.

Engaging with people in your target audience

To solicit advice and guidance from people in your target audience, seek them out and get to know them. You can find and interact with people in your book's target audience in many ways; for example, you can

>> Reach out to family members, friends, or coworkers.

>> Join a writer's group that encourages honest and open interaction between authors.

>> Become active in an in-person book club that's comprised of people in your target audience.

>> Attend in-person events or activities that people from your target audience enjoy.

>> Interact with people online who are members of Facebook groups related to the subject matter of your book or who fit into your book's target audience.

>> Set up social media accounts for your book, and as the author, seek out and interact with people in your book's target audience.

>> Read magazines and blogs, listen to podcasts, and watch TV shows and movies that specifically cater to your book's target audience.

>> Visit and hang out at places where you know people from your target audience congregate.

>> Use Google Analytics (http://analytics.google.com) and similar online tools to determine what specific groups of people are researching or looking up information related to your book's subject matter on the Internet.

>> Reach out to known readers (after you publish your book) to glean specifics about the types of people who are actually reading your book (as opposed to people you thought would be your readers).

Facebook groups (related to every topic you can imagine) are online communities where people can connect, learn, and share with people who have similar interests. After you set up a free Facebook account, you can join an unlimited number of Facebook groups for free.

Follow these steps to easily find Facebook groups that are comprised of members you want to get to know better and interact with:

1. **Log into Facebook (www.facebook.com) by using either your personal account or the Facebook account that you've created to promote your book.**

   Chapter 17 gives you the lowdown on creating a book-specific Facebook account.

2. **Type a keyword or phrase that describes the group of people you want to interact with into Facebook's Search field at the top of your main Facebook page.**

   If you're using the mobile-device version of Facebook, click the Search button at the top-right of the page, then enter your search terms.

   Make sure that your keyword or phrase relates to a specific subject matter, interest, or characteristic that best describes potential readers.

3. **On the results page, scroll down to the Groups section.**

   Here, Facebook directs you to groups comprised of people who match your search term.

4. **Click the name of a group to explore that group's page.**

   You can also simply click Join, which appears to the right of the group in the Groups search results.

5. **If a group seems promising, click the Join Group button on its page.**

   Now, you can post your own messages, respond to posts from others, and freely engage with other group members.

The preceding steps give you a quick way to target niche audiences from the more than 2.9 billion active Facebook users worldwide (as of early 2023).

TIP

Have a clearly defined research goal in mind. When you begin researching your book's target audience to connect with and get to know this group of people better, do so based on the careful description that you created. Also, figure out exactly what you want to accomplish through your research. Determine whether you want to find someone to read a draft of your manuscript and provide feedback, or simply aim to better understand the wants, needs, interests, lifestyles, and personalities of people in your book's target audience.

Focusing on relevant keywords and phrases

After you complete the essential foundation for your book — you pinpoint the subject matter, devise a detailed content outline, and identify your specific target audience — start brainstorming a list of 15 to 25 keywords or phrases that best describe your book, its subject matter, and its audience. Then focus on incorporating these keywords and phrases when you write your book's description and any content that will be used online. This focus will help with SEO, ultimately making it easier for the right people to find your book.

>> Choose the book's title and subtitle (if applicable). See Chapter 10.

>> Write your book's description. See Chapter 10.

>> Compose the sales, advertising, and marketing copy to promote your book. See Chapters 18 and 20.

>> Use hashtags when you create posts on social media to attract more relevant attention. See Chapter 17.

>> Create listings for your book with online booksellers, such as Amazon (www.amazon.com), Barnes & Noble (www.bn.com), and Apple Books (www.apple.com/apple-books). See Chapters 14 and 15.

In Chapter 18, you can find tools to help you compile a list of relevant keywords that people in your target audience might use when looking for a book like yours online. But don't wait; for now, start compiling and writing down a list of relevant keywords and phrases that you think of on your own.

REMEMBER

Everything that you do during the entire self-publishing process should take your book's intended target audience into consideration. Never rely on just your own personal tastes, especially if you don't consider yourself to be part of your book's targeted readership. For example, if your favorite color is neon lime green, but you know your target audience is fairly conservative and at least 10 years older than you, when designing your book's cover, choose a more neutral color scheme that is more likely to appeal to your audience.

The more you know, the better your chances of success

Although brainstorming a great book concept, flushing out its detailed outline, and writing a well-researched manuscript (that someone has properly edited) are all essential for self-publishing success, writing your book with a specific goal and for a specific audience is equally important. Invest the time, resources, and energy needed to research and engage with your book's intended audience so that you can make intelligent decisions that cater to this targeted and niche group of readers.

Following Trends: Pros and Cons

At any given time, a vast number of people become obsessed with certain trends in pop culture. These trends can relate to a news event, a financial trend (such as the rise of cryptocurrency), the release of a TV show or movie, a hobby that suddenly becomes popular, a diet fad, a fashion style, the sudden popularity of a music genre or recording artist, or even the release of a new book series from a well-known author that quickly hits and remains atop the bestsellers list.

REMEMBER

According to Vocabulary.com, a *trend* is defined as "what's hip or popular at a certain point in time." A trend usually refers to a certain style in fashion, music, or entertainment, but it can extend to just about anything related to pop culture or products. Books related to boybands, dystopian fiction, specific dance styles (such as breakdancing), Beanie Babies collecting, Pokémon, the emo subculture, blogging, K-Pop music, and reality TV shows (such as *American Idol*), are all examples of topics that have been or could be popular for a relatively short amount of time.

If you're a self-published author looking for something to write about — and you want some guarantee of being able to make sales — you can find pros and cons associated with chasing and capitalizing on trends or fads:

>> **The biggest pro:** When you choose a hot trend, you know that you have a large and established audience of people interested in that topic. If you create a book that nicely capitalizes on this trend, you could sell a lot of books.

>> **The biggest drawback:** When you jump on a trend's bandwagon to exploit it for book sales, recognize that many trends disappear as quickly as they become popular. So, in the time that you spend to develop, write, publish, market, and distribute a book based on that trend, the trend could be over or falling out of favor among the masses. So by the time you're ready to sell your book, you've lost the audience.

REMEMBER

When choosing your book's subject matter, approach, and target audience, you'll likely achieve better success if you pursue an evergreen topic that has an established audience that you can easily identify. Following a trend or choosing a topic that's seasonal or that will have a limited shelf life is much more challenging because the window you have to create, publish, and sell your book is often short. And after the public latches onto another trend, sales of books that covered the now defunct trend nosedive with little or no chance for a resurgence in sales.

Self-published authors, especially those who have limited resources and budgets, should refrain from pursuing book topics that have a short (or potentially short) shelf life. Of course, you can always find exceptions to this rule, but if you choose to pursue a book that you know will have only a limited sales window, understand that you need to work quickly and market your book heavily to capitalize on that trend's popularity before the trend reaches is peak.

Chapter **4**

Equipping Yourself with the Write Stuff

B usiness executives work from offices (and golf courses); artists and musicians work in studios; and scientists work in laboratories. Each of these professions, along with countless others, requires that the person work within a special environment that's equipped with the tools they need to successfully complete their professional responsibilities. Because writing is an art form, a skillset, and a job, most writers prefer to do their work in a specialized environment. This dedicated writing space allows them to tap into their true creativity, focus exclusively on their writing, and avoid common distractions.

This chapter focuses on how to create the ideal writing environment for yourself and how to gather the right combination of tools, equipment, and resources to ensure that your writing efforts are as productive and successful as possible.

Fix It Up: Creating Your Ideal Writing Environment

Writing takes an incredible amount of focus, concentration, creativity, and (at times) research. Whether you're writing an essay, article, poem, short story, blog, or the manuscript for a full-length book, you need to focus not just on what you're trying to say, but also on how you want to say it. Unfortunately, writing doesn't have a formula or some easy, predefined steps that you can follow to ensure that your finished product is a masterpiece. You can find tools and strategies, however, that can contribute to your success.

REMEMBER

As a writer, you need to follow established rules for grammar, punctuation, and spelling. Plus, if you want your writing to be understood, you need to use words that readers can find in the dictionary. However, writing also involves creativity, organization, structure, and communication exclusively through the written word (as opposed to communication through spoken language, combined with body language and verbal intonations). Each word and sentence that you write needs to convey meaning and emotion, and help the reader form a visual in their mind's eye.

To successfully produce a well-written book and focus your talents on writing as an art form, most writers and authors find it extremely helpful to create a work environment for themselves that allows them to maximize their concentration, creativity, and writing skills. With the help of the following sections, you can create a writing environment virtually any place where you're comfortable, able to think clearly, and relatively free from distractions. That said, some writers and authors thrive on working from a busy coffee shop, airport terminal, or in a shared office workspace where they don't feel so isolated. You determine what works best for you.

Deciding where to work

The first step to creating the ideal work environment is to decide where you want to work: home, office, library, the park, an airplane, a train, coffee shop, shared workspace, or a hotel room. When you choose your location, consider your needs. Ask yourself the following questions about the space you plan to use:

>> Do I have ample space to work without feeling confined or claustrophobic?

>> Does it have appropriate lighting and climate? Can I open windows, turn on lights, and adjust the temperature as needed?

>> Is the environment clean and well organized?

>> What distractions may I encounter? Does the phone constantly ring? Do my children scream in the background? Do people constantly drop by unannounced?

>> What uncontrollable noise might I deal with? Does that noise bother me?

>> What resources and equipment do I need at my disposal? Do I have a reliable Wi-Fi or cellular data Internet connection to conduct online research, backup

files online, and use cloud-based apps as needed? Is everything I need available and within reach? (See the section "Throw Away the Hammer: Assemble the Writer's Toolbox," later in this chapter, for more about necessary tools.)

REMEMBER

The writing space where you work needs to be a place that's comfortable for you and allows you to focus on writing (without distractions). Every person has unique requirements for what constitutes an ideal writing environment. Do your best to define what works for you and then create that environment for yourself.

You can tell if you create the ideal workspace because you can be productive, stay comfortable, and be free of distractions while you work. The proof is in the pudding. If you can write and be proud of the work that you create in the time you dedicate to working, you're in good shape. If your work suffers or you're unproductive, consider modifying your workspace and environment.

Maximizing your chosen space for comfort and productivity

After you establish where you want to write (which you can read about in the preceding section), take control of your environment. Make it fit your personal taste and needs by making the space most conducive to your personal work habits.

REMEMBER

The perfect work environment should allow you to feel comfortable, relaxed, and focused on the task at hand. Make the furniture, décor, lighting, temperature, and ambiance all to your liking. Because you're going to be spending many hours at a time working in this space, pay attention to *ergonomics* (conditions that promote efficiency in a work environment), especially in terms of your desk, chair, computer keyboard, and mouse. Also, keep the environment clean, clutter free, and well organized to help boost your creativity and productivity. Consider adding one or more plants to your workspace to create a more relaxing atmosphere.

TIP

Many office supply superstores and online retailers offer ergonomic furniture specifically designed for home offices:

>> Office Depot/OfficeMax (www.officedepot.com)

>> Staples (www.staples.com)

>> IKEA (www.ikea.com)

>> Levenger (www.levenger.com)

>> Relax The Back (www.relaxtheback.com)

Concentrating on ease and convenience

While you create your work environment, figure out exactly what work-related tasks you're going to do and make sure that you have the tools, resources, and equipment that you need at your disposal:

>> **Voice/video recording:** If you're conducting phone interviews and doing research, have a way to record voice or video calls on your computer or smartphone.

>> **References and files:** You need easy access to any reference books and paper-based files.

>> **Electronics:** If you're setting up your computer and a printer, for example, you need ample electrical outlets and desk space for this equipment and someplace to store your supplies.

I go into detail on what to have on hand in the section "Throw Away the Hammer: Assemble the Writer's Toolbox," later in this chapter.

In addition to ensuring your physical comfort when working, focus on what helps you concentrate and brings about your creativity. Do you work well if you have music or TV playing in the background? Do you enjoy having a cup of coffee or a cold drink on your desk that you can sip throughout the day? Does lighting a particular aromatic candle or incense help you relax and focus? Every aspect of your environment can impact your comfort and creativity.

WARNING

Sitting incorrectly for long periods of time or having your hands at a bad angle when you're typing, can cause back, neck, arm, and wrist pain, which can lead to other injuries. Not having proper lighting may strain your eyes and cause fatigue or headaches. If you're too warm or too cold in your workspace, these factors can decrease your productivity, too.

Paying special attention to your computer setup

Even the smallest things can impact how productive and comfortable you are in your work environment. Because you'll probably use your desktop or laptop computer to write and perform online research, make sure that your monitor is large enough to fully see the application(s) you use and positioned at eye level. For example, is the monitor conducive to multitasking, where you can have your word processor and web browser open and viewable at the same time, or would you benefit from connecting two or more monitors to your computer? Ask yourself whether your setup has any potential irritations. Is there a glare from a nearby window that you find distracting? Do you like your keyboard, or does the clicking noise that it makes sound too loud and annoying?

Especially if you rely mainly on a laptop computer, you may find that using a portable monitor (as a second screen) helps your writing efforts. With this extra monitor, you can

>> Double your screen real estate so that you can multi-task much more easily.

>> Set up almost anywhere in less than two minutes.

>> Transport it easily in your existing laptop bag because portable monitors are thin and weight 2 pounds or less.

The prices of portable monitors powered by your computer that offer at least 1080p resolution cost between $150 and $500 at the time of writing — depending on its screen size, resolution, and brand.

Minimize Distractions and Drains on Your Time

When you need to concentrate and be productive, distractions can really derail your work. Multitasking is hard enough as a writer when you're trying to maintain focus, meet deadlines, be creative, and be productive at the same time.

TIP

Pinpoint what distractions you're most apt to encounter while you're trying to work. Determine, in advance, how you can control or minimize them. Also, consider how you spend your time. Answering the telephone, responding to e-mails, browsing social media, interacting with people via instant messaging, or taking too many breaks can all waste your time and keep you from your writing. I cover the most common distractions in the following sections.

Making comfort a priority

Make sure that you set yourself up with a comfortable and ergonomic desk and chair, ample lighting, and proper room temperature (or adjustable temperature). See the section "Maximizing your chosen space for comfort and productivity," earlier in this chapter, for ideas on setting up a workspace that enhances productivity. Don't forget — even what you're wearing can affect your mood and ability to concentrate. Be comfy!

TIP

If you have the budget to splurge on only one piece of home office furniture, make it an ergonomic, adjustable office chair. Many business professionals use the Herman Miller Aeron Chair (or one like it). These chairs cost a lot to purchase new — around $1,800 at the time of writing (http://store.hermanmiller.com), but you can often find a used one online (via Facebook Marketplace, for example) for between $200 and $300. Ideally, you want an ergonomically designed chair that provides the following options:

>> Swiveling

>> Adjustable height

>> Adjustable arm rests

>> Lumbar support

>> Potentially, a headrest

The chair should also be designed for someone with a height and weight similar to yours.

Crafting a practical workspace layout

When you're working, you want to have a space that's organized and doesn't require you to use extra time to get things done. Here are some good examples of poor workspace situations:

>> **Awkward location of resources:** When your printer is located across the room and you have to stand up and walk 10 feet to pick up your printouts, that's poor design — unless you intend to build in some mandatory breaks, in which case, retrieving your printout would force you to get up and take a few steps.

>> **Inefficient organization:** If you need to move around a lot to access your most important papers and reference materials, you need to rearrange your workspace so that you have your often-used resources closer and better organized.

>> **Chaotic desktop:** Don't clutter your desk or work area with tools or items that you don't use often. For example, how often do you use that stapler that's taking up space on your desktop?

Figure out what tools and equipment you need close by, and then choose a desk and related furniture that allows you to have what you need where you need it. Office supply superstores and furniture stores offer a wide range of home office desks and furniture that allow you to maximize available space. Some of the handy options include

>> **A corner desk or bookcase** that fits that otherwise unusable corner in your workspace

>> **A printer stand** that holds your printer and related paper and ink/toner at a convenient location near (but not on) your desk, but not on your desk

>> **Filing cabinets** near your desk that allow you to keep important papers nearby and well organized

>> **A shelving unit** for storing books and displaying knickknacks that would otherwise clutter your desk

Keeping resources easily available

If you need specific research materials that you don't have at your fingertips, you have to stop what you're doing, find the necessary materials, and then go back to work. This interruption may even include a trip to the local library or a search through your paper-based files for needed information. Again, I recommend using one large desktop computer monitor (which makes viewing multiple windows easy) or a portable monitor connected to your laptop computer so that you can use a word processor or other writing tool on one screen and, at the same time, conduct online research, search the web, or use other apps on the second screen (or split screen) where everything remains readable.

Taming that obsession with e-mail, web browsing, or phone calls and texts

Every day, people receive e-mails (many of which are spam or unsolicited junk). Reading and responding to those e-mails takes time. Plus, you can waste a huge amount of time browsing the web or spending time on social media (for reasons that don't involve promoting your book). Being a writer takes discipline. Unless you're doing research that pertains directly to your work, perhaps you should disconnect your computer from the Internet while you're writing.

In addition, telemarketers, friends, coworkers, relatives, and other people may call or text you throughout the day. You probably find these disruptions extremely inconvenient when you're trying to concentrate on your writing. The easiest fix for this problem is to silence your phone and/or send incoming calls to voicemail while you're writing. Then, when you take a break, check your messages and set aside time to call people back. Another option involves working late at night, but go this route only if you can sleep in the following morning.

Blocking out loud noises

Uncontrollable noise can come from any number of sources: Neighborhood traffic, an air conditioner, nearby appliances, airplanes flying overhead, construction, or neighbors, children, and dogs. Try to find a work environment that's free from these distractions or find a way to deal with them. Here a few suggestions:

>> **Close your door.** If you have children or household pets, make sure that your workspace includes a door that you can shut and lock, if necessary. (Make sure someone else is watching your kids, though!)

>> **Wear headphones or earbuds.** Consider purchasing noise-cancelling headphones or earbuds to wear while you're working. You can find these at consumer electronics stores, such as Best Buy (www.bestbuy.com), or on Amazon (www.amazon.com).

>> **Add a counter-distraction.** Playing music or the TV to drown out other noises is an option for some people; however, you may find this practice more distracting than the existing noise if you're not careful. If you're singing along with a song on the radio or trying to follow the plot of a TV show, you're probably not focused on your work.

TIP

Some authors and writers find it convenient to wear noise-cancelling Bluetooth (wireless) headphones or earbuds, without listening to music, to greatly reduce ambient noise so that they have an easier time focusing in an otherwise loud environment. Companies such as Bose, Apple, Samsung, OnePlus, and countless others make high-quality and affordable noise-cancelling headphones and earbuds.

Taking charge of your workday schedule

Whether you work in an office or at home, if other people are present, set ground rules for when you're working. For example, block out several hours per day when you don't allow any intrusions whatsoever — unless it's an emergency, of course. Consider placing a *Do Not Disturb* sign on the door so that people know not to bother you.

TIP

While you plan your writing schedule, take breaks throughout the day. Breaks can include the following:

>> **Five- to fifteen-minute breaks:** Reward yourself for reaching specific objectives, milestones, or deadlines.

>> **Eating:** Set aside time to eat a healthy meal — not just a granola bar or candy and a soda while you work.

>> **Stretching:** Your muscles get tense, especially if you sit in front of your computer for several hours straight. Make sure that you take a break to stretch your muscles. Consider taking a walk around the block (and bring your dog or children, if you have them).

Negating worries about deadlines and other obligations

Because writing is an art form, you can't rush the process. The more you write, the more comfortable you become with your work habits. Employing good prewriting practices and proper work habits can hopefully lead to meeting deadlines. Here are some practices and habits that can help keep deadline worries out of the writing process:

>> **Do your research upfront.** Before you start writing, make sure that you have your research already done. When you do so, you have the context for what you plan to write.

>> **Create a detailed outline for your book.** Doing so before you actually start writing gives you a head start and a guideline for the writing process. (See Chapter 5 for more information on outlines.) This preparedness gives you more confidence in your ability to focus on delivering the right content during each writing session.

>> **Be realistic with time management.** Don't expect to write a 30-page chapter for a book in two or three hours. Allocate the necessary time in your schedule to accomplish your daily or weekly writing goals.

REMEMBER

If you constantly think about everything else that you need to accomplish, including other personal and professional responsibilities, you may never be able to focus on the task at hand — writing. The best way to deal with this situation involves blocking out a specific amount of time every day to write, knowing that you have the rest of the day to deal with your other obligations.

Throw Away the Hammer: Assemble the Writer's Toolbox

Every job enlists certain tools of the trade to complete the project. Writing is no different. Just like carpenters rely on hammers, surgeons on scalpels, and painters on brushes, good writers need their own set of tools to help them maximize their productivity, organization, and creativity. The following sections help you gather what you need in your writer's toolbox.

TIP

Some of the tools in this chapter can also help you when you set up and run your own self-publishing business. For details on additional self-publishing business supplies, see Chapter 7.

Getting the office equipment you need

Creating the right environment to do your writing is important. (Flip back to the section "Minimize Distractions and Drains on Your Time," earlier in this chapter, for discussion on the right writing environment.) Equally crucial, you need to equip your workspace with the right tools to achieve success. In terms of office equipment and related technology, the following sections summarize what you need to get the job done right.

A desktop or laptop computer that has appropriate software

You'll likely use your computer as your primary tool for writing, page layout and design, and cover design, as well as for generating advertising, publicity, and marketing materials for your book. Depending on your work habits, choose between a Windows PC or macOS-based desktop computer (or laptop computer) based on personal preference and the other equipment you foresee using. You need to determine, in advance, how you plan to use the computer. Here are some software-related tools to consider:

>> **Word-processing applications:** Almost any Windows PC or macOS-based computer can easily run word processing software, such as Microsoft Word (www.microsoft.com/microsoft-365/word) and allow you to browse the web. Microsoft Word, which is part of the Microsoft 365 suite of applications, is the most commonly used word-processing software in the world. If you use other word-processing software, make sure that the files you create are Word-compatible so that any editor or printer can access your files.

Other programs are available for your word-processing needs, including

- *Popular, general purpose, and free word processors:* Google Docs (http://docs.google.com), Apple Pages (www.apple.com/pages), LibreOffice (www.libreoffice.org), and Open Office (www.openoffice.org) are all such applications.

  Some of these apps are cloud-based and require a continuous Internet connection to function, while others require you to download and install an application onto the device on which you plan to use it.

- *Word processors designed specifically for authors:* You need to purchase or subscribe to these applications, such as Scrivener (www.literatureand latte.com/scrivener), Novel Factory (www.novel-software.com), Ulysses (www.ulysses.app), Dabble Book Writing Software (www.dabblewriter.com), Novlr (www.novlr.com), or Novelize (www.getnovelize.com).

>> **Page layout software:** If you use print-on-demand (POD) or short-run offset printing to publish your book, you likely need to handle your own page layout and design. For this process, check out specialized software, such as Adobe InDesign (`www.adobe.com/products/indesign.html`). See Chapter 9 for more about page layout software, Chapter 12 for information on short-run offset printers, and Chapter 13 for details on POD printers.

>> **Specialized e-book applications:** You can choose from several available applications that help you write, layout, and generate professional-looking e-book files. The output files are compatible with the most popular e-readers and e-book reading applications for computers and mobile devices. Vellum (`www.vellum.pub`) is one such application, which you can read more about in Chapter 11. It's used for creating e-book files in all popular file formats.

Software for the brainstorming or research phases

Many writers and authors find mind mapping or outlining software applications useful. These applications can help you during brainstorming sessions to flesh out ideas and organize information in a way that you can easily reference when you write your manuscript. To discover specific applications available for the computer or mobile device that you use, follow these steps:

1. **Visit the app store associated with your device.**

   - Microsoft Store (Windows PC)

   - Apple Mac App Store (iMacs and MacBooks)

   - Apple iOS/iPad OS App Store (iPhone/iPad)

   - Google Play Store (Android devices)

2. **Click in its search field and enter** mind mapping **or** outlining **in that field; then click the Search button.**

   Xmind (`www.xmind.app`) is just one example of a mind mapping application available for all popular computer and mobile device platforms. Meanwhile, Plottr (`www.plottr.com`) is a tool used for fiction writers to visually plan their storylines and character arcs.

3. **Read the application's description, check it's star-based ratings and determine if the app will be useful to you.**

4. **Click or tap on the appropriate button to purchase (if applicable) and download the app onto the computer or mobile device you're using.**

When taking notes is your task

As an author, you may find it easier to take notes and jot down ideas during brainstorming sessions by using a notetaking application instead of a full-featured word processor. For this type of notetaking, you can find specialized applications, such as

» Microsoft OneNote (www.microsoft.com/microsoft–365/onenote)

» Evernote (www.evernote.com)

» Google Keep (http://keep.google.com)

» Notion (www.notion.com)

» Apple Notes (which comes preinstalled on all Macs, iPhones, and iPads)

A tablet for when you're on the go

The latest tablets, such as the Apple iPads, Samsung Galaxy Tabs, the Google Pixel tablet, and Microsoft Surface Pros, are even more portable than a laptop computer, but they have the ability to run a full-featured word processor, connect to the Internet, and also handle a wide range of other productivity, communications, and even entertainment tasks.

And when you use a tablet that has a stylus, you can handwrite, annotate, or draw directly on the screen. Plus, by adding an optional keyboard to a tablet, you gain the ability to touch-type, which can make recording your book-worthy ideas more efficient and accurate than using the tablet's virtual keyboard.

REMEMBER

Many authors find ways to use a tablet in their everyday work lives — whether it's as a notetaking or research tool, or as a full-featured word processor — when it's not convenient to use a laptop computer. For between $400 and $1,500 (at the time of writing), you can purchase a powerful tablet that has the right collection of accessories to meet your needs.

Specialized equipment for writers

When it comes to writing your manuscript, you can easily use word processing software that's running on any desktop computer, laptop computer, or tablet. However, if you also have other apps running in the background, you can get distracted by those apps' alerts, alarms, and notifications. To help writers stay focused, a small company called Astrohaus (www.getfreewrite.com) has developed two versions of portable, battery-powered devices that have a full-size tactile keyboard and a small display that's designed exclusively for distraction-free word processing by authors and writers. The Freewrite Smart Typewriter ($649) and Traveler ($499) are available from the company's website.

If you're on a very tight budget and want to purchase a laptop computer, consider a Chromebook (www.google.com/chromebook). These laptops run by using ChromeOS, a special operating system created by Google. They typically rely on a continuous Wi-Fi Internet connection to give you access to your applications, data, documents, files, and photos. These days, you can find a low-end Chromebook laptop computer starting around $200 that can run a word processor or cloud-based writing application, such as Google Docs or Microsoft Word.

Computers and mobile devices are complex machines that occasionally break down. Therefore, always maintain a current backup of your files in the cloud and/or on an external hard drive — preferably a solid-state drive (SSD) — or USB flash drive. Both of these are easy-to-use external storage for your files. Also, consider investing in the extended service plan offered by most computer manufacturers and computer retailers. If you accidentally spill coffee on your keyboard, you have to pay for the repair unless you add on the extended service agreement at time of purchase.

A printer that has handy features

Because you're a writer who needs to produce a full-length manuscript, invest in a laser printer capable of printing at least 15 to 20 pages per minute. You need this capability so that when you print chapters of your book or the entire manuscript to edit and review, printing doesn't take too long. Seek out an all-in-one laser or inkjet printer that includes the ability to print, scan, photocopy, and maybe even act as a fax machine.

Invest in a smartphone

Whether you conduct voice or video-based interviews, work with your editor over the phone, or discuss your book-printing needs with a handful of publishers, you need access to a telephone. Using a smartphone gives you the most freedom to make and receive calls, send and receive text messages, participate in video calls, manage e-mails, and browse the web from almost anywhere.

Your biggest decision: whether to go with an Apple iPhone or Android-based smartphone, such as one from Google, Samsung, or OnePlus. Base this decision on the equipment that you already use. If you use a macOS-based computer and Apple iPad tablet, stay within the Apple ecosystem and invest in an iPhone. Otherwise, feel free to go with an Android-based smartphone, which might be a bit cheaper.

When choosing a cellular service for your smartphone, go with a plan from a nationwide carrier — such as AT&T, Verizon, or T-Mobile — that offers unlimited talk, text, and data for a fixed monthly rate. Also, consider a service plan that allows the smartphone to act as a personal Wi-Fi hotspot so that you can establish

Wi-Fi Internet access for your tablet and/or laptop computer from just about anywhere.

TIP

If you want to establish your own publishing business (see Chapter 7 for details), invest in a smartphone that can handle two separate phone numbers so that you can keep your personal and business calls totally separate.

Adding tools to enhance your creativity outside the office

A variety of tools exist that writers can use to keep track of ideas, brainstorm, and stay organized. The tools in the following sections can help you organize and document your ideas whenever and wherever they pop into your head.

Notebooks and pens

Did you ever wake up in the middle of the night with a great idea that you didn't write down, and then you forgot it by the next morning? You want to kick yourself, don't you? You never know when a brilliant idea may pop into your head, so have a small notebook and a reliable pen handy, for whenever creativity strikes. Tuck away small notebooks near your bed and in your briefcase, desk, pocket, purse, or car (but don't write while driving!). Alternately, become proficient at using the notetaking app (such as Notes on an iPhone) that comes preinstalled on all smartphones and tablets.

You can also use digital notepads. These devices look like tablets, but you can use a stylus to handwrite or draw directly on the screen to create unlimited notes in custom-named virtual notebooks. Here are some examples of digital notepads that can replace a traditional paper and pen:

>> Amazon Kindle Scribe (www.amazon.com/scribe)

>> reMarkable 2 (www.remarkable.com)

>> Boox Note Air2 (http://shop.boox.com/products/noteair2)

>> Kobo Elipsa 2E (https://us.kobobooks.com/products/kobo-elipsa-2e)

Newer versions of these virtual notepads will likely be available by the time you read this book. If possible, seek out a newer model with a full-color e-ink display.

REMEMBER

In recent years, several companies have created *smart pens* that allow you to write on regular paper, but everything you write or draw is immediately converted into a digital format and transferred to your computer or mobile device, where you can view, print, edit, store, or share it. Yes, writers and authors who love technological gadgets love these tools, but they can help you create digital versions of your handwritten notes even if you aren't tech savvy. While new versions of these technologies are constantly being released, as of mid-2023, examples of these smart pens include

>> Livescribe Echo 2 (www.livescribe.com)

>> NewYes SyncPen 3 (www.newyes.com/collections/syncpen)

>> Moleskine Smart Writing Set (www.moleskine.com/shop/moleskine-smart)

A digital voice recorder

Some writers first prefer to dictate their ideas into a digital voice recorder before they start writing. Other writers record all their in-person and phone interviews to ensure accuracy. You can use your smartphone as a digital voice recorder, and if you download a proper app, you can also record phone calls or video calls.

A camera

Depending on the type of writing you do and whether you plan to incorporate photographs in your self-published book (see Chapter 5 for more about using photos), you may consider investing in a high-end digital camera, although your smartphone's built-in camera may more than adequately meet your photography needs. Ideally, take photos in the highest resolution possible. Some smartphones have main cameras capable of shooting at 50-megapixel (MP) resolution, or even up to 200MP resolution.

TIP

Many writers take photographs for their own purposes to help jog their memory of people they interview, places they visit, or events they experience. These photos may never actually get published, but they provide writers with additional documentation that they can use when writing. When you take pictures by using a digital camera or smartphone camera, you can set it to automatically record the time, date, and location where you took each photo. This *metadata* gets saved with each digital image, and you can use it to organize your digital images quickly and automatically. For example, you can use metadata to search through and find specific images (from a certain location, for example). This capability is especially important if your personal image library consists of thousands or even hundreds of thousands of images.

A dictionary, a thesaurus, and other writing reference books

As a writer or author, you rely on words to communicate. Have a dictionary and thesaurus on-hand when you're writing and get into the habit of using them. In addition to helping you better communicate with your readers, a dictionary and thesaurus can help you build your vocabulary. All word processors now include a powerful built-in dictionary and thesaurus, but some writers prefer having these reference tools on their desk and accessible in book form. You can also access Dictionary.com or Thesaurus.com using any web browser.

Additional writing tools can work in conjunction with a word processor to go well beyond just checking your spelling and grammar. For example, these applications also check for accidental plagiarism and serve as a line editor while you're writing. Here are some powerful, but easy to use apps that can help your writing:

» Grammarly (www.grammarly.com)

» ProWriting Aid (www.prowritingaid.com)

» AutoCrit (www.autocrit.com)

Even if you plan to hire a professional editor, using one of these tools can help you create a polished, easy-to-read, and error-free manuscript. I highly recommend using one of these applications with your chosen word processor.

TIP

You can access *The Associated Press Stylebook* (http://store.apstylebook.com) or the *Chicago Manual of Style* (www.chicagomanualofstyle.or) online and in print formats. Either of these guides can quickly answer common questions about writing style, formatting, punctuation, and the use of common words or terms.

A scheduling or calendar application

You can find a scheduling and time management application that can help you better manage and schedule your time built into your computer, smartphone, or tablet. However, you can also use countless other applications for project management to keep your entire self-publishing project on schedule and keep track of every task involved in the project.

Choose a scheduling/calendar app and/or a project management app that syncs data between all of your computers and mobile devices. Apple users can use the Calendar application, for example, and both Windows users and Apple users can use Microsoft Outlook. Some of the popular project management applications include

» monday.com (www.monday.com)

» Smartsheet (www.smartsheet.com)

» Asana (www.asana.com)

» Airtable (www.airtable.com)

IN THIS CHAPTER

» Figuring out the right way to address your audience

» Preparing an outline and researching your book's content

» Incorporating visual elements into your text

» Adding sections to your manuscript's beginning and end

» Securing the right releases and steering clear of plagiarism

Chapter 5

Creating a Winning Manuscript

When you first sit down at your computer, stare at a blank screen, and know that you need to come up with hundreds of pages worth of interesting, informative, entertaining, and well-written text, it's enough to give anyone second thoughts about becoming an author. Well, don't panic! When you take an organized and disciplined approach to your writing, putting together a book-length manuscript is a manageable task.

While you develop your manuscript, which ultimately becomes your published book, you have a variety of considerations. Assuming that you already know your topic, this chapter provides you with strategies for considering the needs of your audience and creating the most well-organized, informative, and entertaining manuscript possible. I also explain how to effectively research your topic, incorporate visual elements and special sections into your manuscript, obtain permissions, and avoid plagiarism.

Concentrate on Your Readers

You may have already determined the audience to which you're writing. These people are your readers. Most books, whether fiction or nonfiction, cater to a specific audience or demographic. After you specify your target readers, you also need to make sure that the content you're giving them fits their wants and needs. Chapter 3 offers more advice about identifying and focusing on your intended audience.

REMEMBER

The target audience for your book may be somewhat broad. Or your book may be targeted to a niche audience, comprised of people who have a very specific interest. Whatever the case, as the author, you have to understand not only exactly who you're writing your book for, but also what the reader hopes to get out of your book. You need to ensure that you provide that information to your readers in the most enjoyable way possible.

Choosing and fine-tuning content

To ensure that your book targets the selected audience, provides information of interest, and stays on target in terms of the content, ask yourself (and answer) these questions:

>> Specifically, what do I want to teach or convey to the reader? How will my target audience use the content that I'm sharing?

>> Am I writing something that my target audience will be interested in? Will my readers find the content well-written, useful, and/or entertaining?

>> Am I taking into account the information or knowledge that the reader already has and then building on it with my writing?

>> Do I explain key concepts in a way that my readers can understand? If I'm writing fiction, does my reader relate to the characters, plot, and subplots?

>> Do the examples, artwork, charts, or graphics that I plan to incorporate into the book help convey the information? (Flip to the section "What Meets the Eye: Adding Visual Interest to Your Manuscript," later in this chapter, for details on graphic elements.)

>> Does my story tap into the reader's imagination and entertain them?

TIP

When it comes to choosing content for your book, consider what the reader may already know, and then slowly build on that knowledge. As necessary, provide the background information that your readers need to understand fully whatever you're writing about, even if you're writing a novel.

Writing a full-length book is a process. Most writers create multiple drafts of their manuscript prior to getting it published. While you review each draft, follow these tips:

>> Rewrite sections as needed for clarity and focus.

>> Delete unnecessary information, such as irrelevant history or anecdotes.

>> Fine-tune your approach to include information that the reader needs to understand your topic.

>> Carefully analyze each chapter to ensure that the entire manuscript flows smoothly and achieves its objectives.

Who you gonna call? Ghostwriters!

If you're a recognized expert in your field but not a writer, seriously consider hiring a professional ghostwriter who will work closely with you to create your book's manuscript based on information that you provide. Any literary agent can provide referrals for experienced and previously published ghostwriters. When you see a book written by a big-name celebrity, business executive, or athlete, more times than not, a professional writer was the ghostwriter on that book. Check out Upwork (www.upwork.com) or the American Society of Journalists and Authors (www.asja.org) for info on finding a ghostwriter.

Hiring a skilled and experienced ghostwriter may not be cheap, but the results can dramatically improve the overall quality of your book and improve its chances for achieving success. When working with a ghostwriter, remember the following points:

>> **Choose a writer who has relevant knowledge and skills.** Interview ghostwriters to determine whether they understand the intended target audience. And although a talented ghostwriter may be able to write on any topic, hire someone who has knowledge of and previous experience writing about topics related to your book.

>> **Remain close and engaged.** Work closely with the ghostwriter; don't just provide basic information and content that you want in your book. Instead, work with your ghostwriter to create an extremely detailed outline and provide them with your ideas, thoughts, insight, experiences, and knowledge. Remember, the ghostwriter should have enough information to write your book in your voice.

>> **Take care to retain your author voice.** Ensure that the writer you hire communicates the information in your voice by participating in interviews with the ghostwriter during which they should ask you detailed questions pertaining to your book's content, get to know who you are, and determine how you'd like to present information.

TIP

When you think you've found the perfect ghostwriter to work with — before hiring them for the project — invest the time to introduce them to you and your goals. Then, work together to write a sample chapter that represents the project to make sure you two can work well together. Be prepared to compensate the writer for their time and initial work, regardless of whether you ultimately choose to hire them.

ChatGPT OR GOOGLE'S BARD ARE NOT VIABLE GHOSTWRITERS . . . YET

In late 2022 and into mid 2023, an evolving technology called ChatGPT (and shortly thereafter, Google Bard) got a lot of hype; the gist of the hype involved how artificial intelligence (AI) could potentially replace the need for a human writer to compose text about almost any topic.

As an author who's writing a book for other authors, I see the irony in the fact that I need to discuss how AI might replace the need for writers — and someday very well could. But short of replacing human writers, ChatGPT and evolving AI technologies could become valuable tools for writers. In fact, Microsoft will soon be incorporating AI into Microsoft Word and other applications, and other word-processing application providers will no doubt follow suit.

To further explain what exactly ChatGPT is, I went to the ChatGPT website (`http://chat.openai.com`), logged in for free by using my Google account, and at the prompt, typed, "In 200 words, describe what ChatGPT is and how it can help authors." I wanted ChatGPT to describe itself. And within seconds; here's the unedited, word-for-word text it generated:

"ChatGPT is a large language model developed by OpenAI that is designed to understand human language and generate responses that are indistinguishable from those of a human. The model has been trained on vast amounts of data and can perform a wide range of language-related tasks, including answering questions, generating text, and providing recommendations.

For authors, ChatGPT can be an invaluable tool for brainstorming, generating ideas, and refining their writing. By asking ChatGPT a question or providing it with a prompt, authors can receive instant feedback and suggestions that can help them develop their ideas and overcome writer's block.

Additionally, ChatGPT can help authors with language-related tasks such as generating headlines, summarizing articles, and proofreading their work. The model's ability to understand natural language makes it an ideal tool for authors who want to improve their writing but may not have access to professional editors or writing coaches.

Overall, ChatGPT is an innovative tool that can help authors overcome many of the challenges associated with writing. Whether an author is struggling to come up with ideas or wants to refine their language, ChatGPT can provide valuable feedback and support."

After reading this response, I then entered, "In 200 words, describe the dangers of an author relying on ChatGPT," and here's the exact text that was generated by ChatGPT, again in less than 10 seconds:

"As an AI language model, ChatGPT has the capability to generate text that can appear convincing and coherent, making it a useful tool for authors who are looking for inspiration or assistance with their writing. However, relying too heavily on ChatGPT can be dangerous for several reasons.

Firstly, ChatGPT's responses are based on patterns and trends that it has learned from its training data, which means that it can be prone to repeating biases and inaccuracies that exist within that data. Therefore, an author who relies solely on ChatGPT's suggestions may inadvertently perpetuate stereotypes, misinformation or misleading information.

Secondly, ChatGPT is not capable of understanding the nuances of human language and context, and can sometimes produce responses that are inappropriate or offensive. This can lead to legal, ethical, and reputational risks for the author if they use ChatGPT-generated content without thoroughly reviewing it.

Thirdly, relying too heavily on ChatGPT can stifle an author's creativity and originality, as it may limit their ability to develop their own ideas and writing style. Writing is a craft that requires practice, and an over-reliance on ChatGPT may prevent an author from developing the skills and techniques needed to improve their writing.

In summary, while ChatGPT can be a useful tool for authors, it should not be relied upon exclusively. Writers should exercise caution and use their own judgment when incorporating ChatGPT-generated content into their work, and should always strive to develop their own voice and style."

So at least ChatGPT is honest about describing itself and its capabilities. A lot of unknowns exist about how ChatGPT will evolve, and you can find significant controversy surrounding it. For example, the companies creating these AI-based technologies, along with state and federal lawmakers need to address and resolve important issues related to copyright, transparency, privacy, bias, and misuse while this technology continues to permeate the Internet; how people create content and communicate by using ChatGPT, Google Bard, and other AI tools is still developing. However, as authors working in the 21st century, we certainly need to become acquainted with and vigilant about this technology.

Don't Be Sketchy: Creating an Outline

An outline for a book-length manuscript can be anywhere from 1 to 20 pages in length, depending on the level of detail you get into. This phase of the writing process is so important that most major publishing houses require even their most experienced authors to submit a detailed outline for each book before they begin writing. For example, the outline for this book, *Self-Publishing For Dummies, 2nd Edition*, took up 11 pages, and I prepared it (with the help of my editing team) before I wrote the first words of the manuscript.

WARNING

Without proper planning, writers can easily get lost in their manuscript of several hundred pages and lose focus on their true objectives. A lack of focus can lead to disorganization of information, repetition, deletion of key content, and ultimately production of a manuscript that's difficult to read, understand, and enjoy.

TIP

Ensure that your manuscript is organized, flows nicely, and makes sense to the reader by creating a detailed outline *before* you actually begin writing. Also, if you've already started writing your book but find that you can't stay focused and organized, coming up with an outline may help you shape the text that you've already created and get back on track to finish your book.

Understanding an outline's importance

An outline provides a detailed overview of your book's content in just a few pages. The outline that you create divides the information that you plan to present into sections and subsections, which ultimately expand into the individual chapters and sections of your book. Working from a detailed outline forces you to consider every topic you plan to write about within your book. Create an outline for any type of book, whether fiction or nonfiction:

>> **Fiction:** The outline helps ensure that the timeline of your plot makes sense and that plot twists, subplots, or aspects of each character's development happen at the appropriate time in the story.

>> **Nonfiction:** An outline ensures that you first build a foundation of knowledge for your readers, and then, with each subsequent chapter, you appropriately build on that knowledge — one concept at a time, in an organized way, without jumping ahead or repeating ideas from earlier chapters.

Creating an outline organizes your thoughts, research, and content, but it also helps with the following items. It helps you

>> Decide what information to include within your book.

>> Place information in appropriate chapters and make the topics flow smoothly from the beginning of the book to the end.

>> Avoid repetition.

>> Remember to include key content.

>> Consider your book's page count and how much space you dedicate to each topic within each chapter or section.

>> Stay focused and take an organized approach to writing your manuscript.

Ordering your topics

Before you begin writing an outline, consider putting together a detailed list of topics and subtopics to include in your book, and then follow these steps:

1. **Write each idea, topic, or subtopic on a separate index card.**

   By keeping each idea or concept separate, you can reorganize them or build on them with ease while you plan your book's content.

TIP

   Instead of using index cards or Post-It sticky notes, you can find various computer applications and services that help with this process of segmenting topics. For example, the Scrivener software (www.literatureandlatte.com/scrivener) offers a feature-packed outlining tool for writers.

2. **Spread out your collection of index cards on a table and begin moving them around.**

   With each idea on a separate card, you can pinpoint essential information and cluster cards that contain supporting ideas, concepts, or information. You can also find applications such as NoteDex (www.notedexapp.com/index-cards) that handle the virtual index card creation and organization process.

3. **Place each card in an order that makes sense in your book.**

   While you do this placement, the content for each chapter or section within your book begins to take shape. Be willing to tinker with your outline extensively by adding and removing topics, and then moving content around, until you develop a true template for your book.

4. **Arrange your chapters in a logical order.**

   This step ensures that a reader can easily understand your book. The chapters should nicely flow from one topic to the next and build on the knowledge the reader has already gained in preceding chapters.

After you get your index cards properly grouped together, create a detailed written outline for your book (see the following section). You can organize the outline that you create in other popular notetaking apps including Microsoft OneNote (`www.microsoft.com/microsoft-365/onenote`) and Evernote (`www.evernote.com`). Microsoft Word and other full-featured word processors can also help you write and format detailed outlines.

Formatting and polishing your outline

The level of detail that you include in your outline depends on your knowledge of and comfort with the topic. The more detailed your outline, however, the more easily you can keep your manuscript well organized and ensure that you don't accidentally leave out important details, concepts, or ideas. In the following sections, I show you how to format and polish your outline.

Looking at different formats

Outlines typically are divided into A, B, C, D, and even E headings. An *A heading* might be a chapter title. Under each chapter title, record a handful of topics that you want to include within that chapter (referred to as *B headings*). Under each B heading are key pieces of information or content that relates directly to that heading or section. These subdivisions can include C, D, and even E headings, as appropriate. Depending on the topic of your book and your personal work habits, choose an outline format that best helps you organize your manuscript and supports your style of writing. Consider using one of the following styles:

>> **Traditional outline:** To create a detailed template for your book that divides information based on chapters with headings, subheadings, and sidebars. Figure 5-1 shows a traditional outline format. It uses Roman numerals for the main headings (or topics), letters for the subheadings, and then alternates between numbers and letters for the sub-subheadings.

>> **Bulleted outline:** To better organize general ideas and decide where they go within your manuscript. Instead of using Roman numerals, letters, and numbers to list headings and subheadings within an outline, some writers prefer to use bullets, as shown in Figure 5-2.

I.   Main topic, such as a chapter title ("A" heading)

    A. Sub-topic ("B" heading)
        1. Supporting information or content ("C" heading)
        2. Additional supporting information or content ("C" heading)
            a. Sub-sub topic ("D" heading)
                1. Supporting information ("E" heading)
                2. Supporting information ("E" heading)
            b. Sub-sub topic ("D" heading)
            c. Sub-sub topic ("D" heading)
        3. Additional supporting information or content ("C" heading)
            a. Sub-sub topic ("D" heading)
            b. Sub-sub topic ("D" heading)

    B. Sub-topic ("B" Heading)
        1. Supporting information or content ("C" heading)
        2. Additional supporting information or content ("C" heading)
            a. Sub-sub topic ("D" heading)
            b. Sub-sub topic ("D" heading)
            c. Sub-sub topic ("D" heading)
        3. Additional supporting information or content ("C" heading)
            a. Sub-sub topic ("D" heading)
            b. Sub-sub topic ("D" heading)

II.   Main topic, such as a chapter title ("A" heading)

    A. Sub-topic ("B" heading)
        1. Supporting information or content ("C" heading)
        2. Additional supporting information or content ("C" heading)
            a. Sub-sub topic ("D" heading)
            b. Sub-sub topic ("D" heading)
            c. Sub-sub topic ("D" heading)
        3. Additional supporting information or content ("C" heading)

    B. Sub-topic ("B" heading)
        1. Supporting information or content ("C" heading)
        2. Additional supporting information or content ("C" heading)
            a. Sub-sub topic ("D" heading)
            b. Sub-sub topic ("D" heading)
            c. Sub-sub topic ("D" heading)
        3. Additional supporting information or content ("C" heading)
            a. Sub-sub topic ("D" heading)
            b. Sub-sub topic ("D" heading)

FIGURE 5-1: A traditional outline format features Roman numerals, letters, and numbers.

CHAPTER 5 **Creating a Winning Manuscript**   77

- Main topic, such as a chapter title

    - Sub-topic
        - Supporting information or content
        - Additional supporting information or content
            - Sub-sub topic
                - Supporting information
                - Supporting information
            - Sub-sub topic
            - Sub-sub topic
        - Additional supporting information or content
            - Sub-sub topic
            - Sub-sub topic

    - Sub-topic
        - Supporting information or content
        - Additional supporting information or content
            - Sub-sub topic
            - Sub-sub topic
            - Sub-sub topic
        - Additional supporting information or content
            - Sub-sub topic
            - Sub-sub topic

- Main topic, such as a chapter title

    - Sub-topic
        - Supporting information or content
        - Additional supporting information or content
            - Sub-sub topic
            - Sub-sub topic
            - Sub-sub topic
        - Additional supporting information or content

    - Sub-topic
        - Supporting information or content
        - Additional supporting information or content
            - Sub-sub topic
            - Sub-sub topic
            - Sub-sub topic

FIGURE 5-2: This outline uses bulleted items to organize information.

Fine-tuning the details

Invest significant time developing your outline and then fine-tuning it. Don't be afraid to move portions of your outline around, and add or delete sections, until you create a document that serves as a solid foundation for writing the actual manuscript. Here are some other tips to help you polish your outline:

- >> Consider adding actual chapter titles, section headings, and subheadings to help you create a more comprehensive overview. This practice also helps you track which elements within your manuscript belong where.

- >> List specifically where supporting elements of your manuscript go, elements such as sidebars, interviews (quotes), photographs, examples, references, statistics, illustrations, graphs, charts, and checklists.

- >> Think about and record how many pages of your book you want dedicated to each chapter, topic, or section, keeping in mind the total number of pages you plan for your completed manuscript.

- >> Try to keep your manuscript well balanced. Make all your chapters similar in length. (When chapter lengths vary too widely, perhaps you need to look at subdividing or regrouping topics in your outline.) This similar-length-chapters rule isn't steadfast, but it does help with the book's flow. This concept applies to fiction, as well — although, with fiction, focus on making sure that your story flows smoothly and engages the reader.

- >> If you're writing fiction, list what happens in each chapter, what plot twists you introduce, and the relevant details about characters.

TIP

Find a handful of people (say, three or four) who are knowledgeable about your book's topic and have them review your outline and provide feedback. Obtaining someone else's perspective may help you develop a more thorough outline. The more work you do now in terms of organizing and choosing the content for your book, the easier you make the actual manuscript writing process. Unlike the Ten Commandments, your outline isn't etched in stone. You're free to make changes while you go. But, when you make changes, ensure that they make sense when considering the big picture. And don't introduce unnecessary repetition.

Dig for Facts: Doing Research

Even if you're the world's most renowned expert in your field, you may find filling a book with interesting, informative, and accurate information a huge challenge. Either prior to writing your book or while you write, you may need to conduct research and combine that information with your own knowledge and experience in order to create the best possible book.

If you're writing anything that's technical in nature, you especially want to convey accurate information. Even when writing fiction, research helps your story be more believable. Bestselling authors, such as Tom Clancy, Dan Brown, and John Grisham, often credit a handful of experts in their book's respective acknowledgments. These authors rely on experts to provide some of the technical details that allow their fictional stories to be more realistic.

The five popular methods for doing research include

>> Accessing online resources

>> Visiting the library and reading books, magazines, newspapers, and newsletters

>> Buying and studying books and magazines that relate to your topic

>> Seeking out and interviewing experts

>> Listening to podcasts or reading blogs by experts

TIP

Online research can involve using a search engine, such as Google (www.google.com), to discover websites, articles, blogs, podcasts, and other information that's relevant to your book. Before relying on information that you find online, make sure that the content comes from a credible source and that the information is timely and accurate. As the technology continues to evolve, you might soon be able to use ChatGPT or Google Bard, for example, as a research tool, but not necessarily as a writing tool. However, be sure to check all facts, figures, and statistics that the AI tool gathers on your behalf.

Staying away from bad info

Avoid embarrassing errors in your text. No matter what type of research you do, make sure that the various sources you use are timely, reliable, and accurate. Here are some ideas for vetting researched content:

>> Research the origin of each source and whether or not it's reputable and unbiased.

>> Confirm any facts and figures with other sources; find at least one alternative source that supports this information.

>> Make sure that you don't use outdated information by checking the date and time that the source material was posted and looking for later contradictory information.

Keeping track of your resources

Keep one master list of all your reference materials and resources so that you can find and refer back to them later as needed. For each source that you use, gather the following information:

- Title of the article, book, publication, blog, podcast, or reference work

- Copyright or publication date for each printed or online source; specific page numbers, website URLs, or location of information that you use

- Name and contact information for the authors, experts, or other people interviewed

- Date and time of the interviews (see the following section for specifics about all the interview intel to gather)

- Written permission to use the information in your book, if applicable (see the section "Keep It Legal: Obtaining Permission to Use Other People's Materials," later in this chapter)

TIP

When using the Internet as a reference tool, print out the information that you use and keep a file of those printouts. Make sure that the website address and date is printed on the various pages. (You can also create a PDF version of a webpage by using your favorite web browser, and then store that PDF on your computer or mobile device.)

Relying on experts for solid information

If you want to include the most timely and cutting-edge information possible, track down a handful of recognized experts on the topic that you're writing about and interview those people. When conducting an interview for your book, make sure that you gather the following information:

- The interviewee's name (verifying the correct spelling) and a brief biography that outlines the expert's credentials

- How the interviewee wants to be credited within your book, including their company's name and exact job title (if applicable)

- The source of any statistics or research data, for example, that the interviewee provides during the interview

- A signed release stating that you have the interviewee's permission to include excerpts from the interview within your book

- The expert's contact details (e-mail and phone number) in case you have follow up questions or need to clarify something

TIP

Whether you're an accomplished journalist or a first-time author, record all your interviews. Before you start recording, however, make sure that the interviewee is okay with being recorded. Having a recording to refer to while you're writing helps ensure proper quotes in your book and accurate context of the conversation.

You have many ways to track down experts on virtually any topic. For example, journalists and authors alike often use an online-based service called HARO, which stands for Help A Reporter Out (www.helpareporter.com). After you sign up as a journalist (which you can do for free), you can publish queries on the site looking for experts on specific topics. Describe exactly the type of expert you're looking for (someone who has related work experience, for example) and what you need from that expert (such as a 30-minute phone interview). The service then e-mails your request to thousands of public relations firms, companies, and organizations that have a roster of experts on hand. Typically within hours, the experts you need start contacting you based on your query.

What Meets the Eye: Adding Visual Interest to Your Manuscript

As soon as you begin creating the outline for your manuscript, think about what kind of graphic elements you can include for visual appeal. You can acquire and place the graphic elements within the manuscript while you write or during the final page layout and design process. *Note:* After you lay out the pages, however, adding or deleting large amounts of text or graphics requires major layout and design changes, which can cost you time and money.

You can use specific visual elements in your book to help organize information for your readers. Depending on your topic, approach, and applicability, consider using the following elements (which don't apply for a novel) in your book:

>> **Sidebars:** A *sidebar* is a subsection of a chapter that allows you to go off on a tangent without interrupting the reader's train of thought. Sidebars are used in nonfiction books to provide examples, short anecdotes, short interviews, or other information that doesn't directly flow with the main body of the manuscript. But the sidebar does relate to the topic at hand and tends to be short — between a quarter of a page and one full page. (For an example, check out the sidebar, "ChatGPT isn't a viable ghostwriter . . . yet," in this chapter.)

>> **Lists:** You can create a bulleted list, like the one you're reading right now. This kind of list gives you an easy way to communicate information to the reader. Items in a list can be short and concise, and you can write them in full sentences or sentence fragments. Use a numbered list if the reader must follow the elements in a specific order (you can find an example of this sort of list in the section "Ordering your topics," earlier in this chapter) or use bullets to emphasize key pieces of information.

>> **Checklists:** Use a checklist as a tool to help readers make sure that they follow everything in a list of steps or items they need to accomplish. The reader can check off boxes when they complete steps or items.

>> **Charts and graphs:** If you want to communicate a lot of numbers or statistics, a chart or a graph provides a visual, easy-to-understand way to showcase the data. You can create a wide range of charts and graphics by using a spreadsheet program, such as Microsoft Excel, depending on your needs. You can also hire a professional graphic artist to create visual elements for your book.

>> **Graphics:** Graphics, such as illustrations or drawings, communicate information or simply add visual appeal. If you consider incorporating graphics, refrain from using so many that your final laid-out book pages look cluttered. Unless you have strong artistic skills, have a professional artist create the illustrations and drawings that you use. The graphics must look professional and help communicate important information.

>> **Graphic icons:** Throughout this book, you can find graphic icons called Remember, Tip, and Warning. You can use graphic icons within your book, if applicable, to draw the reader's attention to something specific. A graphic artist can help you design these visual elements for your book.

>> **Photographs:** Often, you can most easily convey information through the use of a photograph. Depending on the type of book you're writing, you can often include black and white images within the main body of your book. Some self-publishing options allow you to use full-color photographs, as well. You can take photographs yourself, purchase images from a stock photo agency, or hire a professional photographer to create customized photos for you (each option depends on your needs and your budget).

If you're on a tight budget, consider using images from a stock photo library. To find a library of stock photography, use any Internet search engine and enter the search phrase *stock photo library*. The following list includes four examples of stock photo libraries:

- Getty Images (www.gettyimages.com)

- Shutterstock (www.shutterstock.com)

- iStockphoto (www.istockphoto.com)

- Adobe Stock (http://stock.adobe.com)

When you want to incorporate photographs, charts, or graphics in your book and refer to those elements within the main body of your text, use figure numbers and captions to identify each graphic or image. Figure numbers typically begin with the chapter number, followed by a dash or period, and are in chronological order. The first image in Chapter 3, for example, is labeled Figure 3-1 or Figure 3.1. The second is Figure 3-2 or Figure 3.2, and so on. Below each image, include a one-sentence (or shorter) caption, identifying what the reader's looking at.

Put the Pieces Together: Examining Other Book Elements

If you look at any book — fiction or nonfiction — it typically contains special sections. Many of these sections are standard. Which elements you include within your book depends on your personal preferences and the type of book that you're writing. I cover all the special elements, in order of their appearance in a book, in the following sections.

Copyright page

The *copyright page* lists all the legal information pertaining to the publication of the book, including details about its copyright, publisher, International Standard Book Number (ISBN), Library of Congress Control Number (LCCN), and trademarks used in the book. The copyright page usually appears on a left-handed page, directly after the inside title page.

Author acknowledgments and dedications

The *author acknowledgments* section of your book typically thanks anyone and everyone who helped you write and publish the book. It's also where the author can thank loved ones, friends, coworkers, and even their dog. This section can contain only a few sentences, or it can go up to one page long — but one to two paragraphs is standard. Don't forget to thank the reader for buying your book (not required, but a nice touch!).

It's also a common (but not required) practice for an author to include a dedication within their book as a way of honoring someone. Whether you include a separate dedication is a personal decision. If you do add a *dedication*, it can appear on a separate page and say something as simple as, "For my mom" or "In loving memory of my grandmother [*insert name*]." There are some authors (and I am one of them) who have dedicated one or more of their books to a beloved pet.

Table of contents

A *table of contents* is simply a list of the chapters and major sections within your book and their respective page numbers in a directory-like listing. A table of contents makes it easy for readers to find what they're looking for and skip directly to that section or chapter. Your table of contents can list just your chapters and related page numbers, or it can include subtopics to provide a more comprehensive listing about what's in your book, like this book's detailed Table of Contents.

TIP

E-books can contain hyperlinks within the content, including within the table of contents. When readers tap or click on the link, they quickly jump to a specific location or page within your book. If you plan to publish e-books, you can and should utilize this feature.

Foreword and/or preface

A foreword is typically written as an introduction to your book, but someone other than the main author writes it, such as a famous person, another author, or a well-known expert. In terms of length, a foreword can be one to five pages, and it should contain information about what's included within the book. It can also describe some of the reasons why the book may be of interest to the reader. When you have someone write your foreword, obtain written permission from the foreword writer (see the section "Keep It Legal: Obtaining Permission to Use Other People's Materials," later in this chapter).

A preface contains much of the same information as a foreword does, except that the book's author typically writes the preface. The preface sets the tone of the book and tells the reader what to expect. A book, whether fiction or nonfiction, can have both a preface and a foreword; however, this practice doesn't happen too often. If you have a foreword in your book, you can add any messages for your reader within the acknowledgements or introduction sections without including the preface, too.

Introduction

An *introduction* introduces the content and structure of your book. You can write the introduction in first person so that you, the author, communicate directly with the reader. Don't confuse the introduction with the preface; the intro is typically longer and more detailed than is a preface. The length typically runs one to four pages, but it can be as long as the other chapters in your book if you want.

Here's what to include in your intro for different types of books:

>> **Nonfiction:** Your introduction precedes Chapter 1 and provides the reader with a general overview of what the book is about, who's reading it, and what it contains. The intro can also include a summary of core knowledge that readers need prior to reading your book.

>> **Fiction:** You can use the introduction to set the stage and provide readers with background stories, character information, or plot details that they need before the actual story begins.

Appendixes

Found at the end of a book, an *appendix* can provide a list of resources or the equivalent of a short chapter offering information that relates to your book's topic but that didn't easily fit into the main body of the book. The appendixes can also summarize important information and provide worksheets or additional checklists for the reader.

Appendixes typically appear in nonfiction books, rather than fiction. If you want to incorporate appendixes into your book, plan to have at least three to five of them (although this isn't a steadfast rule). Keep each appendix short (no longer than two or three pages). They're typically titled Appendix A, Appendix B, Appendix C, and so on, although each can also have a short title.

Bibliography

If you rely on many sources of information while writing your book, include a detailed listing of your sources at the end of the book in the form of a formatted *bibliography.* Follow traditional formatting based on the type of source that you quote, excerpt, or paraphrase as a reference.

TIP

The Chicago Manual of Style (University of Chicago Press) offers guidelines that the publishing industry commonly uses for formatting bibliographies. Visit www.chicagomanualofstyle.org for more information.

Glossary

Found at the end of some nonfiction books, a *glossary* is a list of terms and their definitions. The length of a glossary varies, based on the number of terms you want to explain. This section provides a quick reference for readers, so try to keep your definitions short. A glossary is handy if your book contains a lot of technical terms that the reader needs to know to better understand and use the content in your book. Italicize the words that appear in the glossary to indicate to the reader that the term is defined elsewhere.

Index

An *index* is a detailed listing of keywords and topics featured within a nonfiction book. Each keyword also has a specific page reference (or references) where readers can find related information in the book. An index has far more detail than a table of contents (see the "Table of contents" section, earlier in this chapter). Putting together an index takes a lot of time, but your readers can see it as a valuable resource to find specifics quickly within your book.

REMEMBER

Most companies that offer self-publishing services, including print-on-demand (POD) publishers/printers, provide an indexing service for an additional fee. (Flip to Chapter 13 for details on these companies.)

About the author

Some fiction and nonfiction authors like to dedicate an *about the author* page (either in the beginning or end of the book) that includes detailed information about themselves, such as a picture, background, education, company or employer, credentials, or other personal details. Within this section, you can also promote your personal or company website, disclose an email address (so that readers can contact you directly), and share your social media usernames (so that readers can subscribe and follow you on Facebook, Twitter, Instagram, TikTok, and/or LinkedIn, for example).

The about the author section of your book provides more detail than the short paragraph that you include about yourself on your book's back cover. (See Chapter 10 for details about creating your book's front and back covers.) If you're publishing a hardcover book, you can place the about the author information on the book's jacket.

Keep It Legal: Obtaining Permission to Use Other People's Materials

Anytime you incorporate someone else's words, writing, artwork, photographs, or original ideas into your writing, not only do you need to give proper credit where credit is due, but you must also obtain the necessary permission, in writing, from the copyright owner of that material. The written permission that you obtain can be in the form of a *standard release* (a legal document that any lawyer can create for you) or a simple letter stating that you have permission to use the material in your book. Make sure that the letter you obtain spells out exactly how, when, and where you use the material, and have all parties sign and date the letter.

TIP

Consult a lawyer who specializes in copyright laws for guidelines about what specifically you need to do to protect yourself from legal problems after your book is published. Generally, you want to obtain permission for anything you plan to use in your book that's copyrighted, trademarked, or patented. You can find a reputable copyright attorney by contacting your state's Bar Association, for example.

Authorizing interviews

Information from interviews can add valuable text and credibility to your book, but make sure to properly recognize the interviewees in the text and get their okay to include content from the interview. Include the name of the person you interviewed and their likeness (if applicable) within your book. Check out "Dig for Facts: Doing Research," earlier in this chapter, for more details on interviews.

Firming up the foreword

If you ask someone else to write the foreword for your book, make sure to obtain written permission from the writer to use their name and words within your book. Simply draw up a basic release or a letter stating that you have permission to use their words and name in your book, and then have the foreword writer sign the agreement.

Permitting photographs

Depending on the situation, using photographs within a book can be a bit tricky from a legal standpoint, unless you take the photographs yourself and have a signed release from any person (or people) featured within each photograph. If you use someone else's photos, you need the photographer's permission, as well as permission from any people in the photo. If the photo depicts someone's private property, make sure to secure permission from the property owner to use the photograph, even if you took the actual picture.

TIP

If you use stock photos (see the section "What Meets the Eye: Adding Visual Interest to Your Manuscript," earlier in the chapter), for a low flat fee, you can use images without the need for formal releases or the fear of copyright infringements. Aside from photographs, you also need permission to use any type of copyrighted artwork within your book. This material includes drawings, graphics, logos, charts, illustrations, or icons that someone else created.

Concerning the concept of fair use

Depending on what type of material you want to use within your book, if you provide the appropriate credit, you may be able to use copyrighted content without obtaining written permission. This concept is called fair use and applies when you use a small portion of another source (no more than 300 words). You're also allowed, from a legal standpoint, to quote information from press releases issued by companies or individuals. To find out more about fair use, check out this resource: www.copyright.gov/fls/fl102.html.

You're not a copier: Avoiding plagiarism

Plagiarism occurs when you use someone else's words, ideas, or materials and call them your own without giving the person you took the material from proper credit. This practice amounts to stealing. *Remember:* In the publishing world, the offense of plagiarism is a major no-no and can lead to costly lawsuits and also destroy your professional reputation.

Properly document and credit your source(s) whenever you refer to or make use of any of the following information within your book:

>> Quotes from another book, a newspaper or magazine article, a blog or podcast, a TV or radio show, lyrics from a song, a web page, an advertisement, or someone's words from any other published or electronic medium

>> Quotes from someone you interviewed, either in person or on the phone

>> Quotes from someone that you heard while attending a press conference, lecture, or speech

>> Reproductions of any type of artwork or graphic image

You *don't* commit plagiarism when you write about your own ideas, observations, experiences, and knowledge, or when you form your own conclusions about a subject matter or topic. You also can make full use of what's considered common knowledge or generally accepted facts.

Chapter **6**

Fine-Tuning Your Work with Careful Editing

Wut wood you due if you purchased a book that wuz full of errors? Wood you still respect wut the author had to say? Probably not!

A good writer not only strings together the right combination of words, sentences, and paragraphs in their work, but also ensures that these structures adhere to proper grammatical, spelling, and punctuation rules (or break those rules consciously to convey meaning to the reader). Although authors should edit their own work carefully before their book goes to press, they should also have the text professionally edited.

In addition to using text-checking software such as Grammarly (www.grammarly.com), ProWriting Aid (www.prowritingaid.com), or AutoCrit (www.autocrit.com), you absolutely need to have a professional and experienced (human) editor proofread your manuscript *before* the layout and design process, and then one more time just before the book actually gets published. This chapter discusses why your book needs good editing, provides an overview of the author's and editor's roles in the editing process, and explains how to hire a freelance professional editor for your book project.

A Bird's-Eye View of the Editing Process

When you hire a freelance editor, make sure that the editor can and will edit both the original manuscript that you provide, as well as the *galleys* (laid out pages) before they go to press. At a major publishing house, two different people usually perform these functions. The editor edits the original manuscript, and then a proofreader reviews the final pages before publication. Keep in mind that you find different editor titles in the publishing industry; each title indicates a different editorial focus. For example

>> **Line editor:** Proofreads the manuscript line-by-line, focusing on style, syntax, and use of language (word choice) to make sure the manuscript uses tight sentence structure, proper vocabulary, and a voice that's easy to understand and relatable

>> **Developmental editor:** Focuses on the manuscript as a whole, ensuring that it's well-organized and that each chapter or section flows smoothly to the next

>> **Copy editor:** Focuses on spelling, grammar, and language (for example, the English language, if the book is being written in English) to ensure their proper usage

When it comes to self-publishing, although these three editor roles apply different skills to perfect an author's manuscript, you should be able to find one freelance editor who can handle all of these tasks.

WARNING

A poorly edited manuscript can destroy a reader's appreciation and enjoyment of your work, and it can take away from the overall professionalism of the publication. For a book to achieve its objectives, a talented writer should author it, and at least one equally talented editor should review and adjust it. Authors and editors bring together unique skills and often work as a close-knit team.

Just like writing is a skill, so is editing. Editing requires strong knowledge of grammar and punctuation rules and a command of the English language (or whatever language you plan to publish the book in). It also requires extreme attention to detail because an editor must review every line of the manuscript. Without this proper editing pass, a book can easily contain a wide range of errors. While you review your manuscript, here are some common errors that you, the software you use, and your human editors should look out for:

>> **Factual errors:** For example, incorrect names, phone numbers, addresses, quotations, statistics, dates and times, and website URLs.

>> **Grammatical errors:** Including improperly matched subjects and predicates.

>> **Improper page numbering:** This error can show up after layout when content is added or removed from your manuscript, or if content is moved around within chapters or sections of your book.

>> **Improper use of punctuation:** For example, leaving the comma out of a compound sentence.

>> **Mismatched figures and captions:** May happen when figures are added or deleted late In the writing and editing process.

>> **Mistakes in chapter titles or subtitles:** For example, when content is reorganized within the manuscript, but titles or subtitles are not updated accordingly.

>> **Page layout and design errors:** Such as the wrong typeface, type size, or paragraph formatting. For example, having the fonts (typeface, size, and style) vary between the *same elements* can mess up the overall appearance of the pages; one chapter title should look like the next chapter title, top level headings should look alike, and so on.

>> **Incorrect references:** Pointing to specific page numbers, figures, or chapters that don't contain the content you reference.

>> **Spelling mistakes or "wrong word" typos:** Common misspellings (such as *seperate* rather than *separate*) or using a wrong word that's spelled correctly but not what you intended (for example, *they're* instead of *their*).

>> **The accidental deletion of content:** Can happen when either the author or editors are reviewing the text and accepting or rejecting changes.

>> **Writing style mistakes:** Such as constantly switching between past and present tense or first and third person.

>> **Inconsistencies in fiction storylines:** When it comes to details about characters, plots, and subplots.

>> **Long sentences and paragraphs:** You can (and should) break up these long chunks of text in order to make your book more straightforward, objective, and easy to understand.

Editing your own work first

As an author, you have a responsibility to review your manuscript several times before turning it over to a professional editor. During one readthrough, focus on content and make sure that the text flows smoothly. When you read it the second and third times, focus more on the quality of the writing; on the wording you use; and on correcting spelling, grammatical, and punctuation mistakes.

REMEMBER

You can effectively use software applications such as Grammarly (www.grammarly.com), ProWriting Aid (www.prowritingaid.com), or AutoCrit (www.autocrit.com) during both the writing and self-editing phases to help catch manuscript errors. These tools became available just a few years ago, but today, they're indispensable aids used by writers and authors.

Follow these steps to focus your editing efforts:

1. **Create a double-spaced printout of each chapter.**

   You often can much more easily edit a hard copy of your work than review it on a computer screen. The double-spaced format allows room for marking your corrections or annotating the document.

2. **Grab a red pen (or any other contrasting color from your printout color) that you can use to make corrections and start reading.**

   When you go back to make the corrections in your text file by using a word processor, you want to easily spot your corrections on the edited hard copy pages.

3. **Edit one chapter or section of the book at a time.**

   Editing takes time and requires your total focus. If you find your mind wandering or you're getting tired, take breaks in between chapters and continue the editing process later. Never attempt to edit your entire book in one sitting — even if it's a children's book or poetry book that contains just a few hundred words of text. Often, when authors review their own work and aren't properly focused, they miss errors because they know (in their minds) what the text is supposed to say — so they don't pay as close attention to what the text on the page actually says.

4. **After you review your entire manuscript and mark up the pages with your edits, corrections, and changes, incorporate them into your book's electronic document by using your word processor.**

   When you enter each correction or edit, review it and make sure that it works in the context of the manuscript. This process of transferring your edits from paper to electronic format provides you with an additional opportunity to improve the overall quality of your work.

5. **Run the word-processed file through a grammar checking application to make sure that no new problems arose based on your changes.**

   These applications include Grammarly, ProWriting Aid, and AutoCrit.

6. **Create a fresh printout and review it again.**

    Each time you review your work, you may think of potential improvements that you can make to the content or flow of the manuscript. Perhaps you can think of additional examples to include or realize that a specific section is out of place or doesn't really belong in the book after all.

TIP

Working with a professional editor can help you make sure that you don't second guess yourself as an author and wind up over-editing or becoming too critical of your own work. One of the skills you need to develop as an author is knowing when to consider your work completed; you can then turn over the manuscript to an editor and move forward with the production process of your book. If you know what you intended to say, believe you have conveyed your thoughts clearly and accurately, and are generally pleased with how the manuscript turned out, then it's probably ready to be professionally edited.

WARNING

Never rely exclusively on your editor to fix all the mistakes in your manuscript, especially those relating to the accuracy of information. Most editors focus primarily on spelling, punctuation, and grammatical and formatting mistakes, as well as structural and organizational issues, as opposed to actual content-related issues. For checking facts, consider hiring a professional fact-checker or *technical editor* (although not every book requires a technical editor). I explain the job of a technical editor in the section "Do you also need a technical editor?" later in this chapter.

Understanding an editor's responsibilities

The editor focuses on the minute and technical details of a manuscript, but also maintains perspective for the bigger picture. Even experienced writers sometimes make different types of mistakes (such as repeating information or including contradictory material) and lose a sense of their book's overall structure; a good editor can step in and help bring the manuscript back on track.

Typically, you don't hire an editor based on their knowledge of the manuscript's subject matter. Instead, hire them based on their knowledge of written language and how to best use it. The editor should understand the publishing process and what you need to transform a manuscript into a professionally published book.

Therefore, the editor doesn't need expertise in the subject matter of the book (that's your job) — although if they have a basic knowledge of the subject, they can make suggestions on how to clarify key ideas or identify potential accuracy-related errors. You're the expert in terms of the content and information that you want to convey; look to your editor as an expert in making sure that you present the information in the best way possible.

Here are a few editor responsibilities:

>> Reviewing your manuscript sentence-by-sentence, and fixing the spelling, punctuation, and grammatical mistakes.

>> Ensuring the structure and organization of the entire manuscript has a nice flow and rhythm. Checking the manuscript's continuity in terms of the information provided, whether you're writing fiction or nonfiction.

>> Making sure that readers can easily understand your manuscript and that the writing style (your voice as a writer) is straightforward and appropriate for the intended audience.

>> Objectively assisting the writer in fixing problem areas of the manuscript before it goes to press.

>> Certifying that the finished product truly welcomes the reader. A good book should draw the reader into its subject, and to reach that goal, the writer and editor both need to be aware of what the audience expects and needs.

REMEMBER

An editor needs to make sure that you provide all information in a logical sequence so that the reader can understand it. Even if a book is easy to read, the subject matter isn't necessarily simple. A well-written and edited book can take extremely complex or technical information and clearly state it for the reader.

Working efficiently with your editor

All authors and editors have their own style for how they work. So when you begin working with the editor you hire, be prepared to provide them with a word-processed file (created by using Microsoft Word or a word processor that's capable of creating Word-compatible documents). Also, try to ensure that you and the editor are using the same version of the word processor. (This is not absolutely necessary, but it ensures against file compatibility errors, especially when it comes to formatting).

Next, develop a plan for how you want the editor to actually edit the work. Create a plan that ensures ample time for the editor to properly edit the manuscript, and then proofread the galleys again, before you send the book off to the printer or publish it in e-book form. As part of your plan, you and the editor should discuss, in advance, how edits, queries, and communication between author and editor will be handled within the manuscript itself. Be sure you take full advantage of features that track changes and allow commenting, which are built into most popular word processors.

WARNING

If you wait until after you lay out and design the interior of your book to have an editor review it for the first time, you face a rough patch in the self-publishing process. If the editor makes any significant edits or styles changes, or recommends moving content around, these changes can often mean having to redo the entire page layout. This unwelcome situation can cost you in both time and money, even if you're using the latest page layout software, such as Adobe InDesign (www.adobe.com/products/indesign), and working with a skilled graphic designer.

TIP

When a professional editor corrects your manuscript, they often use special symbols and terms associated with publishing. The following website, NY Book Editors, provides a listing of popular editing terms and symbols: www.nybookeditors.com/2013/06/copyediting-marks. Make sure that you understand the editor's comments and corrections — you can always just ask for clarification — before deciding whether to implement them.

After your editor reviews your manuscript for the first time, don't be surprised if they come back with many proposed changes. You're probably extremely attached to your work, but you need to trust the editor enough to allow them to improve your text. These suggestions aren't a personal attack on your writing skills. The editor is simply doing their job: transforming your manuscript into the most professionally written book possible.

The Nitty-Gritty of Hiring an Editor

Hiring your book's editor(s) and proofreader (who can all ultimately be the same person) are important steps in the publishing process. The following sections help you hire the perfect editor(s) for your book and develop a strong and productive working relationship with each of them.

Hiring an editor to optimize timing

Avoid waiting until the last minute to hire your editor, or you can wind up having difficulty finding someone who has time to take on your project or who has to rush to get your manuscript edited. Your level of writing experience can help determine the optimal time to hire your editor. Consider these two divergent, but effective, scenarios and choose an approach that works best for you and the editor:

>> **If you're a first-time author or feel that your writing skills don't meet professional standards,** you probably want to hire an editor early in the writing process and submit individual chapters to the editor as you finish them. This scenario, called *trickling chapters,* allows more time for the editor

to provide you with feedback on the submitted chapters so that you can keep your manuscript organized and properly structured. By receiving feedback from your editor while you're writing, you can cut down on the edits and rewrites that later chapters may need before the book goes to press.

REMEMBER

>> **If you're confident in your writing ability,** and you have other people (such as friends, family members, coworkers, and professional colleagues) who can review your manuscript while you're writing to provide impartial and objective feedback, you can hold off on working with an editor until your manuscript is complete.

After you finish the manuscript, allow up to several weeks for your editor to properly review the entire project and complete the initial editing process. Depending on how much other work your editor has, the length of your manuscript, and the quality of your writing, allocate three to five weeks in your overall publishing timeline for proper editing of the initial manuscript. Then, after whoever is handling your page layout and design work for the interior of your book has created the *galleys* (meaning this person has designed and laid out the pages of your book), give the editor ample time to review the entire book again before you turn it over to the printer or e-book publisher.

WARNING

If an editor tells you that they can edit your entire manuscript in a few days or over a weekend, run in the opposite direction as fast as you can. Find someone else. The editing process takes time and careful attention to detail. You don't want to rush or cut corners on this step. Proofreading the galleys, however, should go much more quickly than the editing because, theoretically, you and the editor have already found and corrected all of the major errors.

Planning for the cost

Like with any professional service, when you hire an experienced editor, you're paying for time, skills, experience, and knowledge. Plan on spending anywhere from $1,500 to $5,000 to have your book-length manuscript professionally edited. A book-length manuscript can range anywhere from 50,000 to 100,000 or more words, depending on the type of book. A children's book, cookbook, or poetry book may be significantly shorter.

REMEMBER

Some editors charge a flat rate for a project, others charge an hourly fee for their time, and still others charge by the word for their editing services. (The price of per-word editing commonly falls in the range of 2¢ to 5¢ per word for a 50,000- to 100,000-word manuscript.) The price you pay for editing services depends on many factors:

>> The length of your manuscript

>> How much work the editor anticipates having to do on the manuscript

>> How closely you work with the editor during the writing process

>> The editor's current workload

>> How quickly you need the editing work done

Finding an experienced editor

When it comes time to find a professional editor to work with you on your project, you have a multitude of choices, but the best way to find someone is through a referral from someone working in the publishing industry. If you don't know anyone firsthand, consider the following options:

>> **Ask for a referral** from the book printing company you plan to use.

>> **Contact members of a local writer's group** or a Facebook group that caters to writers.

>> **Respond to classified ads** from freelance editors that appear within special-interest magazines for writers, such as *The Writer* (www.writermag.com), *Writer's Digest* (www.writersdigest.com), or *Publishers Weekly* (www.publishersweekly.com)

>> **Use an online service** or place ads online for a freelance editor by using resources such as

- Upwork (www.upwork.com)

- ZipRecruiter.com, Indeed.com, or LinkedIn Jobs (www.linkedin.com/jobs)

- The American Copy Editors Society (www.aceseditors.org/resources/job-board)

- The Editorial Freelancers Association (www.the-efa.org/hiring)

- Reedsy (https://reedsy.com)

Even when you work with a self-publishing company that offers a complete solution for publishing your book (such as BookBaby, Trafford Publishing, iUniverse, Issuu Digital Publishing, Barnes and Noble Press, Amazon Kindle Direct Publishing, IngramSpark, or Wheatmark — all of which you can read more about in Chapters 12 and 13), the basic services don't include editing. These companies, however, can refer you to a professional editor for an additional fee. So, make sure that you also allocate funds in your publishing budget to hire an editor (see Chapter 7 for details about budgets).

TIP

Choose the person you hire as an editor carefully. Find an editor who's experienced and well educated, and one you can work well with. Your editor should never try to force their ideas, vision, writing style, or voice into your work. Find someone who can embrace your vision and who understands exactly what you want to accomplish with your book. The best way to confirm that an editor is the right person to work on your book is to set up a phone call, video call, or in-person meeting to discuss their credentials, their approach to editing, and your concept for the book. Of course, you also want to discuss fees and scheduling early on.

REMEMBER

Editing is a technical skill. Ideally, you want to hire an editor who studied editing and/or journalism at a college undergraduate or graduate level and who has experience editing full-length manuscripts for the general trade book market. Most professional freelance editors have no trouble providing you with their credentials and a list of published books they've worked on in the past.

Deciding to add a technical editor, or not

If your manuscript requires a review from a technical editor, find someone who's extremely familiar with the topic or subject matter of your book and who can focus on the accuracy of information — especially if the copy editor you hire doesn't really know the subject matter of your book.

A technical editor's job can be time-consuming and requires careful attention to the subject matter's details within your book. A technical editor, for example, fact checks the book's information, confirming all phone numbers, addresses, website URLs, names, facts, figures, statistics, research materials used, and the accuracy of the cited works. Hiring a technical editor costs considerably less than hiring a developmental or copy editor. Plan on spending anywhere from a few hundred dollars to $2,500, depending on the length of your manuscript and the type of work involved.

2

Pulling Together the Details: Administration and Design

Set up your publishing business in a way that makes sense.

Complete the tasks that identify your book and get it ready for effective sales.

Design the interior of your book so that it's easy to read and appealing to your target audience.

Create a professional-looking book cover that grabs your target audience's attention.

IN THIS CHAPTER

» Looking at the pros of establishing your own company

» Forming your business from the ground up

» Setting up a business office

» Watching costs carefully

» Getting help from business veterans and fellow writers

Chapter **7**

Setting Up Your Self-Publishing Business

When you begin to prepare your book for publication — depending on how you choose to market, advertise, and sell it, and what involvement you have in those processes — you may find that establishing your own publishing company can really benefit your publishing project and overall finances in a positive way. As a self-published author who has only one book title, you may need to establish and operate your business only for the life of this one book — that is, unless you plan to follow up with additional book titles in the future.

This chapter covers the basics of establishing a publishing company as a business entity. It also offers an introduction to the benefits you might realize — from a legal and financial standpoint — as you embark on your self-publishing venture. You also get tips on how to get started setting up a business, how to watch your budget, and how to find the expert help that you might need along the way. (Specifically, be sure to speak with an accountant and/or attorney to get more personalized advice based on your particular needs.)

Understanding the Benefits of Establishing a Publishing Company

Establishing a business that you can use for your publishing venture offers a variety of tax advantages and potential legal protections. Your accountant and attorney can review these benefits with you, based on the state in which you're establishing your business and on your personal situation. Here are a few general benefits:

» **Credibility:** In terms of actually selling your book, obtaining publicity, buying advertising, and coordinating distribution, a legitimate company gives you credibility.

» **Loans:** You can qualify for small business loans or grants.

» **Location:** In most cases, you can operate a self-publishing business from a home, as opposed to an office or warehouse. Although you need to legally establish your business and submit the appropriate forms to the state and federal government (see the section "Legally establishing the right type of business," later in this chapter), you don't need to rent office space, especially if you're running a one- or two-person operation. (But consider opening a post office box for privacy and to keep your personal and business mail separate.)

» **Tax deductions:** By establishing a company, most or all of your legitimate business-related expenses become tax deductible. For example, if you hire people to help with your publishing project, such as an editor or graphic designer, you may find financial and tax benefits to hiring these people through your business (as opposed to as an individual).

Not all self-published authors need to create their own businesses. Instead, they can use certain publishing methods and services that handle many of the tasks and financial transactions involved. For example, if you're writing a book that you plan to publish by using print-on-demand (POD) or your focus is on selling only e-books through services such as Amazon.com, BN.com, Apple Books, and Google Books (http://books.google.com), you may not need to establish your own business. (Chapter 11 focuses on e-book publishing, and Chapter 13 has details on POD publishing.)

If you're a self-published author who wants to sell your own books, before you publish your first book is a good time to establish your own business so that you can reap the financial and tax benefits, and also establish your bookkeeping system appropriately. (Look to Part 5 for more information about the business tasks of publicity and marketing.)

REMEMBER

Prior to establishing any type of formal business, be sure to consult with an accountant and attorney who can review your situation and help you determine the best type of legal business entity to create. See the section "Legally establishing the right type of business," later in this chapter, for information on your business-type options.

Taking Official Steps to Create a Company

Starting an actual business doesn't require a pile of money or paperwork, so establish your business as early in the self-publishing process as possible, especially if you ultimately plan to sell your book directly to consumers. The following sections help you take the necessary steps to determine the best type of business for you and then establish that business.

Legally establishing the right type of business

When it comes to creating your company as a legal business entity, you have a variety of options. Some common types of businesses include

WARNING

>> **Sole proprietorship:** A *sole proprietorship* means that you're the exclusive owner of the business. It's the most inexpensive, quickest, and easiest way to create a legal business entity. While your business grows, you can later transform the company into something more formal, such as some type of corporation. If you have a small publishing business and it only breaks even (so no profits), it can easily remain a one-person company indefinitely. But successful sales of a title (perhaps 25,000 copies sold in one year) may dictate that you expand into a company that has employees or move into a formal office space.

Consider carefully whether you want to form a sole proprietorship because it offers less legal protection and fewer tax benefits than various types of corporations, for example. When you operate a sole proprietorship, you include all profits and losses on your individual tax returns. If a customer sues your business, they may also be able to sue you personally, which makes both your personal and business assets subject to those claims.

>> **Partnership:** When two or more people work together as co-owners of a company, this business is referred to as a partnership. It's like a sole proprietorship from a tax and legal standpoint, but it has multiple people involved, which increases the complexity and the amount of required paperwork.

Keep in mind that partners in a business share unlimited liability: According to the law, each partner is usually responsible for the acts of the other. Also, if someone sues your business, they may also be able to sue you and your partner(s) personally, which makes your personal and business assets subject to those claims.

>> **Limited liability company (LLC):** When you create this type of business, the income goes directly to the owner (or owners), but the owners aren't usually personally liable for the LLC's debts. Therefore, the personal assets of the company's owners are generally protected, and the owners can lose only the money that they invest in the company and the money that the company has earned.

>> **Corporation:** For the maximum amount of legal protection and potential tax benefits, consider establishing a corporation. A corporation is a legal entity, and the corporation holds all business-related liabilities. This practice minimizes the personal liability of its owners. The corporation operates as a business, and registered certificates, called stock, can represent ownership in all or some of the business.

>> **S corporation:** Offers many of the same advantages as a regular corporation. But, unlike a corporation, for income tax purposes, it acts as a *flow-through entity*, which means that, as a company, it pays no income taxes. Instead, the owners or stockholders report all income and losses individually on their personal income tax returns. If your business has fewer than 35 stockholders, consult with your accountant and attorney about this option.

You can find many online services (such as LegalZoom.com) that allow you to form your own corporation in minutes for a flat fee. But you may want to seek the guidance of a lawyer to help you with this process so that you can ensure you do it correctly and make the best decisions based on your personal situation. *Note:* The paperwork that you need to complete and file varies dramatically by state.

For a self-published author, even if you set up a publishing business, you could still be sued personally if something you write and ultimately publish involves plagiarism, defamation, copyright infringement, or trademark infringement. Obviously, refrain from any of these activities.

Starting with a name and an image

Because you plan to launch a business to self-publish and sell your book, you already have an overall objective for your business (which is a starting point for a business plan; see the following section for information about developing a business plan). You need to come up with a business name. Go ahead; think of something that's unique and catchy.

The name that you choose can help establish your publishing company's image. The name needs to sound professional, hold meaning (at least, to you), and establish your credibility in the publishing field. The name can be either specific or general:

>> **Specific name:** If you know you plan to publish only travel books, name your company something like Acme Travel Adventure Publications.

>> **General name:** Go with something generic, such as ABC Enterprises, Inc., which does not reveal anything about what the company does.

If you're providing other services, in addition to publishing books, you may want to reference these services within the general name of your company — or at least refrain from implying in the company's name that it only publishes. A name such as Acme Publishing, Inc. implies that the company exclusively does publishing. Acme Ventures, Inc., Acme Worldwide, Inc., or Acme Enterprises, Inc. don't specifically reference what the business does.

REMEMBER

As a self-published author, for credibility and publicity reasons, don't use your own name as your company's name if your name also appears on your book's cover as the author.

After you come up with a satisfactory business name, do a few things to protect and promote it:

>> **Register the company name:** To ensure that no one else is already using your business name, contact your local County Clerk or Recorder's Office for details about how to complete this process. You need a registered name to establish a company bank account or a P.O. Box, for example.

>> **Register your company name as a website domain name.** Even if you don't have a site designed yet, reserve the name for your site so that no one else takes it from you. See Chapter 17 for more information on this process. To register one or more domain names, visit a domain registrar, such as GoDaddy.com. You need to pay an annual fee for each domain name that you register.

For a company name, always register the dot-com extension because people browsing the web tend to automatically enter this extension when they type an address into their browser. The sooner you register the domain name(s) you plan to use, the better; you don't want someone else taking these names while your book is in development or before you're ready to actually launch your website.

TIP

At the same time that you register the domain name for your company's website, obtain a domain name that includes your own name, as well (www.JohnDoe.com). If someone else has registered your author name as a domain name, come up with an alternative, such as www.JohnDoeAuthor.com or www.TheRealJohnDoe.com.

>> **Develop a logo to promote your identity and image.** A *logo* is a graphic that accompanies your company name. Any graphic artist can help you create a logo, which you can use on all of your book's promotional materials. See Chapter 10 for details on finding a graphic designer.

Developing a business plan

The company that you establish will most likely handle your book's marketing, advertising, distribution, sales, order fulfillment, and other business-related matters. So, you need to create a well-thought-out business plan for the company that you want to establish. In a nutshell, you need to develop a thorough understanding of what the business does. Does the company simply publish and sell books, or does it sell other products or services, as well?

Before investing your time and money in your business and into the publishing of your book, create a detailed business plan that specifically defines your business, identifies its goals, and describes how the business operates. Be sure to include a balance sheet and cash flow analysis as part of the business plan. For more on business plans, check out *Business Plans For Dummies,* 3rd Edition (Wiley), by Paul Tiffany and Steven D. Peterson.

MAKING YOUR MARK

If you use a unique or original company name, or if you create a company logo along with the name, be sure to trademark the name and logo with the United States Patent and Trademark Office (www.uspto.gov). Obtaining a trademark for your unique company name and logo gives you added legal protection and helps keep your competition from using a similar name or logo to confuse consumers. Keep in mind, you can trademark any unique logo, but to trademark a company name, it has to include something special, such as a made-up word or unique spelling of a word. You can't trademark words that appear in the dictionary, for example. Consult with an attorney or the U.S. Patent and Trademark Office to find out more about what can and can't be trademarked.

Keep in mind, if you plan to operate and self-finance your one-person publishing business — at least, initially — creating detailed financial documents (such as a balance sheet and cash flow analysis) for your new business can be beneficial for your own financial planning, but you don't need them. The goal of a business plan is to provide a written road map for you to follow. It can help you keep your activities focused on the business's core objectives.

TIP

If you don't have a financial background, consider hiring (in advance) an accountant or bookkeeper — someone who has the expertise to help you create a financial model for your company (which you may need later to secure a loan or pitch to investors), plus help you set up the financial aspects of your business.

Getting start-up money

After you have your business plan and financial planning in place (see the preceding section), you need to get some money to run that business of yours! The type of business you're forming, and the purpose of that business, determines how much money you need. Plan on spending at least several hundred dollars to complete and file the necessary paperwork to establish your business, especially if you're establishing a corporation, as opposed to a DBA, sole proprietorship, or LLC. Beyond that, you need to calculate the costs associated with writing, editing, printing, promoting, selling, and distributing your book into your business's operating budget.

Where will you get the required funds? You can self-finance your operation, which is a common option. If you have money in your savings, you can start there. However, you can also try getting a small business loan, borrowing money from family or friends, or establishing a crowd-funding campaign. You can even look for private investors.

REMEMBER

Don't take too many financial risks with your personal savings. You don't want to end up in serious personal debt or even bankruptcy if your publishing business for some reason fails.

WARNING

Obtaining cash advances on your credit cards to launch your business can cost you. If the business fails and you can't pay at least your monthly credit card minimum payments, you can find yourself in serious financial trouble and having to pay extremely high interest rates and other fees.

After you establish your business and get it operational — and determine whether you want to operate from your home or an office — you need to make a financial investment in office supplies and equipment. The following sections provide a sampling of the equipment you likely need to properly equip your business's office.

Getting and staying connected

Writers amass a lot of the same tools and infrastructure that any business operator requires, long before they even consider starting a self-publishing company. The important tools that provide your office with access to all-important communications include

>> **A computer that has Internet access:** For your business, a connected computer provides access to many of the tools you will need to write, publish, distribute, and promote our book.

>> **A business e-mail address:** For example, *YourName@YourCompanyName. com,* that you use for everything having to do with your publishing business or self-publishing project. You can often acquire personalized email addresses at the same time you register your domain name(s).

>> **Telephone service with a separate business phone number:** I recommend a separate number because you want to be able to keep your personal and business calls separate.

Getting the right computer software

Your computer is your most important business tool. Figure out what types of applications you need, and then make sure that you purchase a Windows-based PC or Mac-based desktop or laptop computer that can run those applications.

In addition to writing, designing, and laying out your book, you use your computer to perform a variety of other business-related tasks, including

>> **Bookkeeping and handling your business finances:** Applications such as Intuit QuickBooks (`http://quickbooks.intuit.com`) or FreshBooks (`www.freshbooks.com`) can help you keep your money in order.

>> **Dealing with inventory and automating book shipping via FedEx, UPS, USPS, and so on:** Intuit QuickBooks or a simple Excel spreadsheet that you create can help you track inventory, and you can use a separate tool to help automate your shipping processes.

>> **Handling contacts, calendars, and schedules; sending and receiving email:** Many personal productivity apps, such as Microsoft Outlook, Gmail, or Apple Calendar, can help you take care of all these tasks for your business. *Note:* Set up a separate account for your business to keep your personal and business records separate.

>> **Managing a website (or e-commerce website that sells your book online).** See Chapters 14 and 17 for more information on these services.

>> **Researching and marketing online:** Performing online research and engaging in social media activities to promote your book. The software required here includes a browser (such as Google Chrome or Apple Safari or Microsoft Edge) and platform-specific media apps (such as Facebook, Instagram and TikTok).

Gathering other resources that you need

To handle daily business operations, you likely need a wide range of office equipment and supplies. In addition to visiting your local office supply superstore, you can often find low prices by shopping online for items, such as printer ink/toner cartridges. Table 7-1 categorizes some of the furnishings and supplies that you may need for your business office. (This table doesn't offer an exhaustive account of all your possible office needs, but it gives you a start and may stimulate other ideas.)

TABLE 7-1 **Handy Office Furnishings and Supplies**

Category	Examples
Accessories	Power strips, extension cords, wastebaskets
Appliances	Copier/printer/fax machine combo, credit card processing equipment, label printer, paper shredder, postage machine and scale
Customized supplies	Business cards, letterhead, business-size envelopes
Desktop supplies	Folders, paperclips, pens and pencils, paper, scissors, staplers and staples, tape
Shipping supplies	Boxes, envelopes, packing tape, labels
Furniture	Bookshelves, desks, chairs, filing cabinets

Adding essential relationships and insurance

Here are a couple of ideas to consider while you set up your office and go forward with your self-publishing business:

>> **Set up accounts with shipping companies.** After you establish your company (which I talk about in the section "Taking Official Steps to Create a Company," earlier in this chapter), contact shipping companies such as FedEx, UPS, DHL, and/or the U.S. Post Office. If you plan to fulfill your own book

orders, you need to set up a warehouse (in-house or remote), handle inventory control, and establish a shipping department. (See Chapter 16 for details on fulfillment, warehousing, and shipping.)

>> **Acquire adequate insurance for yourself *and* your business.** If disaster strikes, not being adequately insured can quickly put you out of business and cause serious financial hardship. Protect your assets from theft, fire, lawsuits, and other disasters by obtaining homeowner's insurance *and* small business insurance that covers all your equipment, inventory, and other business assets. In terms of your personal insurance, also consider obtaining health insurance, life insurance, long-term disability insurance, and an umbrella insurance policy.

Consult with several insurance companies and independent insurance brokers to determine your needs and find the best deals for the most comprehensive coverage.

WARNING

Homeowner's or renter's insurance does *not* cover your business-related equipment or inventory that you store or use within your home. For this stuff, you need small-business insurance. Likewise, you need different types of insurance if you personally or your business wind up getting sued.

Keeping Costs Tracked and Under Control

The success of your business and publishing venture depends on your ability to manage your money and generate a profit. Allocate the money that you spend wisely. Focus on your company's objectives and how to best use your available funds to achieve those objectives. One of the biggest mistakes start-up business operators make is misallocating their funds so that they run out of operating funds before their company can turn a profit.

Listing your expenses

Successfully launching and running your own business involves many start-up and operational costs. Table 7-2 contains some of the initial business expenses that you need to budget for. Do a bit of research on the cost of these goods and services, and record projected expenses in the table.

TABLE 7-2 **Initial Business Expenses**

Category	Frequency	Projected Cost
Professional Services		
Accounting services	Quarterly or yearly	
Legal services	One time retainer and as needed	
Logo design	One time	
Operational Costs		
Banking fees	Monthly	
Business licenses, incorporation, and filing fees	One time	
Credit card merchant accounts	At startup and ongoing	
Insurance	Monthly or yearly	
Internet service	Monthly	
Phone service	Monthly	
Storage and office rental fees	Monthly	
Infrastructure Investment		
Office computing equipment and software	One time and yearly subscriptions	
Office furnishings	One time and as needed	
Office supplies	One time and as needed	
Phone hardware	One time and as needed	

In addition to listing and tracking business costs in Table 7-2, create a budget for your actual publishing project. Table 7-3 offers a look at some of the expenses you'll have that relate to the development, publication, and distribution of your book.

Implementing a budget

While you plan your business's operating budget for its first six months and then for its first year of operation, allow for unexpected expenses and have money available to deal with them. Your accountant (get one if you don't have one) can help you properly budget for all your anticipated and potentially unexpected expenses. Ideally, you want to launch your business with enough money in the bank to operate for at least six months without generating any revenue. Update your budget as needed, based on how the business grows and develops over time. It's an ongoing process.

TABLE 7-3   **Publishing Project Expenses (Per Book)**

Category	Frequency	Projected Cost
Book Construction		
Editing fees	One time	
Ghost writer fees	One time	
Front and back cover design	One time	
Page layout and design	One time	
Photos and artwork for the book, website, or marketing and advertising	Per image	
Printing	One time or as needed	
Administration and Promotion		
Obtaining copyright, ISBN, Library of Congress card number, and barcode	One time	
Advertising	Ongoing	
Marketing and public relations	Ongoing	
Website development and maintenance	One time and ongoing	
Post-Publishing Overheads		
Order fulfillment	Ongoing	
Shipping/warehousing	Ongoing	

REMEMBER

You have many costs associated with successfully writing, editing, laying out, printing, distributing, marketing, advertising, and fulfilling orders for a self-published book. Establishing a proper budget, and then carefully managing your finances, can help ensure your success. Be sure to have an accounting and record-keeping system in place. Also, maintain at least a monthly balance sheet and income statement (a profit-and-loss statement), while keeping track of all banking records.

Finding Additional Expert Help

When you first came up with the idea to write and publish a book, you probably didn't realize that you might also be a small-business operator. Well, in addition to becoming an author and figuring out how to publish a book successfully, if you plan to launch a business, you need to understand the fundamentals of business administration.

REMEMBER

If you have absolutely no experience working in the business world, don't panic. First, focus on writing and publishing the very best book you can. Then, consider seeking the help of someone who can assist you in setting up and potentially managing your business. You can try the following sources to get some help with your business:

» **Credit-card companies:** Both American Express (www.americaexpress.com) and Visa (www.visa.com) cater to small-business owners through their websites (just select the Business option on the main webpage). These websites include all kinds of helpful articles, links to resources, and online-based tools.

» **Professional trade associations:** These organizations typically offer significant discounts on services and equipment, networking benefits, and informational resources. Consider joining the following publishing industry trade associations:

• *Writers & Publishers Network* (www.writersandpublishersnetwork.com): Formally known as the Small Publishers, Artists & Writers Network (SPAWN), this organization provides information, resources, and opportunities for anyone involved in or interested in publishing. The organization encourages the exchange of ideas, information, and other mutual benefits. On its website, you can also share information on writing, marketing, and publishing.

• *Independent Book Publishers Association (IBPA):* With over 4,100 publishers represented, the nonprofit trade association IBPA (www.ibpa-online.org) is an organization that offers a wide range of resources to small and independent publishers. This organization can help you establish your business, and then obtain discounts on book publishing and marketing services.

» **Service Corps of Retired Executives (SCORE):** Although you can hire someone who has experience as a partner or employee, a cheaper option is to take advantage of the free resources available to small business owners from SCORE. As a nonprofit association comprised of over 12,000 volunteers from across the country, SCORE is a division of the U.S. government's Small Business Administration (SBA) and is dedicated to aiding in the formation, growth, and success of small businesses nationwide. SCORE volunteers serve as counselors, advisors, and mentors to aspiring entrepreneurs and business owners.

You can reach SCORE volunteers in your area by visiting the organization's website (www.score.org), which also offers a variety of free resources to small business operators.

TIP

Facebook hosts a wide range of special interest groups appropriate for writers, self–publishers, and small publishing companies. Members of these groups are open to sharing advice on how to achieve success. To find special interest groups available on Facebook, follow these steps:

1. Point your web browser to www.facebook.com.

2. Sign in by using your existing Facebook account.

If you don't have one or want to have a business-specific account, you can create one for free.

3. In the Search textbox at the top-left of the page, enter the type of group you want to search for, and then press Enter.

You can type in "Self-Publishing," "Writer's Group," or "Author Group," for example.

4. Click on the Groups menu option on the left of the screen that appears.

Alternatively, you can select the See All button that appears below the Groups listing in the main window.

5. Select the title of any of the displayed search results to access the group's page.

Look over the page to determine which group(s) might be helpful.

6. When you see a group that you like, click the Join Group button in the top-right of the group's page.

You can join any Facebook group for free.

To get the most out of the Facebook group member experience, become an active participant in the groups that you join. Don't be afraid to ask questions, solicit advice, and share your own experiences. *Note:* Before following any advice, check the credibility of the source that's offering it by confirming credentials with a quick Google search.

IN THIS CHAPTER

» Obtaining an ISBN and a barcode for your book

» Making sure your book can be found

» Applying for a Library of Congress Control Number

» Securing the copyright for your work

» Setting your book's cover price and publication date

Chapter **8**

Tackling Book-Specific Tasks

I f you look at any commercially available book, the back cover displays the book's International Standard Book Number (ISBN) and barcode, along with the book's price. Within the front matter (which appears right after the title page inside your book), you typically find the copyright page, which lists legal information, including the book's copyright notice and the Library of Congress Control Number (LCCN). The numbers, copyright information, and barcode are required so that bookstores, online sellers, distributors, and other retailers can properly identify your book.

Not all self-published authors have to handle the administrative tasks required to obtain the book's identifying elements on their own. In many cases, your print-on-demand (POD) publisher or traditional short-run book printer obtains the necessary ISBN, barcode, LCCN, and copyright on your behalf — although you may have to pay an additional fee for these services. See Chapter 12 for more information about traditional short-run printers and Chapter 13 for details on POD publishing.

Note: This chapter contains a bunch of legal stuff that may at first seem confusing. Don't despair! In addition to the information in this chapter, also check out the Internet for easy-to-understand legal resources. You can also seek help from an attorney or book printer who has experience in the areas covered in this chapter. Worst case scenario: You attend law school for three years and then self-publish your book (but probably your situation won't come to that).

This chapter focuses on how to obtain the essential identifying elements that are exclusive to your book. You can also find out how to select an appropriate publication date for your book and how to fill out Advance Book Information (ABI) forms (for printed books).

Obtaining an ISBN for Your Book

Any book that's sold anywhere in the world must have a unique International Standard Book Number (ISBN). E-books also have this requirement, but when you opt to distribute your e-book through Amazon, Barnes & Noble, and/or Apple Books, each of these services assign an ISBN number for that specific edition of your book for free. However, for a traditionally printed or POD book, you typically need to acquire an ISBN another way. The following sections describe what an ISBN is, what the number signifies, why your book needs to have one, and how to obtain it.

An ISBN: What it is and why your book needs one

The ISBN system is an internationally recognized book identification system that's been in use since 1970. Booksellers use an ISBN for a variety of purposes, including inventory control; sales tracking; and order processing by booksellers, wholesalers, distributors, libraries, and universities. An ISBN's 13 digits are divided into four parts of variable length, with each part separated by a hyphen (see the description of each part later in this section).

Some books have similar titles, or the same book may have multiple editions published over several years. To help keep track of every edition of every book that's published, each book (in each different format, for example, paperback and e-book) gets a unique ISBN. The ISBN appears on the book's back cover, inside the book's interior on the copyright page, and sometimes on the inside front or back cover, as well.

WHEN PUBLISHING IN THE U.S., CONTACT ISBN.ORG

According to ISBN.org, "An ISBN is a number, not a bar code. One agency per country is designated to assign ISBNs for the publishers and self-publishers located in that country. The U.S. ISBN Agency cannot assign ISBNs to publishers and self-publishers located outside the United States and its territories.

"The ISBN identifies the title or other book-like product (such as an audiobook) to which it is assigned, but also the publisher to be contacted for ordering purposes. If an ISBN is obtained from a company other than the official ISBN Agency, that ISBN will not identify the publisher of the title accurately. This can have implications for doing business in the publishing industry supply chain."

Throughout the world, 160 ISBN agencies are assigning numbers; each agency is responsible for assigning unique ISBNs to new books published within a specific region. The U.S. ISBN Agency (www.isbn.org) handles the United States, the U.S. Virgin Islands, Guam, and Puerto Rico.

The ISBN for the print version of *Self-Publishing For Dummies*, 2nd Edition, is 978-1-394-20127-3. The five parts of an ISBN-13 like this one offer the following information:

>> **The prefix:** This three-digit number (in this book's case, *978*) identifies the book publishing industry.

>> **Group of country identifier:** This digit (for this book, it's *1*) indicates the country where the book was published.

>> **Publisher identifier:** This part of the number is a unique code given to every individual publishing company or book packager that publishes books on a self-publisher's behalf (see the section "Applying for a prefix and single ISBN or block of ISBNs," later in this chapter, for more on this code). For this book, the segment numbers *394* identify the publisher.

>> **Title identifier:** This part of the ISBN is unique to every book and identifies the particular title or edition of that title. This second edition of *Self-Publishing For Dummies* is identified by the numbers *20127*.

>> **Check digit:** This single digit at the end of the ISBN (for this book, it's *3*) validates the number as it relates to the centralized ISBN database. In some cases, this could be the capital letter X (the Roman numeral for the number 10).

REMEMBER

Without a proper ISBN, most booksellers and retailers can't order or sell your book. If you're using a POD publisher or a publisher that offers a turnkey self-publishing solution to authors, that publisher/printer typically obtains an ISBN on your behalf. The company that distributes your e-book also handles the ISBN. You need to acquire your own ISBN only if you plan to self-publish your book entirely by yourself and establish your own publishing company to do so.

Getting ISBNs on your own

Only established book publishers can acquire ISBNs for books that they publish. If you're self-publishing a book without the help of a POD publisher or another type of turnkey publishing solution (as described in Chapters 12 and 13), you first need to establish a publishing company; see Chapter 7 for details on going into business for yourself. As soon as you have your company established, contact the U.S. ISBN Agency at 800-662-0703 or online at www.isbn-us.com.

Applying for a prefix and a single ISBN or block of ISBNs

Even if you represent a small publishing company and plan to publish only one or two book titles, you still need to acquire an ISBN publishing prefix, along with at least one ISBN. This process takes approximately 15 business days; however, for an additional fee, you can request Priority Processing (two-day) or Express (one-day) service.

As of mid-2023, the price of one ISBN is $125 (without the accompanying barcode; I talk about barcodes in the section "Ordering a Barcode for Your Book," later in this chapter). However, you have some options in bundling your ISBN purchases:

>> 10 ISBNs (to be used by the same publishing company) cost $295.

>> 100 ISBNs cost a total of $575.

Packages that include an ISBN and corresponding barcode are also available, starting at $150 for one ISBN and barcode combo.

To acquire an ISBN publisher prefix and purchase a block of ISBNs (and corresponding barcodes), complete and submit the appropriate forms as the author/self-publisher (the section "Establishing your publishing company and its titles," later in the chapter, has more about this process). You can submit these forms online by visiting www.isbn.org/buy_isbns.

If you're a self-publisher who needs just one ISBN number, visit www.my identifiers.com, then select Publish Your Book ⇨ Self Publishing Discount Packages from the top menu to access a page that details your self-publishing options. You can do this instead of working with isbn.org.

Accounting for the cost of ISBNs

WARNING

All fees that you pay to isbn.org are nonrefundable (you can pay by using a major credit or debit card). In addition, you can't transfer, sell, or reassign ISBNs because a portion of the 13-digit number represents the individual publishing company.

TIP

Include the cost of acquiring a publishing prefix, ISBN(s), and corresponding barcodes in your overall budget. Keep in mind, if you publish the same book content, but in different formats (such as paperback, hardcover, and e-book), you need a different ISBN number and corresponding barcode for each version of that book.

Establishing your publishing company and its titles

After you submit your application forms to secure ISBNs and establish your company as a publisher (which you can read about in the section "Applying for a prefix and a single ISBN or block of ISBNs," earlier in this chapter), the ISBN website asks you for a wide range of information about your company, including

>> The company/publisher name and contact information (address, phone number, e-mail address, and website).

>> The year the company was founded and started publishing.

>> The names of the Rights and Permissions Contact and the ISBN Coordinator within the company, each person's title, and their phone numbers. (Because you're self-publishing, these roles probably all fall to you, the self-published author.)

>> The type of products produced by the company (books, e-books, audiobooks, software, and so on) and the primary subject areas covered.

>> Information about how your products get distributed (see Part 4 for book distribution details).

After you obtain your ISBN publisher prefix and assign individual ISBNs to your upcoming books, you can then list each title with Bowker's Books In Print. (See the section "Adding Your Book to the Books In Print Directory," later in the chapter.) Booksellers, libraries, schools, universities, and other institutions use this comprehensive database and directory of all current and upcoming books to search for and pre-order books. By using this service, the buyers can decide which books they want to carry in advance of the publication date. Check out the Books In Print website at www.booksinprint.com. If your book is being published using a POD publisher, this process will likely be handled for you.

REMEMBER

According to the organization's website, "Books In Print combines the most trusted and authoritative source of bibliographic information and includes powerful search, discovery, and collection development tools designed specifically to streamline the book discovery and acquisition process."

Ordering a Barcode for Your Book

In conjunction with each ISBN issued for a book (see the section "Obtaining an ISBN for Your Book," earlier in this chapter), you should order a corresponding barcode, which gets printed on the back cover of your traditionally printed book. (You don't need a barcode for e-books.) This barcode primarily helps with retail inventory control and sales. It recreates the book's ISBN and cover price.

You can see a barcode for yourself on this book's back cover.

You can obtain your barcode from Bowker Barcode Service at the same time you acquire ISBNs. Each barcode comes in a camera-ready, digital format — in 2400 dots per inch (dpi), 99.26 percent magnification. You receive a *vanilla barcode* (white background and black text) with an accompanying price add-on. Contact Bowker Barcode Service (www.bowkerbarcode.com) for additional details.

REMEMBER

The barcode that appears on your book's back cover uses a different format than a Universal Product Code (UPC) barcode that appears on retail products. The book publishing business uses its own unique barcode system tied to each book's ISBN. Many publishers include the Price Code extension onto their barcode, as well, which displays the cover price of the book so that consumers can easily see it (using a standard format, such as $19.99), but the price also appears in the barcode itself.

When designing your book's back cover, position the barcode near the bottom of the back cover and accompany it with the book's ISBN printed in a readable font. The barcode should also appear on the inside front cover of *strippable* paperback books. (When retailers return the books for credit, they rip off the front cover of the book and send it back — hence the term strippable.) Chapter 10 has additional details about incorporating a barcode into a back cover's design.

INCLUDING BISAC SUBJECT AND AUDIENCE INFORMATION

Created by The Book Industry Study Group, a professional trade association comprised of companies and individuals working in the publishing industry, the Book Industry Standards and Communications (BISAC) Audience categories and Subject categories are industry-standard, and your book must fit into at least one of them. These classifications help booksellers display your book in the appropriate section, based on subject matter and target audience.

Have your book's BISAC Subject and/or Audience classifications printed (in small type) on the back cover of your book, either near the barcode or in the upper-right or -left corner of the back cover. You also need this information when submitting listings to online booksellers (see Chapter 14) and selling your book to distributors or wholesalers (see Chapter 16). This is only necessary if you plan to have your book distributed through retail bookstores. It makes it easier for the bookstore to know in what section to display your book.

For a comprehensive list of BISAC subjects and subcategories, point your web browser to: www.bisg.org/complete-bisac-subject-headings-list. In addition to choosing a Subject that's most appropriate for your book, you can further classify your book by using a subcategory. For example, a book about Yorkshire Terriers fits into the subject *Pets,* with the subcategory *Dogs.* Therefore, next to the barcode on the book's back cover, you *Pets/Dogs.*

The BISAC Audience categories refer to the intended readers for the book. Ideally, use only one audience code for your book. Two industry standards exist for classifying books by audience; they are

- **The X.12 system:** Audience codes include COL (College), JUV (Juvenile), PSP (Professional and Scholar), TRA (Trade), and YA (Young Adult).

- **The Onix Code:** Has the categories 01 (General/Trade), 02 (Children/Juvenile), 03 (Young Adult), 04 (Primary & Secondary/Elementary & High School), 05 (College/Higher Education), 06 (Professional and Scholarly), 07 (English as a Second Language), and 08 (Adult Education).

For more information about BISAC Subject and Audience classifications, and how to choose the right category and subcategory for your book, visit www.bisg.org/selecting-a-bisac-code.

Adding Your Book to the Books In Print Directory

After your book has its own ISBN (flip back to the section "Obtaining an ISBN for Your Book," earlier in this chapter, for the details on getting an ISBN), complete the Advance Book Information (ABI) form so that your title can be listed within the Bowker's Books In Print directory. R. R. Bowker provides the appropriate forms for submitting your book title(s) on their website, at `www.bowker.com/self-publishing-solutions`. *Note:* If you're using a POD publishing service or another turnkey self-publishing solution, the company or service that you use most likely obtains an ISBN on your behalf and completes the necessary ABI paperwork to get your book listed.

If you're handling ABI paperwork yourself, Bowker offers the online BowkerLink service that allows publishers to create and update listings in the company's databases. Registered publishers can use this free service, which replaces ABI paper forms. To register for this service, visit `www.bowkerlink.com` and set up an account.

REMEMBER

Only recognized publishing companies can gain access to this BowkerLink service. After you establish a publishing company (see Chapter 7 for details on getting your business going), complete the registration form.

After you register, select the Add Title menu option to add information about specific book titles. After you complete the online form, the information appears in the Bowker Books In Print database within one to two business days. You need to provide the following information about each book title that you want to list in the Books In Print database:

- >> BISAC Subject and/or Audience categories
- >> Book title and subtitle
- >> Description of content (in 25 to 200 words)
- >> Format details: Binding type, language, page count, trim size
- >> ISBN
- >> Price
- >> Publication and ship dates
- >> Publisher and publisher imprint (if applicable)

Publishers have the option of including additional details about their book titles, which the BowkerLink website prompts users to enter, if it's applicable. You can (and should) also include a cover image.

Securing a Library of Congress Control Number

The Library of Congress assigns a Library of Congress Control Number (LCCN) to your book, which libraries use for numbering and cataloging books. The LCCN, which started back in 1898, includes the year of publication and a unique serial number for each book title. Make sure that you obtain your LCCN prior to the book's publication because this number should appear on the copyright page of your book.

CAN I HAVE IT? CATALOGING IN PUBLICATION

Major publishing houses use a Cataloging in Publication (CIP) number, which serves the same purpose as an LCCN but follows a slightly different format. Books can have a CIP record filed with the Library of Congress. This bibliographic information consists of details about books that allow libraries to catalog them quickly, including information about a book's title, publisher, author, trim size, binding, copyright, and table of contents. CIP compiles the bibliographic information from the book or manuscript itself, not from forms submitted by the publisher.

Prior to a book's publication, the publisher electronically submits the full text of the publication to the Library of Congress, which then creates an original bibliographic record (CIP data). The Library of Congress then returns the record to the publisher so that they can include the CIP number within the front matter of the book, usually right after the title page.

At the same time, each library that acquires the book has immediate access to information about the book, which ultimately saves librarians time and expense when it comes to cataloging the book within their collections. Librarians also use pre-publication data from the Library of Congress to order books.

Here's the kicker, though: Only U.S. publishers that publish titles most likely to be widely acquired by U.S. libraries can participate in the CIP program. Self-published authors need to utilize the Preassigned Control Number program (www.loc.gov/publish/pcn), which offers the same benefits in terms of making information about your book readily available to libraries across the country.

Obtaining an LCCN doesn't cost a thing. To get one, visit `www.loc.gov/publish/pcn` — where you find the page for the Preassigned Control Number Program (PCN) — and complete the necessary form online. You must first acquire an ISBN for your book to participate in this program. (The section "Obtaining an ISBN for Your Book," earlier in this chapter, discusses getting an ISBN.)

TIP

Most POD and turnkey self-publishing solutions handle acquiring the LCCN for you. When researching which self-publishing solution you want to use (you can find solutions covered in Part 3 of this book), inquire whether they automatically offer this service. If not, you need to obtain a LCCN for your book on your own.

It's Mine, All Mine! Copyrighting Your Work

When you write a book, it's an original work, whether its fiction, poetry, a collection of essays, a cookbook, or any sort of non-fiction. You're probably very proud of the work that you've done, and you want to ensure that your work remains your own, and that no one misuses or steals it. Therefore, make sure to properly copyright your book. As an author, you can copyright any original work, including literary, dramatic, musical, artistic, and certain other intellectual works.

REMEMBER

The most important reason to copyright your work is to prevent anyone else from stealing or *plagiarizing* it (calling it their own and publishing it under their own name). After you copyright a work, that work is protected for the life of the author, plus 70 years. In some cases, the duration can be for 95 or even 120 years after the author's death. Contact the United States Copyright Office (`www.copyright.gov`) for details on which situation applies to your book.

In the following sections, I show you how to create a copyright notice and give you steps for registering your copyright.

Including a copyright notice in your book

All versions of your work should include a legal copyright notice. When you formally publish your book, the book's copyright page typically goes right after the title page as part of the book's front matter.

A legal copyright notice should contain these three main elements:

» The copyright symbol — the letter *c* in a circle (©) or the word *Copyright*

» The year of first publication

» The name of the owner of the copyright

A one-line copyright notice reads: ©2023 *Jason R. Rich. All rights reserved.*

TIP

For details about creating the appropriate legal wording for your book's copyright page, contact an attorney who specializes in copyright law or consult with your book printer, who may also be able to provide guidance.

Registering your copyright

The purpose of actually registering your copyright (as opposed to just printing a copyright notice in your book) is to create a public record of your book's existence and to announce your ownership of the copyright. Your copyright also establishes an official date when your ownership of the work began. To find out more about the protections offered by filing the appropriate copyright forms for your book, visit the Library of Congress Copyright Office's website at www.copyright.gov.

REMEMBER

Registering the copyright for your book is a fast, inexpensive, and simple process. Simply submit the following three elements to The Library of Congress Copyright Office:

>> **A completed copyright application form:** You can obtain the appropriate form (which is Form TX for a literary work) online at www.copyright.gov or by calling 202-707-3000.

The author or someone representing the author (such as the copyright claimant, the owner of exclusive rights to the manuscript, or a duly authorized agent of the author or copyright claimant) must complete the form.

>> **The nonrefundable fee:** The current fees are listed at www.copyright.gov/about/fees.html.

>> **A copy of your complete manuscript:** This can be in digital or printed form.

To begin the online process for filing a copyright for your book, visit http://eservice.eco.loc.gov and click the Log in to eCO button. Alternatively, you can hire a third-party agency, such as LegalZoom (www.legalzoom.com), to help you with this process (for an additional fee above and beyond the filing fees charged by the copyright office).

TIP

For more information on how to copyright a book yourself or to use a service to help you, visit these websites:

>> **Legal Zoom (www.legalzoom.com):** On the main page, select Resources from the top menu. In the screen that appears, enter "How to Copyright a Book" in the search text box and click Search. Select the article from the list that appears so that you can see the LegalZoom words of wisdom on copyrights.

>> **SelfPublishing.com** (`www.selfpublishing.com`): From the main page, click the Search button in the upper-right corner and enter "How to Copyright a Book" in the text box that appears. Click Search, and then click to open the article in the results that appear.

Increasing Profits by Setting the Right Cover Price

Prior to printing your book and officially announcing its publication, you need to set its *cover price* (the retail price of your book), which readers have to pay to purchase it — regardless of whether they're buying from you, an online bookseller such as Amazon or BN.com, or from a retail bookseller.

Setting your book's cover price is an important business decision that you make based on accurate market research, knowledge of the publishing industry, and educated predictions about how many copies of your book you'll sell. Handling this aspect of the publishing process correctly could mean the difference between generating a profit and losing money on your self-publishing venture. In the following sections, I explain several factors to consider when you choose a cover price.

TIP

If you're working with a POD publisher, rather than a short-run or offset traditional printer, the POD company probably either helps you set your cover price or sets it for you. See Chapter 12 for the scoop on traditional short-run printers and Chapter 13 for more about POD publishers.

Calculating your publication costs

Base your publishing cost calculations on mathematical estimations and budgeting. Determine how much money you've invested (or plan to invest) in your publishing project to write and publish your book. Every aspect of the publishing process involves a wide range of costs and service fees. Here are the costs that you specifically need to determine, which directly impact your cover price:

>> **Fixed expenses:** Such as writing, editing, and design costs.

>> **Printing and listing costs:** Based on the *print run* (the number of copies) that you order. (See the following section for details on print runs and Part 3 for basics on printing.) If you plan to publish e-books, determine what percentage of the cover price e-book sellers (such as Amazon, Barnes & Noble, and Apple Books) charge you.

Depending on how you print your books, your printing costs can vary greatly. The more copies of your book that you have printed at the same time, the lower the cost per copy. Keep in mind, although a book from a major publisher may sell for $19.95, a self-published author might have to sell a similar book for $24.95 to make any money. This pricing depends on how you print or publish the book. Using a POD publisher often requires a higher cover price, regardless of the competition, because the POD company charges extra fees for their printing and distribution services.

>> **Promotional and distribution costs:** Including shipping, warehousing, advertising, marketing, and public relations for your books.

TIP

Use a spreadsheet application, such as Microsoft Excel, Google Sheets, or Apple Numbers, to create a detailed budget, track expenses, and calculate your break-even point while you begin to determine the cover price of your book. Look to Chapter 7 for more ideas on budgeting and tracking expenses.

Gathering market information

Do your market comparison research. Look at already published books from other authors and publishers that have a similar size, format, and topic to your book. Make sure that you don't underprice or overprice your book for the current market.

If you plan to directly sell most of your book inventory at personal appearances or through your own e-commerce website, you may be able to price your book higher than the market average. If you're sending a substantial proportion of your books to bookstores (or you plan to sell them through online-based sellers, such as Amazon or BN.com), be price-competitive.

Predicting demand

Accurately anticipating the demand for your book helps you predict sales and calculate potential revenues. You find a huge difference between having anticipated sales of 1,000 copies of your book (which targets a very niche audience) and sales of 25,000 copies or more for a general interest book that attracts a mass market audience.

Keep these audience differences in mind:

>> **A niche-oriented audience:** Limits sales potential, so you may want to have a higher cover price for your book to ensure profits.

Selling your book directly through in-person appearances or via your own e-commerce website can save you a lot of money and allow you to keep a greater portion of your book's cover price as the result of each sale.

>> **A mass-market audience:** Requires an expansive marketing, advertising, and promotional campaign, which you have to pay for. If you plan to sell a lot of books, you can reduce the cover price somewhat to earn higher profits based on sales volume.

REMEMBER

Doing proper market research, knowing the size of your audience, and having realistic expectations helps you anticipate demand for your book. Begin by researching the sales success of previously published books that have similar topics and marketing campaigns. You need to market your book directly to readers and determine the best ways to reach them. Chapter 3 helps you better understand your target readers.

If you plan to sell a small number of books or want to keep upfront publishing costs down, consider using a POD service. But POD publishers have a very high per-copy cost. However, if you use a short-run printer to print 100, 500, or 1,000 copies of your book at the same time, the more copies of the book you print, the lower your per-copy cost and the more profit you make per copy sold. However, you have a much higher upfront investment in printing and warehousing the books that you create through a short-run printer when compared with using POD, for example.

Considering wholesale and discounted pricing

Depending on how you plan to sell your book, you may need to calculate potential profits based on the wholesale or discounted price for which you plan to sell your book. (Also consider sales commissions and royalties that you may need to pay for certain distribution opportunities.) For example, booksellers, distributors, and wholesalers may purchase your book in large quantities, but at a discount of 40 to 60 percent off the cover price. If you plan to sell your book through Amazon or BN.com, for example, these services also take a nice chunk of the cover price in the form of their fees.

REMEMBER

Unless you plan to sell your book directly to readers, via your own website or when you make appearances or do lectures, plan on selling it at a significantly discounted price. See Chapter 15 for details about distributing your book through traditional channels.

Determining your book's perceived value

How much are people really willing to pay for your book? Some nonfiction special-interest trade paperbacks have a retail price of $39.95 or higher because the intended reader perceives the information that they contain as valuable. Knowing your audience helps you evaluate how much they may be willing to pay for your book at retail. However, for a novel, a reader might be willing to pay only $9.99 (or even less), based on what major publishers charge for similar works.

Here are some considerations when determining your book's perceived value:

TIP

>> **For exclusive content:** If your book provides information, facts, statistics, or other content that readers can find only in your book, those readers may consider that content extra valuable. So they may pay a slight premium based on their perception of value — especially if you offer them an opportunity to learn from a recognized expert on the book's topic (that's you!).

>> **For a work of fiction:** Perceived value doesn't really apply to fiction. Readers expect to pay under $10 for a fiction paperback or e-book. Even if the novel is a bestseller, readers won't pay a premium for it. Mass-market paperbacks (novels) typically have a relatively low cover price compared to nonfiction trade paperbacks for this reason.

>> **For comparable titles:** After performing your own financial calculations (which you can read about in section "Calculating your publication costs," earlier in this chapter) and sales projections, take a look at competing book titles already on the market to determine their pricing and how the sales history is trending for those titles. Use this competitive-research information to determine whether your book's intended cover price is too low or too high:

- **Too low:** If any book is priced much lower than its competition, potential readers may think that book possesses less valuable information.

- **Too high:** If the book is priced much higher than the competition, the potential reader may opt to purchase the less expensive book.

WARNING

With so much hype around books written by artificial intelligence (AI), such as ChatGPT, readers will be wary of purchasing a book from a non-credible author. You may foresee get-rich-quick schemes for self-publishing books created by using AI, which could theoretically save time and money on the writing and editing processes. But following this practice can be a slippery slope that causes you to destroy your reputation as an author or expert in your field. The perceived value of your book will be low if readers feel that they could acquire the same information for free by doing a quick Google search, or if they find out that you had the book written in under five minutes by using an AI-based text generator. If a book appears to be written by a non-human, contains inaccurate or out-of-date information, or otherwise comes across as disreputable, the potential reader will likely opt to buy a book that seems more credible.

Putting everything together to come up with a magic number

After you calculate the total cost per book to have it printed (flip back to the section "Calculating your publication costs," earlier in this chapter), use this important piece of information to help you create your book's cover price. If you'll be publishing the book exclusively in e-book formats, your costs include writing, editing, layout/design, marketing, and potentially paying a hefty commission to Amazon, BN.com, and/or Apple Books — but you don't have any printing costs whatsoever.

Your *cost per book* is the total amount of money you need to spend to have each copy of your book printed. To determine your cost per book, simply add together all of your publication costs and divide it by the number of copies you plan to have printed. I can't offer you a set formula to figure cover price based on cost per book, though. Everyone has a totally different way to figure their book's price, based on how they plan to print and publish the book, which distribution method(s) they want to use, and who their target audience is.

REMEMBER

You do need to consider how you plan to sell the book and what distribution methods you plan to use. Depending on these choices, you may earn the entire cover price of the book, or just 40, 50, or 60 percent of the cover price. Check out the chapters in Part 4 for a look at booksellers and distribution methods.

Note: The calculations in the following sections don't consider any advertising, marketing, or public relations costs associated with promoting your book to its intended audience.

For direct sales

If you're selling your book directly to consumers at its cover price, you can calculate your profit by subtracting the cost per book from the cover price. For example, if you set your book's cover price at $19.95 and your total cost per book is $6, your profit — if you sell your book directly to a customer for the cover price — is $13.95 ($19.95 − $6) per copy. If you sell your entire print run of 2,000 books directly to customers (through your own website or when you make appearances), your total profit for that print run will be $27,900 (2,000 x $13.95).

For selling through others

If you plan to sell your book through retailers, booksellers, wholesalers, or distributors, you often sell it for 40 to 60 percent off the cover price to those entities. You also need to calculate any additional sales commissions or fees that you need to pay.

So, say that you want to make your book's cover price $19.95, and the total cost per book is $6. You're selling the book to a retailer at 40 percent off the cover price at $11.97 ($19.95 x 0.6), so your per copy profit will be $5.97 ($11.97 − $6). If you sell your entire print run of 2,000 books through booksellers and retailers, you'll earn $11,940 (2,000 x $11.97).

Choosing printing and distribution options wisely

REMEMBER

Choosing the most competitive printer, negotiating your best printing deal, and accurately anticipating demand so that you can determine the most appropriate size of your print run helps you keep your costs down and increases your book's profit potential.

Print-related factors, such as trim size, page count, paper type, cover stock, and binding, all impact your printing costs. For example, you can cut costs by hiring a traditional short-run printer to publish a trade paperback book (as opposed to hardcover) with a less expensive paper stock, a larger trim size, and fewer pages. However, you don't want to jeopardize the professional look of your book.

The printer that you hire needs to understand what your book is about, its intended audience, how you plan to distribute it, and your budget, so that the printer can help you make appropriate printing-related decisions. See Part 3 for more about your self-publishing printing options.

If you plan to sell your book directly to consumers or retailers, you may need to charge sales tax. Every state has different guidelines, so be sure to consult with your accountant to ensure that you collect the appropriate amount of sales tax on applicable sales. As for shipping charges, you don't need to calculate those into the cover price of your book. When people place an order for your book — for example, from your website — they probably anticipate paying extra for shipping and handling. However, most avid readers tend to buy books from Amazon or other online booksellers that don't necessarily charge shipping costs for their sales.

TIP

To help encourage sales from your website, consider offering free shipping to be competitive with other online retailers potentially selling your book or similar books.

The Right Time: Selecting Your Book's Publication Date

Part of taking a well-organized and well-thought-out approach to self-publishing involves determining the best time of year to release your book. Consider the time it takes to complete each stage of the publishing process (taking into account lead times and processing times needed by editors, layout people, graphic designers, proofreaders, printers, distributors, order fulfillment houses, and so on) and plan your release date accordingly.

REMEMBER

Your publication date is the date your book goes to press. Your *street date* or *release date* is the day your book becomes available to the public. After you set a firm release date for your book, begin accepting pre-orders via your own website or through online services such as Amazon, BN.com, or Apple Books. However, after you begin to accept pre-orders, you absolutely must make your book available on its release date.

TIP

If your book has seasonal interest or must be released in conjunction with a certain holiday or date, scheduling becomes that much more critical. Missing that date could cost you sales.

Choose a date to release your book that's achievable and that makes the most sense in terms of generating the highest possible sales, based on your audience; the topic of your book; and your writing, production, printing, distribution, advertising, public relations, and marketing schedules. Here are a couple of examples:

>> If you're releasing a book about decorating your home for the Christmas holiday, a good time to release the book would be early fall (two or three months *before* Christmas), not after the holiday season.

>> January or February provides a great time to release a book about dating or romance because you can tie in your promotional efforts with Valentine's Day.

Chapter **9**

Coming Up with Creative Page Design and Layout

When readers open your book, they expect to see each page professionally designed. In addition to the content being free of spelling and grammatical mistakes (something a professional editor helps you with; see Chapter 6), from a visual standpoint, each page should look appealing and easy to read.

If you plan to create a printed book, making its interior look good involves laying out each page and converting the final pages into a PDF file before it goes to press. The formatting and design that you apply to your book's interior directly impacts how your book looks when you ultimately print it. (If your focus is on publishing e-books, see Chapter 11 for more information on how to layout and design those formats.)

Many companies that offer all-inclusive publishing solutions, such as print-on-demand (POD; see Chapter 13), include basic page layout and design services. But if you're handling your self-publishing project entirely on your own, you must also decide how to make your book visually appealing by using other methods.

This chapter focuses on your manuscript's layout and design, the software you can use for that task, and the help you can find to ensure that the book's interior looks professional and appealing. If you're not proficient in using a popular desktop publishing software package — such as Adobe InDesign or QuarkXPress, for example — you can hire a professional graphic designer to handle this aspect of the book publishing process for you.

Delving into Do-It-Yourself Page Design

A book's interior pages must contain the proper information, displayed in headline and body text fonts that are easy to read. If your book includes pieces of artwork, you must properly format this content and place it on the appropriate pages (with applicable captions and in-text references). A properly designed book also includes all the elements common to professionally published titles in the front and back matter. In the following sections, I guide you through considerations for choosing your fonts (typeface, point size, and style), deciding on a few upfront design considerations, and creating the body of your book.

TIP

Full-featured word processors, such as Microsoft Word and Apple Pages, have features and templates that you can use to lay out and design the interior of a book, and then convert the content into the required PDF format. However, if you want complete creative control, use page layout and design software that's designed specifically for this purpose. This kind of software is called *desktop publishing software,* and you can find packages for both PC and Mac platforms. (Jump ahead to the section "Using Popular Desktop Publishing Software," later in this chapter, for an overview of your software options.)

Offering design instructions in a word processor

Authors create most manuscripts by using a word processor, such as Microsoft Word. Unless the person who does your page layout and design tells you differently, within your manuscript, you can add basic formatting instructions, telling the layout and design person where headings, subheadings, sidebars, photos, illustrations, and other elements go. (The actual text of your manuscript doesn't need any formatting instructions.)

For example, while you're writing, you can add the line ⟨BEGIN SIDEBAR⟩ and ⟨END SIDEBAR⟩ into your manuscript to tell the design person where a sidebar begins and ends. For a level-one heading (the biggest heading you use), you can use the code [H1] followed by the heading. For a *subheading* (a heading smaller than a level-one heading), you could use the code [H2] or [H3] followed by the heading text, as appropriate.

A level-one heading created in a word processor looks like this example:

[H1] This Is a Sample Level-One Heading

When the designer starts doing their job, they transform the heading to look something like the heading of the section "Delving into Do-It-Yourself Page Design," earlier in this chapter (although you can choose the typeface and point size; see the section "Choosing fonts," later in this chapter).

REMEMBER

The more direction that you provide within the manuscript itself, the more easily any graphic designer you work with can create the book's internal layout to match your vision.

Making some upfront design decisions

When you embark on the page design process, focus on your book's target audience and what's appropriate for the type of book that you're publishing. Begin with good decisions about these all-important factors:

>> **Font (typeface, point size, and style):** The font can make your book more visually appealing but can also set a tone for the reader's experience. Using a font that's too small or a type style that's difficult to read can make it much harder for the reader to appreciate and understand the content.

>> **Content distribution:** Putting too much content on each page can also make the overall book more challenging to read. Set proper margins and allow for adequate white space on each page. Also, recognize that if you choose a body font size that's too small, the result can be lines of text that contain too many characters and look cumbersome.

>> **Purposeful design:** In the same way that creating the content for your book is a creative and well-thought-out process, so is the layout and design of your book. The creativity and rigor that you incorporate into this phase of the publishing process can determine how well your book sells and whether your readers will enjoy looking at the pages while they're reading.

Setting up the design's foundation

With the important factors from the preceding section in mind, follow these steps to establish other foundational design elements:

1. **Choose the *trim size* (dimensions) for your book.**

   This step sets the width and height dimensions of each page and helps you figure out how much actual content fits on each page.

   Note: At this stage, don't aim for a certain page count for the total book; wait and see how your choices affect the book's length before tweaking anything within the layout.

2. **Determine your use of color.**

   Figure out how many colors you want to include and how you plan to use them within the book.

   Many books use black ink on white pages, and black-and-white photos within the book's interior. You can, however, opt to include a second or third color or utilize full-color printing throughout your entire book, using additional colors to highlight headings or specific content. You might print the text in your book in one color but display the drawings, charts, or illustrations, for example, in a different color so that they stand out more and are easier to read.

   Note: This color decision affects your production costs dramatically: More colors, more money.

3. **Outline the specific order for major elements of your book.**

   See a listing of major book elements and their placement in the following section.

4. **Decide how you want each element to represent your book's look and feel.**

   This relates to the book's overall appearance and, if it's a physical book, how it will feel in someone's hands. The thickness of the book cover and the paper used for the inside of the book impact how it looks and feels.

Knowing and sequencing your book's elements

The front matter and back matter of your book typically require more formatting than the main body of your book because of their unique and specific content. The front matter includes

» Title page

» Copyright page

- » Acknowledgements and dedication

- » Table of contents

- » Foreword or preface

- » Introduction

The back matter can include

- » The appendixes

- » Bibliography

- » Glossary

- » Index

- » Author bio

REMEMBER

The type of book that you're publishing doesn't necessarily require all of these elements. If you're using a POD printer or an offset printer that offers a turnkey publishing solution, the printer typically formats the front matter and the back matter for you.

Designing the Body of Your Book

Based on the type of book that you're publishing, your target audience, and your own sense of style, you need to make decisions about the overall look of your book's interior. These decisions should reflect the foundational elements from the preceding section and remain consistent from page to page. They determine how your book ultimately looks when it's printed.

Coming up with the right page design means incorporating a bit of creativity into the process and focusing on each element of your book's interior. You need to select headline and text fonts, which include the typeface, point size, and style (bold, italic, and so on). For this chapter, you find the following terms used for the text elements in your book:

- » **Typeface:** The name that describes a character set of one design (Arial, Garamond, and so on)

- » **Point size:** The numeric designation that describes the size of typeface

>> **Style (or type style):** The treatment that distinguishes versions of a typeface (bold, italic, underline, and so on)

>> **Font:** The term that describes a combination of the typeface, point size, and type style factors

You also need to decide on a master page design so that all the interior pages are consistent in terms of margins, layout, and overall appearance. I cover these topics in the following sections and provide some handy hints for creating chapter title pages and incorporating artwork into your book.

Choosing body and heading fonts

In the world of graphic design and typesetting, typed characters are measured in *points.* There are 72 points in one inch. This measurement means that the smaller the point size of the font, the smaller it appears on the printed page. If you make the text too small, your readers may struggle to read your words. If the text is too large, your book may look childish and amateurish. Text that's too large also boosts your page count, which in turn increases your printing cost and later the shipping cost of your book.

TIP

For the main body text within your book, use a type size of between 10 and 12 points, unless your book is targeted to young children or adults who are visually impaired (in which case, you may want to use a larger point-size type, such as 14- or 15-point type.) Make your chapter titles and headings larger than your body text and display them in a bold style.

The fonts that you choose for body text and the ones you choose for chapter titles or headings don't have to be the same typeface. Figure 9-1 showcases how Garamond (a common text typeface) looks in several different point sizes: 9 points, 10 points, 11 points, 12 points, and 13 points. Also in Figure 9-1, you find several different sizes and styles of the Georgia typeface, one of many that you can use for headings because it stands out visually and is easy to read.

REMEMBER

Decreasing the point size of your font, even by a small amount, decreases your book's page count dramatically (resulting in lower production costs) because more text fits on each page. But remember that a standard 10- to 12-point font is much easier to read than a smaller 9-point font.

This is a sample of Garamond displayed in a 9-point size. As you can see, it's a bit difficult to read.

This is a sample of Garamond displayed in a 10-point size. For certain types of books, when you're trying to make a lot of words fit on a page, this point size is appropriate.

This is a sample of Garamond displayed in an 11-point size. This point size is much easier to read and more pleasing to the human eye.

This is a sample of Garamond displayed in a 12-point size. Most people will have no trouble reading this size type. It's suitable for the body text of almost any type of book.

This is the Georgia font displayed in 17-point type. It's ideal for level-one headings.

This is the Georgia font displayed in a bold, 17-point type. It's also ideal for level-one headings.

This is the Georgia font displayed in a bold and italicized 17-point type. It's another way of displaying this font when using it for a level-one heading.

This is the Georgia font displayed in a bold, 15-point type. It's ideal for level-two headings.

This is the Georgia font displayed in a bold and italicized 10-point type. It's ideal for level-three headings.

FIGURE 9-1:
Choose the fonts
for your main text
and headings
from a variety of
point sizes.

The font — typeface, size, and style — that you choose for your book's main text should be easy to read, based on the look that you're trying to achieve for your book, and on what appeals to its intended audience. Serif-based fonts tend to be popular for interior text in books:

>> **Serif fonts:** Use short lines, curves, or embellishments, called *serifs*, that project from the top or bottom of a letter's main stroke. This style of font helps guide the reader's eyes in a straight line across the page.

>> **Sans serif fonts:** Use less curves and embellishments. They're great for headings but can make reading more difficult when used as a main text font because the text will look more complex on the page.

TIP

See Figure 9-2 for a sampling of common text fonts. Visit the Adobe Type Library online (http://fonts.adobe.com) to see a sampling of over 20,000 fonts — some of which can work well in books. From this website, you can see samples of each font, with the typefaces shown in various sizes and styles.

TIP

Make sure that you can format the typeface that you choose in a variety of styles, including normal, **bold,** and *italics.* (Refer to Figure 9-2 for examples of fonts in all three styles.) Having this variety gives you the most flexibility when laying out your body text.

Focusing on formatting

Formatting refers to how the text is positioned on the page — the page margins, page numbers, and running heads — as well as the structure of paragraphs (for example, spacing between lines of text, use of indentation, and justification). A reader has more trouble reading a cluttered page, and they potentially can find the clutter confusing. Using white space effectively on each page helps make your book more visually appealing.

Follow these steps to format your book's text:

1. **Set the margins for each page.**

Make all of your margins consistent for similar elements. The book's trim size, in part, determines what margins you use, along with the length of the manuscript and your desired page count. Also, you may choose a slightly different set of margins for the first page in a chapter to distinguish it from the other pages (see the following section for discussion of chapter title pages).

Your printer or professional designer can help you choose appropriate margins —there are no hard rules.

2. **Decide whether you want your book to have a running head.**

   Your book's *running head* is text that appears across the top of each page (or every other page) and can consist of the book's title, chapter title, and/or the author's name. If you study other books, you may see that some books display the book's title on the left pages and the chapter title on the right pages. What you include within the running head is entirely up to you.

3. **Decide where you want the page numbers to appear.**

   You have a number of choices: At the top of the page in the center, upper-right corner, or upper-left corner; or at the bottom of the page in the center, lower-right corner, or lower-left corner.

This is an example of Garamond, one of many popular body text fonts. It's displayed here using a normal 12-point font size. **This is what it looks like displayed in bold.** *This is the same Garamond 12-point font displayed in italics.*

This is an example of Times New Roman, one of many popular body text fonts. It's displayed here using a normal 12-point font size. **This is what it looks like displayed in bold.** *This is the same Times New Roman 12-point font displayed in italics.*

This is an example of Baskerville, one of many popular body text fonts. It's displayed here using a normal 12-point font size. **This is what it looks like displayed in bold.** *This is the same Baskerville 12-point font displayed in italics.*

This is an example of Goudy, one of many popular body text fonts. It's displayed here using a normal 12-point font size. **This is what it looks like displayed in bold.** *This is the same Goudy 12-point font displayed in italics.*

FIGURE 9-2:
Garamond, Times New Roman, Baskerville, Goudy, and Bookman Old Style are common serif-based typefaces.

This is an example of Bookman Old Style, one of many popular body text fonts. It's displayed here using a normal 12-point font size. **This is what it looks like displayed in bold.** *This is the same Bookman Old Style 12-point font displayed in italics.*

TIP

To help you develop design ideas, examine a handful of books that target a similar audience — because you *should* keep your audience in mind when making all layout and design decisions. Scrutinize the different design elements that those books have incorporated. Pick and choose elements that you like from those books — but be sure to add your own personal creativity when finalizing your book's design.

Crafting chapter title pages

You can include chapter title pages on the first page of each new chapter. The title page for a fiction or nonfiction book displays the chapter number and title (optional in fiction). For nonfiction, you may also want to include some type of graphic and/or a short paragraph (or bullet points) describing the subject of that chapter.

TIP

Depending on your creativity, you can jazz up your chapter title pages (see an example in Figure 9-3) in several different ways:

» Using a different typeface and larger point size than your body text

» Altering the typeface and/or size of the first few words or the initial letter at the beginning of the first paragraph of each chapter

» Creating a special graphic that goes on each chapter title page

When you create chapter title pages, you're free to use your own creativity; however, make all the chapter title pages in your book similar in their formatting to maintain continuity throughout the book. And don't forget, you have the option of eliminating differently formatted chapter title pages from your book altogether, and simply displaying the chapter number and title on the first page of each new chapter.

Some publishers insist that all chapter title pages (or the first page of each chapter) be on the right side of the open book (called a *recto page*) and include a blank or partially filled left-side page (called a *verso page*) prior to it. This is a tradition that not all publishers adhere to, so ultimately, you can decide whether you want to follow that practice. Generally, running heads and page numbers don't appear on chapter title pages.

Chapter 10

This Is the Title for Chapter 10

....

This is a graphic element to signify the beginning of Chapter 10.

....

This is the first paragraph of Chapter 10 that shows the use of an initial letter with a different typeface and larger point size. This differs from the normal body text of most of the chapters' paragraphs. Beginning a chapter with a page design that includes formatting unique to the first page is a good way to give readers a point of reference for starting and stopping their reading session.

FIGURE 9-3: Unique treatments for a chapter title page.

Incorporating artwork

Depending on the type of book that you're publishing, artwork — in the form of photographs, graphs, charts, tables, figures, illustrations, or clip art — adds visual appeal and helps you better communicate information.

To enhance the impact of your artwork, make sure that each graphic element is sized and formatted properly and placed on the appropriate page in your book:

>> **Sizing:** Size the images, charts, illustrations, and other graphics of your book so that your audience can easily read them. Depending on the trim size of your book, you may want to allocate at least a half-page per photograph, chart, or graphic. Some charts or graphs, however, may warrant a full page if they contain a lot of detailed information.

>> **Formatting:** When it comes to incorporating any type of artwork into your book, that artwork must first be translated into a digital format (if it's not in a digital format already), and then imported into the desktop publishing software that you (or your graphic designer) use to lay out your book's interior pages (see the section "Surveying software packages," later in this chapter, for the lowdown on your software options). You may need to scan photographs or other images and/or use specialized software to edit or fine-tune the digital images to meet the resolution requirements and technical specifications provided by your printer.

Don't use low-resolution artwork in your book. If you don't create or scan the photographs and artwork in high resolution, the printed version will appear blurry or *pixilated* — meaning that the picture appears like a bunch of dots, rather than one smooth image. This error can dramatically detract from the professional appearance of your book. Ideally, reproduce photos at 300 pixels-per-inch (ppi) resolution, although a higher resolution could make the images look better, depending on the printing method being used. Contact your printer for details about specific file-format and printing requirements for artwork that you plan to include within the interior of your book.

>> **Placement:** Place all artwork in the appropriate location, after the text that references that artwork. You can reference figure numbers within the text and display the corresponding figure numbers with the artwork to help readers understand where to look for the image that corresponds to the text that they're reading. For example, in Chapter 1, you could label the first figure Figure 1-1 (or Figure 1.1), the second figure Figure 1-2 (or Figure 1.2), and so on.

Also, never cluster too much artwork together because that can detract from or interrupt the flow of text and look messy.

To help you edit artwork and prepare each image for inclusion within your book, you can use a graphics program, such as

>> **Adobe Photoshop:** www.adobe.com/photoshop

>> **Adobe Photoshop Express:** www.adobe.com/products/photoshop-express.html

>> **Adobe Lightroom** (www.adobe.com/products/photoshop-lightroom.html)

>> **Any photo editing and enhancement application,** such as Apple Photos, Google Photos, or Coral PaintShop Pro. For portraits or photos containing people, Portrait Pro is a powerful and easy-to-use option.

Using Popular Desktop Publishing Software

If you plan to handle your book's page layout and design yourself, you need to first select a desktop publishing software package. In the following sections, I discuss the most popular package and give you a quick rundown on laying out your book by using templates.

Surveying software packages

After your manuscript is created by using Microsoft Word or another popular word processor (see the section "Offering design instructions in a word processor," earlier in this chapter), import your text into a desktop publishing software package so that you can lay out your content. This step is called creating the *galleys*, which show exactly what the pages within your book will look like when you see them printed.

You have several choices when it comes to powerful desktop publishing software. I cover these options in the following sections:

>> **Adobe InDesign:** www.adobe.com/indesign

>> **Affinity Publisher 2:** http://affinity.serif.com/publisher

>> **Apple Pages:** www.apple.com/pages

>> **Microsoft Publisher:** http://www.microsoft.com/microsoft-365/publisher

>> **QuarkXPress:** www.quark.com/products/quarkxpress

>> **Scribus:** www.scribus.net

Adobe InDesign

InDesign, Adobe's comprehensive desktop publishing solution, features all the tools and functionality that you need to expertly create your book's interior layout and design. This software is also compatible with a wide range of graphic development and editing programs, such as Adobe Photoshop, Apple Photos, Google Photos, or Coral PaintShop Pro (used for editing photographs and other graphics). This application has one major benefit: Instead of purchasing it outright, you can pay a monthly subscription fee to use it and pay for only the duration of time that you need it.

WARNING

Adobe InDesign was created for professional graphic designers and relies on the user's working knowledge of graphic design to use it properly. If you're not yet an experienced user, you can expect a steep learning curve, so you may want to use a pre-created template that comes with the InDesign software to save you time (see the section "Utilizing templates for maximum layout ease," later in this chapter).

Affinity Publisher 2

According to the software's designers, "Affinity Publisher is the next generation of professional page layout software. From books, magazines and marketing materials to social media templates, website mock-ups and more, this incredibly smooth, intuitive app gives you the power to combine your images, graphics, and text to make beautiful layouts ready for publication." You can get it for a Windows PC or a Mac for a one-time payment of $70.

Apple Pages

Available exclusively for Apple-based computers and mobile devices, Apple Pages is a free full-featured word processor that also includes basic page layout and desktop publishing elements. It's one of the easiest applications of this bunch to use. But if you plan to use it for desktop publishing, stick with the Mac version (not the iPhone/iPad version) because it lacks important features and it's very difficult to do page layout work on a small size display.

Microsoft Publisher

Microsoft Publisher is desktop publishing software that's part of the Microsoft 365 family of products. You can use this software for designing and laying out the interior of virtually any type of book.

You may find an advantage to using this software because its interface and tools are very similar to all the other applications in the Microsoft 365 suite of products. So, if you already know how to work with Word, Excel, or PowerPoint, the learning curve for mastering Publisher may be much shorter than with other publishing software. It's among the easiest to use of the desktop publishing applications that I recommend.

REMEMBER

Out of the desktop publishing applications described in this chapter, Publisher is the easiest to use, but it offers limited functionality and leaves out features included in some of the others.

QuarkXPress

Ever since page layout and design went digital, QuarkXPress has been on the forefront when it comes to this aspect of publishing. Book and magazine publishers often choose this software to handle a wide range of desktop publishing needs.

QuarkXPress was created for professional graphic designers to use, and it offers a large assortment of tools and features that you can use to create extremely complex page designs. This comprehensive tool can handle all aspects of page layout and design. You begin by loading your basic text into this software, and then if you know the tricks of the trade to use it correctly, you wind up with a fully designed book ready to go to press.

REMEMBER

QuarkXPress has a steep learning curve, especially if you don't have a publishing background. It's also rather expensive. If you're undaunted, it's one of the most powerful desktop publishing and page layout design applications currently available.

Scribus

Scribus is an open-source application that's available for all popular computer operating systems. In addition to being rather powerful, it's also 100 percent free to download and use. Scribus is designed to handle layout, typesetting, and preparation of files for publication.

Using templates for maximum layout ease

Templates reduce the number of design-oriented decisions that you need to make. They also help minimize design errors and ensure that your book has a professional appearance. Depending on which desktop publishing application you wind up working with, you may discover a comprehensive library of free or low-cost book design templates available to use specifically with that application.

Using a template can save you a lot of time and effort. Open your application and follow these simple steps:

1. **Choose a professionally created design template from the options that your application offers.**

   Find a template that resembles how you want your book to look.

2. **Import your text and artwork into the template.**

   Depending on the software you use to create your text, you may cut and paste your book contents into the desktop publishing application. Alternatively, you may need to import text-based files using the application's Import command.

3. **Customize the template to better meet your own design needs.**

   You can make changes to the template to adjust margins or fonts, for example.

4. **Save each chapter of the book as a separate laid-out file.**

   You can more easily manage smaller files. Plan to keep each chapter file separate until you merge them after you complete and look over the layout and design for all chapters.

TIP

For Adobe InDesign, you can find a nice selection of book templates by visiting http://stock.adobe.com/templates. For virtually all desktop publishing applications, you can also find a selection of book design templates at these websites:

>> **Envanto Elements:** http://elements.envato.com/graphic-templates/print-templates/book

>> **48 Hour Books:** www.48hrbooks.com/free-book-templates

>> **BookBaby:** www.bookbaby.com/book-printing/templates

>> **Book Design Templates:** www.bookdesigntemplates.com

Converting Laid-Out Pages into Printer-Friendly Files

After you design and lay out the interior of your book by using a desktop publishing software application (see the section "Using Popular Desktop Publishing Software," earlier in this chapter), you need to convert that file into a version that your printer can use for printing.

Portable Document Format (PDF) files

You can use Adobe Acrobat or a compatible program to create a PDF file. You hand the PDF file over to the printer, along with your cover design (see Chapter 10 for details on covers). The offset printer or POD publishing company that you use gives you the technical specifications for providing your entire book in PDF format; see Chapters 12 and 13 for more about these professional printer options.

The Adobe Acrobat application (www.adobe.com/acrobat) takes virtually any type of file, such as a document created by using Microsoft Publisher, InDesign, or QuarkXPress, and translates it into a digital PDF file. After you convert your book into a PDF format, it basically contains the ready-to-publish galleys for your book. Each page appears exactly how it will look when printed.

TIP

Some programs, such as InDesign, have the ability to create PDF files without using the Adobe Acrobat (or similar) software. If you're hiring a professional graphic designer to handle the layout and design of your book (see the section "Hiring a Professional Graphic Designer," later in this chapter, for discussion of these pros) or using a POD or short-run printer, they can probably handle this phase of the publishing process for you.

PostScript PRN files

A PostScript PRN file is similar to a PDF file and is compatible with printing equipment used by book printers and publishers. Most desktop publishing software packages can export a file into the PostScript PRN format. Your printer will provide specific guidelines on how to create the right type of file to meet its needs for printing.

Hiring a Professional Graphic Designer

If you don't feel comfortable with handling the design and layout of your book (and/or the cover design), consider hiring a professional graphic designer to help you out. This person has experience working with visuals and knows how to choose elements — fonts (typefaces, point sizes, and styles), color schemes, and graphic images — that all work together to help communicate your book's content in a visually appealing way.

REMEMBER

Graphic designers are typically born with natural artistic ability, which they then supplement with several years of training. These people also know how to work with complicated software-based graphic design tools, such as InDesign, Photoshop, and QuarkXPress, that the publishing industry uses. Designers have experience creating content that's compatible with what your book printer needs so that they can publish the most professional-looking book possible.

In the following sections, I give you guidance on finding a graphic designer and providing your designer with proper information on the layout that you envision. For specific information on working with a graphic designer to create your book's cover, head to Chapter 10.

Finding the right expert

You need to hire the right expert to help you lay out and design your book if you want your book to look professional and truly appeal to readers. Even if you have the most fascinating and engaging content for your readers, if the book doesn't have a professional appearance, you lose credibility amongst your readers and potential book reviewers.

Hiring the right designer means finding someone who has experience in layout and design work for books (preferably the type of book that you want their help with). Look for someone who has top-notch design skills and creative, artistic abilities. Also, look for an impressive portfolio of previous work.

Knowing where and when to find a designer

You can easily find a professional graphic designer — really, you can. Ideally, look for someone who comes highly recommended by someone you know. However, you can also find freelance graphic designers on the Internet by visiting these sites:

>> www.upwork.com/hire/book-designers

>> www.guru.com

>> www.99designs.com/book-design-services

Start the process of finding a graphic designer early in the self-publishing process — ideally as soon as you finish writing and editing your manuscript. It takes time to track down suitable candidates, evaluate their respective portfolios, communicate your needs, negotiate a price, and then allow the chosen designer ample time to work on your book.

Also, begin putting together ideas for the design of your front and back covers (see Chapter 10) as soon as you decide to write the book.

Here are two important time-related considerations when hiring your designer:

>> **Turnaround time:** Ask your designer about the timeframe in which they can work to ensure it fits with your publishing schedule. Depending on the workload of the designer, designing and laying out your book properly (as well as working on the covers) can take anywhere from a few days to several weeks.

>> **Corrections:** Leave ample time to make corrections and tweaks to the design after your graphic designer completes the initial draft of your book's interior and covers.

Evaluating designers' work

After you develop a creative vision regarding how you want your book to look, interview a handful of graphic designers and review their portfolios of work. Find someone whose work resembles your vision or who seems capable of taking your vision and transforming it into a professional-looking book.

TIP

While you interview designers and evaluate their portfolios, ask the following questions:

>> How and where were you trained?

>> May I see your portfolio of sample work?

>> Do you understand my book's subject and what kind of readers it targets?

>> How much experience do you have with book layout and design (and/or creating book covers, if you also would like to use this person for that task)? Specifically, do you have experience doing book layout for my intended target audience?

>> Do you know how to use popular software tools to create laid-out pages and covers that are compatible with the technical requirements of my chosen printer?

>> Are you willing to make multiple versions of the page and cover layout, and then make changes as I fine-tune the design?

>> Can you complete the book's layout and covers within the timeframe I need?

>> What are your rates, and how do you bill?

Graphic designers are only as good as the work they create. Having an impressive educational background is useful, but having natural artistic ability and the skills to create high-impact designs is far more important. Examine the designer's portfolio of work and use that as your main criteria when making a hiring decision.

Setting a fair price

The cost of hiring a graphic designer to lay out and design your book's interior can cost anywhere from $500 to several thousand dollars, depending on the design-er's experience and how much time they need to invest working on your project. You get to use your negotiating skills when finding an acceptable fair price with the graphic designer. Consider these factors when proposing and agreeing on the graphic designer's fee:

>> **Find the best.** Find a graphic designer whose work you really like and who you believe can do the job, and then negotiate a price.

>> **Work directly with the designer.** You can often have much better luck negotiating a lower price with an individual designer or freelancer, as opposed to someone who works for a graphic design agency.

>> **Set a flat rate.** You can often save money by negotiating a flat rate for the project, rather than an hourly rate.

Deciding how many graphic designers you need

Many graphic designers can do both interior page layout and design, as well as cover design. However, some designers specialize only in one area. If you hire designers who have specific areas of expertise or you have a very tight deadline, consider hiring separate designers to handle the interior design and the cover. Discuss your requirements with the initial designer you're interested in hiring and determine whether they're capable and comfortable handling both tasks.

TIP

In some cases, if you use a turnkey POD solution, the publisher/printer provides both interior design and cover design services. In this situation, allow the publisher to handle the book's interior design, but still hire your own graphic designer (at an additional expense) to design the book's cover. As you can discover in Chapter 10, you definitely don't want your book cover to look less-than-professional or reflect the use of a generic-looking template.

Supplying your layout preferences and design feedback

Most graphic designers don't sit down and read your book in its entirety. So, you have to properly educate the designer you hire about your book and its intended audience. Be prepared to tell the graphic designer specifically what you want in terms of

>> The look of the interior of your book (the use of white space, possible separate chapter title page design, and specifics of paragraph formatting, for example)

>> Fonts — typefaces, point sizes, and styles — that you want to use

>> How you want the designer to incorporate artwork, graphics, and other visual elements

>> The elements to include in the front and back matter

>> The use of running heads and placement of page numbers

>> Any other creative input you have in regard to page layout and design

TIP

Make sure that you plan your publishing schedule to give the designer ample time to go back and revise the book based on your comments and new ideas. Book layout is a highly creative process that involves plenty of tweaking and fine-tuning while you get it just right. While the graphic designer begins to provide you with drafts of the layout, give them your open and honest thoughts and criticisms. Communicating your desires ensures that you wind up with a layout that you really like. Expect to go back and forth multiple times before you wind up with a final design.

REMEMBER

You also need to allow time for your editor/proofreader to go back and re-read the entire book after your graphic designer lays it out to ensure that neither you nor the designer inadvertently introduced new errors.

IN THIS CHAPTER

» Coming up with a snappy book title

» Discovering the elements of a good-looking front cover

» Putting together a stellar back cover

» Getting the skinny on your book's spine

» Hiring a professional designer for your book's cover

Chapter **10**

Crafting (and Judging) Your Book's Cover

D o you know that saying, "You can't judge a book by its cover"? Well, forget you've ever heard it! In truth, intended readers of your book are your jury, and these people *will* judge your book by its cover. In fact, they often make their buying decision based on how well the cover captures their attention. So, for a verdict in your favor — in this case, a sale — create the best front and back cover possible, plus brainstorm to come up with the best title and subtitle (if applicable).

If you want a Grade-A cover, you probably have to hire a freelance graphic designer who has book cover creation experience. You'll find the additional investment in hiring a graphic designer worth it because having an incredible cover that stands out favorably translates into more sales and enhanced credibility. In this chapter, I discuss working with a professional graphic designer to craft an impressive book cover.

Also, this chapter focuses on the importance of having an awesome title and subtitle, and delves into how to create attention-getting front and back covers that do everything possible to help you sell books. You can also discover how the book's spine acts as a powerful sales tool, especially when it comes to bookstore or other retail sales.

Brainstorming a Catchy Title

What makes a catchy title? Some authors and publishers believe it's a clever play on words or something memorable. Others believe it's a short combination of words that communicates exactly what the book is about. But I know of only one rule when it comes to creating a title for your book: Capture the reader's attention!

For works of fiction, creativity in a title is more important than communicating a clear message about the content. However, for nonfiction, the title and subtitle should quickly educate the reader about the topic of the book and who it appeals to. Think of your book's title as the main headline of a breaking news story. If the person wants to discover more, instead of tuning in for the newscast at 11:00 p.m., they can flip the book over and read the back cover. Then, when they're ready to delve into the topic, they can purchase the book and read it in its entirety.

REMEMBER

Generally, fiction books, such as novels, don't have subtitles. However, if your book is nonfiction, creating a catchy and informative subtitle definitely helps you sell books. Get creative when deciding on your book's main title, but write your subtitle (for works of nonfiction) so that it explains exactly what the book is about or offers a really compelling reason why someone should read it. In the following sections, I show you how to create a clear, concise, and memorable title for your book.

Keeping your title short and clear

Potential readers find long book titles confusing. Long titles don't usually look good on a book's cover, and they seldom help to actually sell a book. Make your main title short and sweet. The shorter, the better. Meanwhile, keep the subtitle (if you choose to use one) to a short explanatory phrase.

TIP

Ideally, keep your main title to under five or six words, which allows you to display the title by using a large font. On the front cover, make the main title of your book large enough for a potential buyer to easily see and read it from up to 6 feet away. (See the section "Selecting the right font and placement for the title," later in this chapter, for more about displaying your book's title effectively.) Also, if you plan to primarily sell your book online, the main title of your book should include one or more keywords that are likely to show up when someone searches for your book using Google or another search tool.

While you develop your title, think about your intended audience (see Chapter 3 for more on targeting certain readers) and create a title that appeals to those people. Consider the following questions when you create your title:

>> Who does the book target, and what do you need to get their attention?

>> Why would someone want to read your book?

>> What does the book offer?

>> What's unique about the book?

>> What can someone discover or learn from reading your book?

>> What problems can the book help solve?

>> What keywords — that potential readers would likely search for online — can you use in the title?

The title of your book is a sales tool. When people hear or read the title, it should immediately capture their attention, and they should want to find out more about your book. Using a play on words in your title as an attention-getting device may often boost sales. Examples of this tactic include *Tequila Mockingbird: Cocktails with a Literary Twist* by Tim Federle, *The Twelve Dogs of Christmas* by David Rosenfelt, or *The Pun Also Rises* by John Pollack. *Note:* If you use a play on words in your nonfiction title, make sure that your book has a subtitle that clarifies what the book is about.

For fiction books, create a title that captures the reader's attention or that somehow relates to the storyline. For nonfiction books, the title should offer a clear benefit or solution, worded in a straightforward way that requires no interpretation or assumptions by the potential reader. Need inspiration? Take a trip to your local bookstore (or visit Amazon.com or BN.com) and check out the book titles for books that relate to yours in terms of audience or subject matter. Also, review the bestsellers lists.

REMEMBER

Of course, don't copy a book title from another book, but you can use your first-hand research (at bookstores and online) to get a good idea of what types of titles work well. It's important that your book have an original title that does not violate someone else's copyright.

Making your title stand out

Your book may be competing with at least a few others for a reader's attention — that is, unless your book covers a topic that's so targeted to a small niche market that it has absolutely no competition, which happens very rarely. Your book's title acts as its first line of defense against someone turning to a competitive book rather than choosing yours. Therefore, make your title stand out from the competition and make the potential reader immediately think, "Hey, I need to read this!" or "This book could really help me."

Creativity sets your book apart from the dozens (or thousands) of others that potentially focus on the same topic, which are available on the bookstore shelves or in online stores. After you capture someone's attention with your title, the book's back cover copy and design should sell the potential reader on actually buying the book (see the section "Turning to Your Book's Back Cover," later in this chapter, for details).

If you need help creating a catchy title, try one of these free website title generators:

>> **Reedsy:** `http://blog.reedsy.com/book-title-generator`

>> **Copywriting Course:** `http://copywritingcourse.com/book-title-generator`

>> **RanGen:** `www.rangen.co.uk/names/titlegen.php`

Here are a few tips to help you come up with an attention-grabbing title:

>> **Create a title for your book after you complete some or all of the manuscript.** While you delve deeper into your own manuscript, you have a better understanding of exactly what it's about, the actual content it contains, and what readers may find most engaging. Use this information to help you narrow down a good title. *Note:* You can much more easily create a title based on a finished book than you can create a manuscript around a pre-created title.

>> **Ask others for help.** Write out and distribute a list of titles to friends, coworkers, relatives, or people who might be interested in reading your book. Ask for their thoughts on the various titles, and then slowly narrow down the list based on the feedback that you receive.

>> **Incorporate action verbs and avoid clichés.** Use powerful words and specific phrases to help sell:

  • *Choosing action verbs can add intensity or impact to a title* and help the reader relate better to the subject matter. Action verbs can also draw in the potential reader and demonstrate what the book is about.

  • *Using a cliché in your title takes away from its originality* and detracts from the potential reader's perception of the overall content of your book. After all, if the title is unoriginal and uninspired, what does that say about the content of the entire book?

>> **Examine other book titles.** Again, visit any bookstore, check out the *New York Times* bestsellers list, or visit Amazon.com or BN.com to carefully look at other book titles. Ask yourself what makes those titles work. Why did the authors and publishers choose them?

Keeping a Close Eye on the Front Cover

A lot goes into a book's cover and into creating a positive first impression on the prospective reader. Whether consciously or subconsciously, the reader focuses on the following when they first see your book's cover:

>> The wording of the title and subtitle (if applicable)

>> The title's placement, size, color, and overall appearance

>> The author's name and credentials

>> The cover's color scheme and image

>> The cover's overall design

>> The hardcover or paper stock used for the book's cover

All the elements that make up your book cover should present a visually appealing design and color scheme. If you use a graphic or photo on your book's cover, that image should also communicate a strong message, have meaning, and relate to your book's content. The font that you choose for your book's title and subtitle should complement that image, not compete with it. For example, pair a modern-looking photo with a modern-looking title font. Don't let the artwork overpower your title. You don't want the title to get lost in the cover design. Remember, make your cover a powerful selling tool for your book, not an art project where you expect the audience to appreciate or reward abstract design.

REMEMBER

To really bring together engaging elements for your book's front cover, you need a great title and subtitle (see the preceding section) along with a superb cover designed created by a skilled graphic designer (see the section "Working with a Design Expert to Create Your Cover," later in this chapter). And unless you plan to use one or more photographs acquired from a stock photo agency, line up a professional photographer and/or illustrator to create your cover's main image(s). In the following sections, I give you tips on highlighting the book's title and the author's name on your cover, show you how to select a cover image and a color scheme, and explain how to pull together an attractive cover design.

Showcasing the front cover's text

Your book's cover should attract the reader's attention by incorporating an eye-catching visual design and text that quickly draws in and inspires the potential reader. The actual words used on your front cover (the title, subtitle, and so on) are important. But equally important is how the text appears. Carefully consider the typeface, color scheme, and point size of the text, and its placement in your cover design.

Selecting the right font and placement for the title

Just as important as the actual title on the front cover is the font you use for that title to create visual appeal. Choosing the right font can add emotion and power to the title, just like music and sound effects add mood and ambiance to a movie. Based on the topic of your book, the title, and the intended audience, choose a font that grabs attention and makes a statement.

You can choose from literally thousands of typefaces. After you find the perfect typeface for your title, you can then adjust its look by displaying it in bold or italics, or by changing its color. Here are a few considerations when thinking about fonts:

>> **Typeface selection:** The typeface that you choose can convey emotion, give meaning to the title, and add visual appeal to your book's cover design. To display your title, choose an eye-catching, yet appropriate, font that will appeal to your book's target audience. For example, if your book is targeted to kids, using a playful-looking font is appropriate. However, a highly technical book for a niche audience of adults should use a more traditional and formal-looking font.

>> **Type style:** After you select the actual typeface, decide whether you need to enhance its look by using **bold,** *italicized,* or <u>underlined</u> text. Using bold or italics for one word in the title or the entire title can help draw the reader's attention. For example, if your book's title is *Stop Smoking Now! 20 Proven Ways To Quit,* you could use bold font to highlight the words ***Stop Smoking*** if doing so enhances the appeal of your cover design and attracts the attention of smokers who want to quit.

>> **Point size:** The size of the typeface determines how much space it takes up on the cover. In most cases, you want to display the title of your book in a large point size and give it considerable space on the front cover. However, if you also incorporate a relevant graphic on your cover, adjust the point size to ensure that all the cover's elements fit together nicely and don't look cluttered.

>> **Color:** Choosing the right color scheme goes a long way toward making your cover visually pleasing. Using bright-colored type can really make your title stand out. Make sure that the color you choose works to enhance the overall design and appeal of your cover and doesn't clash with the other visual elements that you incorporate in your cover.

TIP

Check out these websites to help you select a font:

>> **1001 Fonts** (www.1001fonts.com): This website includes a selection of fonts that you can use on your book's cover.

>> **Adobe Fonts** (http://fonts.adobe.com): Offers over 20,000 different typefaces and typestyles, which you can preview and purchase online. You can enter a short phrase, such as your book's title, to see how it looks displayed in hundreds of different fonts.

Highlighting the author's name and credentials

Typically, you want to make the book's main title the most prominent element of your book's front cover. But, of course, there are exceptions to every rule:

>> **When the author is the draw:** If you're well known and people are buying the book because you wrote it, showcase your name and even your photo along with the book's title because these tactics may help you sell books. On the covers of many books written by well-established and well-known authors, you often see the author's name displayed in a larger type than the title because the author's name and reputation sell the book. For example, on the hardcover edition of a Stephen King novel, you typically see his name displayed much larger than the book's title.

>> **Promoting your achievements:** If you're an expert in your field or a well-known person, promote it on the front cover. For example, you can say, "From the bestselling author of [*insert title*] . . ." or "From the CEO of [*insert company name*] . . ."

Your credentials, as the author, and whether those credentials can help you sell books determine how large you want to present that information on the book's front cover. Make your credentials easily visible but display them in a smaller font size than your name on the book's front cover. However, the size of the font used to display the book's title, author's name, and their credentials is a creative decision — not a design rule that you must follow.

Using attractive images

The cover graphic that you choose has a huge impact on the appeal of your cover. So whether you choose to include one or more photographs, pieces of clip art, illustrations, or any combination of these graphic elements, think about how readers will perceive your book and its cover. There are no hard-and-fast rules for choosing an image to display on your book's cover, but follow these guidelines because they can help make your book more commercially viable.

>> **Make the image relevant to the book's topic** and ensure that it conveys information about the content. For example, if your book is about dog training, it should include an image of at least one dog.

>> **Make a statement with any graphic elements,** but don't let them distract from the book's title. You could use a brightly colored graphic, but you don't use colors that clash with or distract someone's attention from the book's title.

>> **Use visually appealing and attention-getting images.** For example, the artwork should look professional and avoid using clip art (or other non-unique art) that will make the cover design look amateurish or generic.

TIP

Whether you use a photograph, illustration, or some other type of graphic on your book's cover is entirely your creative decision. You want to create a book that looks highly professional, though, and one or more photographs often help to convey a more professional look than do other types of graphics (such as generic clip art).

When it comes to acquiring artwork for your book's cover, you can take your own photograph(s), find relevant stock art or photos to license (for example, at ShutterStock, www.shutterstock.com), or incorporate an appropriate illustration. Depending on your budget, you can also have these graphic elements custom-created specifically for your book by hiring a professional photographer, artist, or illustrator, in addition to a graphic designer (see the section "Working with a Design Expert to Create Your Cover," later in this chapter).

Choosing colors carefully

Certain colors attract attention and create a certain mood or convey an emotion. For example, red signifies passion or desire, while yellow can be used to convey joy or happiness. Consider reading an introductory book about graphic design to discover how colors help to create a mood or emotion, and what color combinations may appeal most to your intended readers. The Color Meanings website (www.color-meanings.com) offers a discussion of the meaning behind specific colors and offers examples for when to use specific colors.

Pulling together the overall design

A cover's *overall design* refers to how all the cover's elements come together to give it visual impact. The design includes the placement and appearance of the cover's text — title and subtitle, and the author's name (and credentials, if used). It also incorporates the use of images, such as photographs, stock art, or illustrations, and applies a distinct color scheme.

The cover's design conveys a message. It can

>> **Attract positive attention.** A well-designed cover will make people want to learn more about the *book* it covers, which is what you want it to do.

>> **Just blend in.** So the potential reader passes by your book and picks up a competing title.

>> **Get attention for a negative reason.** You don't want someone noticing your cover and thinking to themselves, "Man, that's ugly!" or "What was that author thinking?" or "I have no clue what this book is about."

Because you're so close to your own work, before choosing a final title and cover design, get some input about the design that you're considering. You can try getting feedback from total strangers, or salespeople and managers at bookstores, as well as librarians. Consider the people you ask for feedback as your own mini focus group. Include five to ten people you don't know and who fit into the book's target demographic (or are involved in the publishing industry). Ask these people what they think about the book's title and cover design. After showing them the book's title and cover design, ask the group members specifically what they think the book is about and who they think it targets. Also, ask them what they like and don't like about the cover.

If you get responses such as "What's this book about, anyway?" or "I don't get it," go back to the drawing board. If the intended audience for your book doesn't understand what you're trying to say with your cover, the title, and/or the design, you need to rework your ideas before publication. (See Chapter 3 for more about determining your book's target audience.)

The thickness of the cover and whether it has a glossy or matted finish also impacts its appearance and showcases its quality. The most popular cover stocks are 10-point or a thicker 12-point, which is coated on one side in either a glossy or laminate finish.

Turning to Your Book's Back Cover

After your book's front cover grabs the readers' attention (see the section "Keeping a Close Eye on the Front Cover," earlier in this chapter), then hopefully, that convinces your potential readers to flip the book over to read what's on the back cover. When someone takes the time to make the flip and read the back cover copy, you now have your big chance to make a sale! You have to work fast, though; you may have that person's attention for only a few seconds. On the back cover of your book, include important information that further influences the potential reader — beyond just grabbing their attention. Also, adopt the same overall color scheme that the front cover uses for the back cover. In the following sections, I describe the back cover elements and explain how to pull them together into the overall design.

REMEMBER

If you plan to sell your book via an online seller, such as Amazon or BN.com, consider the book listing's main description as equivalent to the back cover copy of a printed book.

The elements of a back cover

If you plan to sell your book through bookstores or retailers, or want it to look extremely professional, incorporate the elements described in the following sections into your back cover design.

The book description

Effective back-cover text must convey all of the important information that a potential reader wants and needs in order to decide whether to buy your book. You have limited space on the back cover, so every word, phrase, and image must have meaning and communicate the importance of your book.

REMEMBER

The description of your book that appears on the back cover should provide a summary of what your book is about and who it appeals to. Also, make the content concise and visually appealing in the way that you lay it out (see the section "The overall look of a back cover," later in this chapter, for more discussion of back-cover layout). In one or two short paragraphs, the back cover needs to

TIP

>> **Explain exactly what the book is about.** To save space on the back cover, use a bulleted list when describing key features or content. If your book is fiction, use the description to offer a brief synopsis of the plot and main characters, without revealing too much. Obviously, never reveal the ending!

>> **Describe what the book offers and what makes it unique.** Take the most marketable, appealing, or valuable aspects of what the book offers and describe this information by using the most sales-oriented but believable words possible.

>> **Inform the reader who the book is targeted to.** Adapt content from the marketing materials (such as the press release) that you create for your book to identify the target audience. (Chapter 18 focuses on how to create a cohesive marketing message to promote your book.)

>> **Establish credibility with the reader.** Be clear and honest with your book's description. Never make statements or promises that you can't keep, and don't create expectations that the content of your book can't live up to.

>> **Create demand for the book and its content.** Make your back-cover text sales-oriented, well-written, upbeat, easy-to-read, informative, and attention getting.

WARNING

Remember to accurately describe your book's content. If readers buy your book based on lies, promises, or intentional embellishments of the facts, they will likely feel ripped off, and you'll lose credibility. This situation can lead to negative reviews, and when people are shopping for books online, such as from Amazon or BN.com, positive reviews are essential. If your book is informative, well written, and well researched, you don't need to make false claims about what your book offers.

Information about the author and an author photo

You don't have to include an About the Author section on the back cover, but it can give you a powerful tool for establishing credibility with the reader:

>> **Nonfiction:** If you write a nonfiction book, you can list your primary qualifications, credentials, or educational background. This information helps portray you as knowledgeable about the topic of your book.

>> **Fiction:** Readers are less concerned about the author's credentials for fiction works. Write an About the Author section that readers relate to. It can contain more personal information about you, such as hobbies, interests, and details about family and pets. It can also list literary awards that you've won, or reference your past work by saying, "From the author of [*insert previous book title*] comes . . ."

Within the author bio section, some authors opt to include a small publicity photograph (a *head shot*). Many readers appreciate seeing a photo of the author simply to satisfy their curiosity. Books also customarily include an author's photo on the inside back cover, inside a hardcover's jacket, or within the About the Author section within the book (although you don't have to include a photo if you don't want to).

TIP

If you have a website for yourself or your publishing company, and you're active on social media, briefly list this information (website addresses and social media accounts) within the About the Author section on the back cover. Even if potential readers decide not to buy your book on the spot, they may still visit your website later to order the book online or choose to follow you on Facebook, Instagram, or Twitter. See Chapter 17 for more about creating your own website and social media accounts.

The barcode, ISBN, and price

If you plan to sell your book through bookstores, online-based booksellers, or through any retail stores, you must display a barcode in black ink with a white background (called a *vanilla barcode*) at the bottom of every book's back cover. Within this area, you also have to include the book's ISBN in a readable font. (Publishers also often print the barcode and cover price for the book within the inside front or back cover of the book.)

You can work the cover price of your book into the barcode through the *price add-on*. This smaller barcode appears immediately to the right of the ISBN barcode. The price add-on begins with the number *5*, which represents that the price is stated in U.S. dollars, and is followed by the four-digit price of the book. For example, a book that costs $18.95 would be listed as *51895* in the price add-on section of the book's barcode. Print the cover price of the book in a font that consumers can read. You can place the cover price in the upper-left or -right corner of the back cover, or in the lower-left or -right corner.

See Chapter 8 for more information on securing your book's ISBN and barcode, and on establishing a cover price.

TIP

To discover more about the technical specifications for reproducing your book's ISBN and related barcode on the back cover, visit the U.S. ISBN Agency's website (www.isbn.org) or visit the Bowker Barcode Service's website (www.bowker barcode.com). When you receive your barcode, it will be formatted in the following standard specifications: 2400 dots per inch (dpi), 99.36 percent magnification, vanilla barcode, and price add-on.

Technical stuff: You receive a barcode from Bowker Barcode Service at its full size. However, according to the organization's website, you can reduce it to 92 percent, or even 80 percent. The standard 92-percent symbol needs a total area of 2 x 1.25 inches. The smaller ISBN Bookland *EAN symbol* (the European version of an ISBN) is an 80-percent symbol, which needs a total area of 1.75 x 1 inches.

The BISAC Subject and Audience codes

As you can discover in Chapter 8, selecting and choosing appropriate Book Industry Standards and Communications (BISAC) Subject and Audience codes helps booksellers and libraries categorize and display your book in the appropriate section. For help choosing the appropriate BISAC Subject and Audience code for your book, visit the Book Industry Study Group's website (www.bisg.org).

The BISAC Subject and Audience categories typically appear in small type on the upper- or lower-left or -right corner of the book's back cover. Some publishers opt to display this information near the barcode, and others avoid including it altogether. If you plan to sell your book through any retail store or bookseller, or make it available through libraries, by not including this information, you run the risk of stores or libraries displaying your book in the wrong area or section. This misplacement makes your book harder to find and may result in lost sales or fewer readers. Never assume that the title of your book is obvious enough that a bookseller or librarian can automatically display it in the right section. You'd be surprised how often categorization mistakes occur because the book didn't display the appropriate BISAC Subject and Audience code.

Publisher imprint information

The publisher of your book usually displays its name and logo somewhere on the book's back cover, typically in the lower-right or -left corner. In addition to its name and logo, some publishers (including self-published authors who create their own publishing company) also display their website on the back cover.

Reviews and quotes

One or two excerpts of positive reviews of your book (from established media outlets) or endorsements in the form of quotes from well-known experts, celebrities, business leaders, or trade associations give you a powerful sales tool; proudly display them on your book's back cover (if you get such reviews or endorsements). These quotes quickly enhance your credibility and show the potential reader that your book has already received praise from others. See Chapter 19 for more about reviews.

The overall look of a back cover

You get to decide the placement of your book's back cover elements from a creative and design standpoint. But keep the following issues in mind while you settle on a design for your back cover:

>> **Spacing:** Don't make the description look too cluttered or take up too much space on the back cover. Use white space liberally to ensure that the copy is easily readable, inviting, and visually appealing.

>> **Completeness:** The back cover must contain all the necessary elements, including the book's description, information about the author, the barcode, price, publisher information, and book category details.

>> **Consistency:** Always carry over the design used for your book's front cover (in terms of color scheme and font selection) onto the book's back cover.

>> **Appeal:** Use your back cover copy as a powerful marketing tool. In five to ten seconds, you want to convince a potential reader (who's part of your target audience) to purchase and read your book. If your back cover copy doesn't meet that goal, you haven't properly designed the back cover.

TIP

Hire an experienced graphic designer who has a flair for creating visuals, and have them put the title, text, and pieces of the front and back covers together into one visually appealing, professional-looking, and cohesive presentation. The graphic designer you hire to create your book's cover should have experience with this type of work. See the section "Working with a Design Expert to Create Your Cover," later in this chapter, for more about working with a designer.

Although I don't recommend it (because the end result often winds up looking amateurish), you can also create your own cover design by using software such as Photoshop (www.photoshop.com) or Canva (www.canva.com).

Remembering Your Book's Spine

You can use the book's spine as a highly effective marketing and sales tool, especially if you sell your book in bookstores or through retail stores. When you visit any bookstore, most of the books are displayed sideways in order to conserve shelf space, so all a potential reader can typically see is a book's spine. Dozens of titles may be crammed onto a single shelf, with your book stuck in the middle. How can your readers find you?

If someone's looking for a book about a specific topic, they may browse a shelf in a bookstore that contains multiple titles. Most people glance at the title printed on the book's spine, and then they pull out only the few books that truly capture their attention, based on the title and/or its appearance on the spine of each book. For more info on catchy titles, see the section "Brainstorming a Catchy Title," earlier in this chapter.

REMEMBER

Most importantly, display on your book's spine — in the largest possible typestyle and font — the book's main title. Also, display the author's name and the publishing company (but print these elements in a much smaller type size than the title). Choose a font color and spine color that stands out to capture the attention of a casual browser. Make sure that the spine design is cohesive with the design of the front and back covers.

TIP

Go to any bookstore, stand in front of the section where your book would fit, and examine the spines of competing titles. Determine which books' spines stand out and capture your attention; then figure out why. And when designing your book's spine, add panache that makes it stand out more than the competition.

Working with a Design Expert to Create Your Cover

Throughout this chapter, I stress how important it is to hire a professional graphic designer to create your book cover, even if the printer or publisher that you choose to work with offers a basic cover design service as part of the publishing package that you're already paying for. When you utilize the cover design services of a print-on-demand (POD) company (see Chapter 13), for example, someone may create your cover quickly, using a previously created template. In some cases, the person designing your cover may not even have professional graphic design experience.

WARNING

Whatever you do, refrain from using a generic book cover template. More often than not, using a template is a dead giveaway that you're self-publishing your book and haven't professionally created it. That said, you can use an application, such as Canva (www.canva.com), to fully customize a book cover yourself if you have basic graphic design skills.

REMEMBER

Hiring your own graphic designer ensures that your book's cover gets the right amount of personalized attention and that the person creating your cover adheres to your creative vision. If you have no artistic flare or even ideas about how you want your book's cover to look, a professional graphic designer can use their artistic skills and creative visions to create an appropriate cover, based on information about your book that you provide. I offer general information on hiring a graphic designer in Chapter 9.

Suppose that you find someone to create your cover — great! Now what? Start off by spending some time with your cover designer (in person or via a video call) and describe your book in detail. Make sure that the designer understands what your book is about and who specifically your target audience is. Your designer probably won't take the time to read your entire manuscript due to time constraints or lack of interest, so you need to provide them with a good summary. In order to supply your designer with all they need to know about your book, give them the following information:

>> The book's title and subtitle

>> A detailed description of the book and its audience, and perhaps a completed outline (with as much detail as possible) and a sample chapter

>> The exact information that you want on the book's front and back cover

>> A rough sketch or description of what you want the front and back cover to look like, with as many specifics as possible

>> Any graphic assets that you already have, such as photographs, illustrations, or stock art, that you want incorporated into the cover design

WARNING

The fee you pay the graphic designer reflects your demand for their time and skill. If the designer needs to acquire artwork, such as photographs or illustrations, you probably have to pay separately for licensing those graphic extras.

TIP

When you receive drafts of the cover design, share your likes and dislikes with your designer. Open communication ensures that you end up with a product that you love. Expect to go back and forth multiple times before you settle on a final design. Remember, you're paying the designer to help make your book shine, so don't hesitate to say what you like and don't like. From a financial standpoint, in this area of the self-publishing project, you don't want to cut corners just to save a few bucks.

After they complete the work, have the graphic designer put into writing that their work is 100 percent original and that you (the author/publisher) take full ownership of their work, including its copyright.

If you or the graphic designer use stock photography, artwork, or other copyrighted material in the creation of the cover, you need to have permission to use those assets and proof that you or the graphic designer paid the proper licensing fees and acquired written permission to use those assets. You get this permission from the stock photo agency, photographer, or illustrator after you pay the licensing fee or stock agency subscription fee.

3

Start the Presses! Examining Printing Choices

Tap into the thriving e-book market and sell digital versions of your book.

Discover the benefits of short run book printing and why it appeals to so many self-published authors.

Use print-on-demand (POD) as your book printing, publishing, and distribution solution to sell through Amazon, Barnes & Noble, and other major online booksellers.

IN THIS CHAPTER

» Examining the technology and benefits surrounding e-books

» Determining why you should self-publish e-books

» Understanding e-book file formats

» Formatting your manuscript as an e-book

» Publishing and distribution options for e-books

Chapter **11**

Creating and Publishing E-Books That Sell

An *e-book* is a book published and distributed in a digital (not print) format. It's designed to be read using an e-reader or an e-book reading app running on a mobile device or computer. The pages of an e-book simulate printed pages, and the overall layout mimics that of a traditional book. However, for readers and publishers alike, e-books offer a handful of benefits that traditional printed books don't.

According to research published by Statista (www.statista.com), e-book sales are there will be expected to reach $14.21 billion by the end of 2023. And by 2027, Statista anticipates upwards of 1.12 billion e-book readers throughout the world. In fact, in January 2023 alone, the Association of American Publishers reported that there was a 3.7 percent increase in e-book sales, representing $85 million in revenue. And as of early 2023, Amazon dominates the e-reader market with its Kindle product line. It represents 72 percent of the e-reader market (as of early 2023).

The good news for you is that self-published books make up around 30 percent of all e-books sold. As a self-published author who wants to be able to reach the broadest audience of potential readers, publish your book in all popular e-book formats if at all possible. In this chapter, you can find out about the various e-book formats, e-booksellers, distribution, and the tools that you need to design and publish e-books. And if the turnkey publishing solution, print-on-demand (POD) printer, or short-run printer that you use to create your printed book doesn't offer an e-book publishing option, you can easily handle e-book publishing yourself.

Looking at E-Readers for E-Books

An *e-reader* is a stand-alone device that looks like a small tablet. It's designed mainly for reading e-books and playing audiobooks. Most e-readers offer a monochrome display, which replicates a traditional, paper-based book-reading experience that's easy on the eyes. The batteries in most e-readers last for weeks at a time, and each e-reader can hold hundreds or even thousands of books.

A bit about e-reader technology

Leading the e-reader market is Amazon. It offers the Kindle lineup of e-readers, which range in price from well under $100 to around $350. However, Barnes and Noble offers its Nook e-readers, and Rakuten sells its own lineup of Kobo e-reader devices. Meanwhile, you can also use all smartphones, tablets, and computers as e-readers if you install an appropriate e-reader app — which makes e-books accessible to most readers.

The majority of e-readers offer a monochrome *e-ink display*, which people also sometimes refer to as a *Paperwhite display* (named after the Kindle Paperwhite e-reader — sort of like calling all tissues *Kleenex*). This screen technology greatly reduces the strain on a reader's eyes and eye fatigue, as compared to a tablet or computer screen. But this type of screen lacks the ability to display any color. As a result, readers see an e-book's color text or images (including photographs) in black and white (and shades of gray) on the e-reader's screen. However, if they read the same e-book on a smartphone, tablet, or computer screen (or on an e-reader screen that has a color display), they see full-color content as intended by the author or publisher.

Consumers can find many e-bookstores where they can purchase e-books via the Internet. As an e-book publisher, you can distribute your own e-books via your own website. However, the most popular e-bookstores are operated by Amazon, Barnes & Noble (www.bn.com), Apple Books (www.apple.com/apple-books), Kobo, and Google. So, if you make your e-book available via these e-bookstores (see the section "Digging Into E-Book Formats," later in this chapter), you make your book accessible to virtually anyone who wants to purchase and read it in an e-book format.

REMEMBER

Although *ePub* is an industry standard e-book file format, each brand of e-reader also uses a proprietary e-book file format. Thus, an e-book formatted to be read on a Kindle isn't compatible with a Nook or Kobo e-reader (but it is compatible with the Kindle app that's available for smartphones, tablets, and computers).

Recognizing e-book and e-reader benefits

Readers who use e-readers reap the benefits of the technology, including the convenience of easy access to and storage of their many e-books. Publishers and authors also see benefits that offer multiple distribution opportunities and directly affect their bottom line.

For readers

Specifically, the benefits of e-books and e-reader technology for readers include

>> **Internal linking:** You can insert hyperlinks into an e-book. So, you can make a book's table of contents, for example, interactive. If someone taps on a specific chapter number or heading, they jump to that location within the digital version of the book.

>> **External linking:** You can also incorporate hyperlinks into a book's text, allowing readers to access webpages (if their e-reader is connected to the Internet).

>> **Automatic bookmarking:** E-readers automatically keep track of digital bookmarks and remember where a reader leaves off (so they can start from that spot when they come back to the e-book). Digital bookmarks also allow readers to restart a reading session at their previous location within a book. For example, if someone has an e-reader and also uses an e-reader app on their mobile device or computer, certain settings allow bookmarks (and reading progress) to automatically sync between devices.

>> **Built-in dictionary access:** A reader can tap on any word in an e-book to look up its meaning.

>> **Easy note-taking:** Readers can insert digital annotations into a book while they're reading.

>> **Available listening:** Some e-readers can use a computer-generated voice to read the contents of an e-book aloud. To use this feature, you typically need wireless (Bluetooth) headphones or earbuds.

>> **Adjustable typeface and point size:** The reader can typically adjust the font (typeface and size) that comprises an e-book at any time. For example, the reader can increase or decrease a type size, or change the typeface altogether and choose one that they prefer or can more easily see on their e-reader's display.

>> **Reading location tolerance:** Most e-readers have a backlight or side-light and glare-free screen, which allows you to use the devices in bright sunlight or in a dark room. Also, many e-readers are waterproof, which makes using one in a bathtub or poolside a lot more worry-free than reading a paper-based book (which warps if it gets wet).

>> **Massive content storage:** An e-reader can hold hundreds or thousands of full-length e-books, depending on its internal storage capacity or ability to use optional memory cards.

For publishers

The benefits of e-book technology for publishers include

>> **Accessible updating:** Publishers have the option of updating their manuscripts and having those updates automatically accessible (for free) to everyone who has previously purchased that e-book.

>> **Convenient distribution and storage:** e-books can easily be found and purchased by readers via online bookstores. The e-book file gets stored on their device, and they can then read it at any time, even if they don't have Internet connection at the time (such as on an airplane or while sunbathing on a secluded beach).

>> **Efficiency and cost-effectiveness:** Publishers and authors can create e-books much more cheaply than they can publish traditional paper-based books because e-books have no printing costs involved. Plus, services such as Amazon, BN.com, Apple Books, Google Books and the Kobo bookstore handle sales and distribution on the publisher's behalf (for a commission, of course).

REMEMBER

As a self-published author, you have to write, design, and format your book, make it available in popular e-book formats, choose from which service(s) to sell it, and then promote the book on an ongoing basis. The e-bookstores do the rest, including paying you your sales revenue monthly.

>> **Merchandising control:** Publishers and authors can set the price of their own e-books and then easily offer limited-time discounts or promotions to help increase sales.

Gauging likely advances in e-reader acceptance and technology

E-reader manufacturers know that most readers prefer using an e-reader over a tablet to read e-books because they generate fewer distractions than a tablet (such as alerts, alarms, or notifications pertaining to other apps, or incoming e-mail messages). Soon (or perhaps by the time you read this book), I predict that the industry will see major technological advancements made to e-readers, such as

>> **Improved displays:** *E-ink displays* built into e-readers that replicate the printed page will likely be able to display full-color (as opposed to just monochrome content) at a lower cost than the high-end e-readers that do so now. Also, the resolution and clarity of e-reader displays will improve so that they generate even less eye fatigue than they already do in any lighting situation — from direct sunlight to a dark room.

>> **Lower prices overall:** The prices of e-readers will continue to drop — making them more affordable.

>> **Increased convenience:** E-readers will become smaller, lighter, and more durable (and *all* will likely be waterproof). And battery life will be extended.

>> **Additional core functionality:** E-readers will likely expand what they can do, beyond just serving as a device for reading e-books or listening to audiobooks. For example, e-readers will continue to offer improved technologies that allow users to handwrite directly on the device's screen by using a stylus — either to annotate the e-book or content that they're reading, or to better use the e-reader as a versatile digital notetaking tool.

Publishing E-Books Easily (and Cheaply)

If you know how to use a word processor, you already have the skills needed to write, design, and publish an e-book by using a specialized computer application, such as Vellum (find out more in the section "Choosing The Right E-Book Design and Publishing Tool," later in this chapter). This type of software allows you to take your text-based manuscript (written by using a word processor) and design and format it into an e-book, which you can then export to various formats and upload for distribution through the major e-bookstores.

REMEMBER

You still need to create a book cover and have your manuscript edited and carefully proofread, and then market and promote your e-book after you publish it.

Getting your e-book content ready for prime time

Chapters 3 through 6 offer detailed information about preparing a manuscript for publishing. And the steps below give you a bird's-eye view of the process that you go through to get your book idea ready for publishing in an e-book format. *Note:* Many of these steps apply to preparing a book for printing, as well.

1. **Do the necessary research and planning needed to compose your book's manuscript.**

2. **Write your e-book by using a word processor or online writer's tool.**

3. **Gather photographs and/or artwork that you want to include within the book.**

   Alternatively, you can determine what art you want to commission

4. **Create a cover for your e-book and export it into a JPG file.**

   For the exact resolution and file specifications that you need for your cover image, see the publishing requirements outlined by each e-bookstore.

5. **Edit your manuscript and then carefully proofread it.**

   Consider hiring a professional editor and proofreader to handle these steps for you.

6. **Layout and design your e-book by using specialized software.**

   See the section "Choosing the Right E-Book Design and Publishing Tool," later in this chapter, for more information about e-book creation software options.

7. **Figure out which e-bookstores you want to sell your e-book through and determine what commission you need to pay on each sale when using that service.**

   For example, a typical e-book commission runs about 30 percent of the book's sale price.

8. **Export your e-book to each e-bookstore where you plan to sell your book.**

   Make sure you use the compatible file format for each particular e-bookstore.

9. **Set a price and release date for your e-book.**

   Consider the commission that you must pay the e-bookstore on each sale when determining the price. Base the release date on your planned advertising and marketing strategies, as well as when you plan to release the printed version of your book (if applicable).

Setting yourself up with publisher accounts

REMEMBER

Before you can publish your e-book, you must create a free publisher account with each e-bookstore that you want to sell through, or you can use a fee-based service to do this account creation for you. (See the section "Distributing E-Books through Popular E-Bookstores," later in this chapter.)

After you set up a publisher account with an e-bookstore and upload your book, it ultimately receives a listing within each e-bookstore that you submit it to. After the e-bookstore approves it, your e-book then becomes available for sale — typically within two to five business days. At the time that you submit your e-book to each e-bookstore, you need to provide information about your book, including its full title, subtitle, author's name, publishing company name, and the e-book's price.

As the author/publisher, you also have to submit a detailed description of your book (which is the same marketing information that you'd include on a printed book's back cover, as I discuss in Chapter 10). And you need to submit a digital version of your e-book's cover.

TIP

Just like when publishing a printed edition of your book, have a custom e-book cover designed by a professional graphic artist, as opposed to using a template to design a generic and unprofessional-looking book cover yourself.

MAKE YOUR E-BOOK EASY TO FIND

At the time that you submit and upload your e-book to each e-bookstore, that e-bookstore prompts you to choose from a list of book categories and subcategories that your book fits into. This is an essential step because each e-bookstore's search tools (not to mention Internet search engines) use this information (along with the book description text that you provide) to help potential readers find your book when they search by something such as book category, topic, title, relevant keywords, or the author's name.

After you submit your e-book to the e-bookstores through which you want to sell it, you must make your book easy to find. Promote and advertise your book to drive a continuous flow of potential readers to the unique link that your e-book receives within each e-bookstore. When someone places an order, the e-bookstore collects the money (at the price you set) and allows the customer's e-reader to download your e-book instantly.

Raking in the revenue

Undoubtedly, e-book sales will continue to grow in the years to come, while the sale of traditionally printed books will continue to slump as peoples' lifestyles change and e-reader technology becomes even more widely adopted. Because anyone can create and sell e-books so affordably now — and they don't have to deal with the more time- and labor-intensive process of printing and selling traditional books as a self-published author — don't overlook this revenue-generating opportunity.

REMEMBER

Each e-bookstore takes a commission on each sale that's made through its platform. Then, the e-bookstore automatically transfers your net profits monthly to the bank account that you set up with them when you create your account. Although an author typically needs to pay a commission of around 30 percent of the book's sale price, how much each e-bookstore charges varies. However, you also have the option of making your e-book available for public library members to digitally borrow for free via an online service, such as OverDrive's Libby app (www.overdrive.com/apps/libby).

You can make a much higher profit from e-books sales than from printed book sales, in part because you don't have to pay any printing and book shipping fees. You do, however, need to consider the percentage of the e-book's sale price that the e-bookstore takes and the investment that you make in the creation, advertising, and marketing of your e-book.

Digging into E-Book Formats

E-book publishing gets a tad confusing when you try to understand all the different e-book file formats that you probably need to contend with. The publishing industry established an e-book file format standard, called *ePub*, which all e-readers are compatible with. However, if you want to sell your e-book though the most popular e-bookstores, such as those operated by Amazon, Barnes & Noble, Apple, Google, and Rakuten, you need to make your e-book available in the proprietary e-book file format used by each of these e-bookstores and their respective e-readers and e-book reading apps.

Presenting your e-book in multiple file formats

Here's the good news: The e-book publishing software that you likely use to convert your text-based manuscript into a professionally designed and formatted e-book also allows you to export the same completed e-book file into each different e-book file format. Software such as Vellum or InDesign can handle this task for you; flip to the section "Choosing the Right E-Book Design and Publishing Tool," later in this chapter, for more on this type of software. You can then easily upload the files in the correct format to each e-bookstore.

You also have the option of using a service (such as a POD printer you're working with; see Chapter 13) to prepare your e-book in multiple file formats, and then have that company submit your book to multiple e-bookstores on your behalf.

Alternatively, each e-bookstore offers formatting and file conversion tools for authors and publishers to use to take a text-based or PDF version of their e-book and convert it into the specific file format used by that e-bookstore. If you plan to sell your e-book via only one or two e-bookstores, using those e-bookstore's tools may not require too much work. But for more than two, using each e-bookstore's own toolset can make the process of converting your e-book to each proprietary format more time consuming than using one application that enables you to convert your e-book into any popular file format.

Protecting your e-book with digital rights management

Digital right management (DRM) encrypts your e-book file in a way that allows its display on the e-reader or e-book reading app used to purchase the e-book, but it prevents the person who purchases the secured version of the e-book from copying, sharing, or printing it. Yes, make your e-book available in the standard ePub and PDF formats so any e-reader device will support it. However, when you create your e-book in these formats, the e-book file, by default, isn't copy protected in a way that can prevent readers from sharing your e-book file with others.

WHAT ABOUT ISBNS FOR E-BOOKS?

When creating e-books for sale through the major e-bookstores, each e-book sales/distribution service automatically generates a different ISBN for your book. Each file format that you use to distribute your book gets a different ISBN. Thus, the edition of your book sold through Apple Books has a different ISBN than the ISBN assigned by Amazon to the Kindle edition of your book. On the plus side, as the author/publisher, you don't have to pay an extra charge to have unique ISBNs assigned to your book by the e-bookstores or e-book distribution services.

To prevent unauthorized sharing, you can incorporate DRM into the digital e-book file, which you can most easily do (if you plan to sell your e-books directly via your own website or by using shoppable posts on social media) by offering your e-book as a PDF file (not an ePub file). All popular e-readers support PDF files. You can secure these PDF-based files by adding DRM yourself via a fee-based tool, such as

>> **Locklizard:** www.locklizard.com

>> **CopySafe PDF Protector from ArtistScope:** www.artistscope.com

>> **Adobe Acrobat Pro:** www.adobe.com/acrobat

WARNING

When you incorporate DRM security into a PDF file, the content's layout is fixed. In other words, the reader can't adjust the typeface or point size, and then have the e-book automatically *reflow* (reformat) to accommodate those changes. Although a reader can change the display size of a PDF file's content, doing so can negatively impact the reading experience by requiring them to scroll side to side if they make the content larger, for example. Plus, a PDF-based e-book might not be compatible with some of an e-reader's other built-in tools or features.

Because most readers prefer having access to the reflow feature that's built into all e-readers, you can offer reflow with your e-book (that you plan to sell directly via a website or through social media posts), but you need to distribute it as an ePub file. This format supports reflow, but not DRM. And so, a reader could potentially share your e-book with others without paying for those additional copies.

REMEMBER

As an author/publisher, you must decide whether protecting your work is more important than offering your e-book in a format that allows readers to reflow the content to accommodate how they prefer to see text displayed on their e-reader screen. Amazon, Barnes & Noble, Apple Books, and other major e-bookstores automatically add DRM to all e-books sold through their platforms.

Choosing The Right E-Book Design and Publishing Tool

Although some word processors, such as Microsoft Word and Apple Pages, have built-in tools that enable you to export your document into the ePub or PDF file format, most don't offer the ability to export your file into a specialty e-book file format used by an e-bookstore platform. Plus, most word processors don't offer advanced layout and design tools suitable for e-books.

If you don't want to handle your own e-book design and file conversions, you can pay an e-book turnkey publishing solution or service, such as IngramSpark or Draft2Digital, to handle these tasks.

But if you plan to create your own e-book files after you do the necessary writing and editing by using your favorite word processor, you need to utilize an e-book creation tool. You can find a bunch of them available for Windows PCs and Macs, but my personal preference for the Mac is Vellum (`www.vellum.pub`) because it's versatile, supports all e-book file formats, and is no more difficult to use than a word processor. It's also affordable.

This application allows you to write your e-book within the software and format it at the same time. However, I find it easier to create e-book manuscripts by using a word processor, and then importing one chapter file at a time into Vellum while I'm designing and formatting the e-book. At the same time, I import photographs and graphics into the e-book file and incorporate them into the page design using simple tools.

Letting software help you design your e-book

E-book creation applications, such as Vellum, walk you through the e-book creation and design process (after you go through a short learning curve), so you need only basic word processing skills. While you create and do the design work for each chapter of your e-book, the Vellum software helps you out by walking you through the process and automatically verifying that your entire manuscript is properly and consistently formatted. This verification is something that most e-book formatting and page design tools do on your behalf, and they help you by

>> Automatically creating an interactive table of contents

>> Leading you through formatting a title page, as well as other front matter and back matter, that you want to include in your book

>> Offering design elements from which you can choose, such as how chapter titles appear and what information you want to include as part of the running headers and footers

When you use Vellum, while you do the design work for your e-book, the software displays an accurate preview of how your e-book will appear to a reader who's using various types of e-readers, tablets, smartphones, or computers. With this advantage, you can tweak formatting or the overall design to better accommodate elements such as photograph placement, size, and caption length. *Note:* This software supports reflowable content, which allows readers to customize the appearance of your content on their e-reader by selecting a typeface and point size that they like.

Generating the various e-book formats

After you fully design, lay out, proofread, edit, and preview your e-book, then you're ready to export it into various file formats. Simply click on Vellum's Generate option and choose in which file formats you want your e-book. By purchasing the more expensive version of the software, you also get formatting options for printed books, so you can select the book's trim size, for example, before Vellum exports the book into the PDF file format that print-on-demand (POD) or short-run printers use to print your book.

REMEMBER

You can purchase Vellum outright for $199.99 or $249.99, as of the time of writing. The less expensive version can handle the design and file exporting of e-books exclusively, but the more expensive version (which I recommend) also allows you to design printed paperback books that you can publish using a short-run printer or POD services (see Chapters 12 and 13, respectively). Both versions enable you to create an unlimited number of books, and both come with lifetime software updates. You can even download the software for free, try designing your own e-book, and then pay for the software so that you can unlock the ability to publish your content in the e-book or paperback format(s) you choose.

Considering other e-book creation software

Of course, you have other e-book software creation options beyond Vellum (see the preceding section), whether you use a Windows PC or Mac. Table 11-1 shows you a few of the more popular options.

TIP

If you're thinking of giving Adobe InDesign a try, for $84.99 per month, you can subscribe to Adobe Creative Cloud All Apps, which gives you full access to InDesign, Photoshop, Lightroom, Acrobat Pro, and other powerful applications that you can use to handle various aspects of the e-book (and printed book) publishing process.

TABLE 11-1   ## Software for E-Book Creation

Software	Platforms	Cost	Features
Adobe InDesign	Windows PC or Mac	$29.99 monthly subscription	A professional tool, powerful and feature-packed for e-book design and publishing, as well as for printed book design work. The learning curve is somewhat steep; consider watching tutorial videos or taking a class.
			`www.adobe.com/products/indesign.html`
Designrr	Cloud-based for Windows PC or Mac	$27.00	Requires no graphic design skills and uses basic tools and templates (100 included) to easily create e-books as PDF files. Free video and text-based tutorials; free access to a vast stock photo library.
			`www.designrr.io`
KitaBoo	Cloud-based digital publishing	Costs vary by user needs	An advanced tool for creating, securing (with DRM), and delivering interactive e-books in a variety of file formats. Then create your own branded website for directly selling your e-book(s) that you create by using the KitaBoo platform.
			`www.kitaboo.com`
KotoBee Author	Windows PC or Mac	Starts at $150	Creates e-books in more than a dozen popular file formats, including ePub and proprietaries for Kindle and Apple Books. One-time purchase offers a lifetime license to create an unlimited number of e-books, access to a stock photo and video clip library to provide visual content in your e-books with no additional licensing fees required.
			`www.kotobee.com`
Marq	Cloud-based for Windows PC or Mac	Free or $10-per-month subscription	The free software has limited features with a fee to unlock more advanced features. Makes design easy with heavy use of more than 1,000 e-book templates to choose from.
			`www.marq.com/pages/templates/ebooks`
Mobipocket Creator	Windows PC	Free	Easy-to-use application for designing and creating e-books by using imported content from Word (.doc), text (.txt), or PDF files. Features are limited.
			`http://mobipocket-creator.freedownload scenter.com`
Scrivener	Windows PC or Mac	$60	Full-featured word processor specifically designed for writing books. It comes bundled with a wide range of e-book design templates that you can use while writing or after you complete the manuscript. Exports e-books into ePub, PDF, or file formats compatible with Kindle and/or Apple Books.
			`www.literatureandlatte.com/scrivener`

Figuring Out Self-Managed E-Book Distribution Options

If you or your publishing company plan to sell your book through your own website or a website that you create specifically for your e-book, you can find tools that make designing, customizing, and publishing professional-looking websites easy. These sites can sell e-books directly to readers. For example, WordPress offers the tools needed to set up a site that has sales capabilities, even if you have minimal website design skill.

Using website creation and hosting tools

If you want to create a custom website to sell e-books by using WordPress, visit www.wordpress.com/go/website-building and browse the articles to get a sense of how selling through WordPress works. For selling-specific information, enter "sell an e-book" in the Search text box and select Search to access articles.

Although WordPress allows you to set up your website to sell, you'll likely find it easier to hire a professional website designer or graphic designer who has website-design skills to handle this task for you.

But if you want to sell eBooks directly using other website creation and hosting platforms, here are three other possible options:

>> **Sellfy:** www.sellfy.com/auth/signup

   For direction on how to use this platform to create a website capable of directly selling your e-books, visit http://blog.sellfy.com/sell-ebook-on-your-website.

>> **Shopify:** www.shopify.com/ppc/website/website-to-sell

>> **Wix:** www.wix.com/ecommerce/sell

Other affordable online-based services make it easy to set up a website for the sole purpose of selling your own e-books. These typically template-based services provide the programming and tools that you need to process and fill online orders. Some of these services include

>> **Artistscope:** www.artistscope.com

>> **EditionGuard:** www.editionguard.com

>> **Koji:** www.withkoji.com

>> **SamCart:** www.samcart.com

Selling directly through social media

If you're active on social media and plan to use social media advertising (on Facebook, Instagram, and other services), you can sell e-books directly through an ad (using a sales tool called *shoppable posts*), without having to set up a separate e-commerce website. Check out Chapter 20 for the scoop on shoppable posts.

Although you can invest the time to figure out how to set up social-media e-book sales yourself, services such as Ecwid by Lightspeed (www.ecwid.com) can cost-effectively set up this functionality for you.

Distributing E-Books through Popular E-Bookstores

If you want to easily sell e-books and make them readily available to the largest audience possible, work with the top e-bookstores, including Amazon, Barnes & Noble, Apple Books, and Rakuten's Kobo store. Although the established e-bookstores charge you a commission to distribute your book on your behalf (handling all financial transactions), you don't have to pay any fees to get your book listed. Flip to the section "Establishing Yourself as a Publisher with Each E-Bookstore," later in this chapter, to find out how to set up publisher accounts.

Other options include making your e-book available through Smashwords (via a service called Draft2Digital), as well as through independent e-bookstores and services that make e-books available to borrow (for free) through public libraries.

Reaping the benefits of your e-book's exposure

By making your e-book available through at least a few of the popular e-bookstores, you reap the benefits of these services' powerful search tools. These tools enable potential readers to easily find your e-book, even if you don't reach them through your own advertising and marketing efforts.

If you set up your e-book listing correctly within each e-bookstore, when someone uses that service's Search field and enters the appropriate subject matter, one or more relevant keywords, the title of your e-book (or words in your title), or your name (as the author), a search result that contains information about your book (as well as similar titles) appears. After it appears in a search, the e-book's description, cover, and price (all of which you control) can convince the perspective reader to purchase your e-book.

When a reader has an account with a popular e-bookstore that's compatible with their e-reader, if they find a book that they want to purchase, the e-reader already has that reader's account and payment information stored, so the purchasing process literally requires just a few on-screen taps. After the e-bookstore processes the payment, the customer's e-reader automatically downloads the e-book, and that e-book becomes available to the reader in about a minute. Because of this speed and convenience, many readers prefer to shop for e-books by using the e-bookstore that their e-reader supports.

Making a sample chapter available

One of the free marketing tools available to you when you sell e-books through the major e-bookstores involves giving a prospective reader the opportunity to read a sample chapter (or portion of a chapter) for free, and then purchase the book after they read the sample (if they like it). This opportunity replicates the experience of being in a bookstore, opening a book, and getting a preview by reading a small sample. Offering at least a sample of your e-book (beyond just the cover and table of contents) as a free preview can help convince the reader that your book is well written and contains information that they find interesting.

Generating positive ratings and reviews

Readers who shop for e-books from the major e-bookstores understand the importance of ratings and reviews, so if you want to sell books, you need to take reviews seriously. Every person who purchases your e-book from Amazon, Barnes & Noble, Apple Books, or one of the other major e-bookstores has the option of giving your book a rating of between one and five stars (with five stars being the best). They can also write a text-based review of your book for all to see. As an author/publisher, you have no say whatsoever or control over ratings and reviews. The e-bookstore automatically displays this information with every e-book listing they have.

You need to generate at least a handful of five-star ratings as soon as your book gets published with each e-bookstore. You can help get these positive reviews by giving out free copies of the e-book to friends and asking them to publish a review. After all, potential readers pay careful attention to a book's average star-based rating and how many ratings that average is based upon. Thus, if someone sees that an e-book has an average of 4.5 to 5 stars, based on hundreds or thousands of ratings, they know most people who have purchased the e-book liked it. However, if your book has only a few ratings and/or text-based reviews posted, a potential reader may be less inclined to purchase that e-book (unless the author already has a positive reputation based on the publicity they've generated for the e-book).

WARNING

Negative ratings and reviews can cause sales of your book to plummet. An e-book that has an average star-based rating of three or fewer stars faces a huge challenge because potential readers immediately become wary of investing their money in a book that other people haven't enjoyed. If your e-book starts to get negative reviews, pay attention to what any text-based reviews say and seriously consider updating your book — offering a new edition that addresses and fixes all the negative complaints.

Pricing your e-book to sell

You need to understand your competition and take that competition into account when you set the price of your e-book. Especially if you're selling a work of fiction, if you price it too high, potential readers simply seek out a more affordable book to read. Thus, when it comes to pricing, stay in line with competing titles. The exception to this rule applies if you can accurately promote that your book has a perceived high value to the reader — perhaps because of your expertise or reputation as the author, or due to the exclusive information in your book.

TIP

If you plan to sell your book at a higher price than competing titles, you must create a perceived value for the book quickly and effectively. Convince the potential reader by using the text-based description for the book, showcasing a high-quality and attention-grabbing cover, and offering a free sample chapter so that the potential reader can get a preview of what to expect from reading your book in its entirety.

Creating an author page

Some of the most popular e-bookstores, including Amazon, allow authors to create a separate author page. On Amazon, this feature is called Amazon Author Central (http://author.amazon.com). It offers you, as the author, an additional opportunity to share information about yourself with readers and to promote your book(s). You can create an Amazon author page for free by clicking the Join for Free link on the main Author Central website. In addition to sharing as much information about yourself as you want, you can also include a photo and/or video.

After you set up an Author page within Amazon's Author Central, you also get access to tools that you can use to allow readers to follow you online, track your own book's sales ranking, and view customer reviews, among other things. If you plan to sell e-books (or printed books) through Amazon, set up an Author Page: It's worthwhile and free, and it doesn't require more than 30 to 60 minutes to create and publish.

TIP

For information about how to set up an author page on Barnes & Noble's website, visit http://help.barnesandnoble.com, and then select B&N Press ⇨ Vendor Accounts ⇨ Creating an Author Page on BN.com.

Establishing Yourself as a Publisher with Each E-Bookstore

Before you can start selling your book through any of the popular e-bookstores, you have to prepare your e-book, and then prepare the e-bookstores for your e-book. Although you can use a single software application to design and lay out your e-book and prepare it for publication on all the popular e-bookstore services, you must set up a free publisher account with each e-bookstore separately. *Note:* If you plan to use (and pay for) a turnkey e-book publishing service, that service can handle this setup and other related tasks for you.

Knowing the costs associated with e-bookstores

You can set up a publisher account with each e-bookstore for free. However, for each sale made, you automatically pay a predetermined percentage of the book's cover price to the e-bookstore. The percentage of each sale that you have to pay to the e-bookstore varies, but it's usually between 30 and 70 percent.

As of early 2023, Barnes & Noble and Apple Books charge a flat 30 percent of your e-book sales revenue, regardless of the book price that you set. Amazon has two main distribution options:

>> **Option #1:** Charges a sales commission of 30 percent (so you, as the author/publisher, get 70 percent of the price)

>> **Option #2** Charges 65 percent (which means you receive 35 percent of each sale)

Several factors determine which fee structure you can qualify for.

TIP

By selling your e-book directly through your own website, you typically don't need to pay a sales commission on each sale (see the section "Figuring Out Self-Managed E-Book Distribution Options," earlier in the chapter). But you probably lose potential sales from people who might find your book by using the search tool of a popular e-bookstore.

REMEMBER

If you offer the book for free, you don't have to pay sales commission to the e-bookstore, but you also don't make any money, either. Giving your e-book away from free works only if you plan to use your e-book as a sales/marketing tool for your existing business or product, so you aren't concerned with generating revenue from the sale of the e-book itself.

Meanwhile, if you opt to use an independent turnkey e-book publishing service, such as BookBaby (www.bookbaby.com/ebooks), you typically need to pay an upfront fee so that the company handles many of the tasks associated with creating the e-book files from your manuscript and making the formatted e-book files available to the e-bookstores on your behalf. This fee ranges from around $100 to well over $1,000, depending on the editing, design, file conversion, cover design, and distribution tasks that you hire the service to handle on your behalf.

The nuts and bolts of setup in e-bookstores

To get started working with the major e-bookstores, set up a free publisher account, and then have each e-bookstore begin selling your e-book(s). Keep in mind, after you have your e-book and its cover formatted specifically for each e-bookstore, you need to use that service's proprietary online-based submission tool to upload your book and create the listing for it. You have access to this tool only after you set up and activate your publisher account.

Follow these steps to get your book listed and sold through a particular e-bookstore:

1. **Set up a free author/publisher account with the e-bookstore.**

   Each e-bookstore has its own specific prompts that you have to follow to create your account.

2. **Use the e-bookstore's proprietary tool to convert the e-book's file to the appropriate format (if you've not already done so).**

3. **Upload your e-book and book cover in the appropriate file formats.**

   In general, your book cover will need to be uploaded as a JPG graphic file.

4. **Create a detailed description page for your e-book and provide all the information that the e-bookstore's setup prompts ask for.**

   Again, the specific information that you need to provide and prompts that you have to follow vary depending on which e-bookstore you use.

5. **Enter appropriate subject categories and related keywords for your book.**

TIP

   Don't forget that when creating your e-book's listing, you need to compose a well-written description, specify the most appropriate subject categories that your e-book falls into, and provide a detailed list of relevant keywords that readers might use to find a book like yours while using the e-bookstore's search tool.

6. **Check and recheck (proofread) all aspects of the e-bookstore listing.**

   Specifically, be very sure that the e-book's description is accurate and attention-grabbing, and communicates all the information you want potential readers to know about your book.

7. **Submit the book for publication.**

   After the e-bookstore reviews your e-book and its listing, they make it available for sale.

REMEMBER

   This review and approval process takes several days, so plan your publication date accordingly. However, when you work with most popular e-bookstores, you can accept preorders (starting on a date that you specify) for e-books not yet published.

8. **After the e-book appears as active and for sale on the desired e-bookstores, begin a marketing blitz.**

   Start heavily promoting your book and drive potential readers to the unique URL that leads to your e-book's listings on all the e-bookstores you're working with.

Taking a look at individual e-bookstores and services

If you plan to sell your e-book through only one major online bookseller, go with Amazon; some independent research shows that Amazon now handles up to 83 percent of all e-book sales worldwide. That said, you can find a number of e-bookstores and services where your e-book might make a splash. I cover these e-book retail options in the following sections.

Amazon Kindle Direct

Out of all the e-bookstores in the world, Amazon is the most popular, in part because its Kindle e-readers offer the features avid readers want. In fact, as of early 2023, Amazon offers an impressive selection of e-readers — ranging from the basic Kindle (priced less than $80) to the mid-priced Kindle Paperwhite Signature Edition ($140), to the Kindle Oasis ($250) and Kindle Scribe ($340). Each Kindle e-reader offers a different set of features, but they all rely on the same ability to search for, download, store, and display e-books purchased from the Amazon Kindle e-bookstore (www.amazon.com/kindle-dbs/storefront).

REMEMBER

Anyone can use the free Kindle app to read Kindle-compatible e-books on any smartphone, tablet, or computer.

TIP

You can find detailed information about formatting Kindle e-books and their covers by going to http://kdp.amazon.com, selecting Help in the upper-right part of the page, and then clicking Format Your eBook from the Help Topics options on the left of the page that opens. You absolutely must follow these guidelines exactly to ensure that your e-book looks perfect on a Kindle screen and accesses all of the e-reader features available to readers.

Here are a couple of unique Amazon publishing services for your e-book:

» **Kindle Unlimited:** To increase the potential readership for your e-book, consider making it available as part of Amazon's Kindle Unlimited subscription service. According to the Kindle Direct Publishing website:

"Kindle Unlimited (KU) is a subscription program where customers can read Kindle eBooks and keep them as long as they want, for a monthly subscription fee. When you enroll in KDP Select, your Kindle eBook is automatically included in Kindle Unlimited (KU). Your Kindle eBook will still be available for customers to buy, and you'll continue to earn royalties from those sales. To be included in Kindle Unlimited (KU), you must meet the KDP Select requirements and enroll your Kindle eBook in KDP Select. If you don't want your Kindle eBook in Kindle Unlimited (KU), you have the option to remove it from KDP Select."

TIP

» **Kindle Vella:** If you don't want to offer your full-length e-book to readers all at once, Amazon also offers a way to serialize your content through the Kindle Vella service (www.amazon.com/kindle-vella). This opportunity might allow you to earn more revenue or build a more loyal following amongst your readers.

To help you get started publishing e-books on Amazon through the company's Kindle Direct Publishing service, check out the vast amount of useful and up-to-date information you can find by following these steps:

1. **Go to** http://kdp.amazon.com.

2. **Select the Help link in the upper-right portion of the webpage.**

   The KDP Help Center Home Page opens.

3. **Scroll down to the User Guides section of the left column of links.**

4. **Click the appropriate link to access the information that you need.**

   - *Kindle Publishing Guidelines* offers detailed information you need to properly format your e-book and make sure it meets all of Amazon's regulations.

   - *KDP Jumpstart* takes you to a quick reference guide that walks you through publishing e-books for use with Kindle e-readers.

   - *KDP University* shows you an in-depth, online course that teaches you how to become an e-book publisher by using the Kindle platform.

Apple Books

Following behind Amazon in the e-book selling business is Apple, with its Apple Books e-bookstore (www.apple.com/applebooks) and e-book reading application that now comes preinstalled on all iPhones, iPads, and Macs. To submit your e-book to Apple Books, follow these steps:

1. **Format your e-book so that it adheres to Apple Books' formatting and file format guidelines.**

   You can find these guidelines at http://help.apple.com/itc/applebooksstoreformatting.

2. **Set up a free iTunes Connect (publisher) account with Apple Books by going to** http://authors.apple.com.

3. **Log into your iTunes Connect (Apple Books publisher) account through iTunes Connect.**

   Use online-based tools offered by iTunes Connect service to list and promote your book online, generate promo codes, or see sales reports. (http://itunespartner.apple.com/books).

TIP

E-book publishers can use the service Apple Books Digital Narration. Instead of hiring a voiceover actor to go into a recording studio (at your expense) to read and record your e-book as an audiobook, this service uses a computer-generated voice that sounds rather human (as opposed to sounding like a robot) to read your book aloud to people who have purchased it and who use the Apple Books app to read (or listen) to it. To get the details on this feature, go to http://itunespartner. apple.com/books/articles, and from the menu on the left of the window, choose Audiobooks ⇨ Apple Books Digital Narration.

However, if you want to go through the time and expense of creating a traditionally recorded audiobook version of your e-book, you can sell that audiobook through Apple Books (and most other e-bookstores).

B&N Press

Once upon a time, Barnes & Noble was second only to Amazon as a pioneer in e-book sales and distribution. Although Barnes & Noble remains the largest chain of retail bookstores in America, interest in its Nook e-readers has dramatically fallen. However, the company's Nook e-bookstore (go to www.bn.com and click eBooks in the top menu) still gives you a viable place to sell your e-book after you format that book for a Nook e-reader or the Nook app on a smartphone, tablet, or computer.

To self-publish and sell e-books through BN.com, follow these steps:

1. **Set up a free publisher account with B&N Press.**

    Go to http://press.barnesandnoble.com and click the Get Started button, then follow the prompts.

2. **Format your e-book to adhere to the Nook file format.**

    You can do this from the Barnes & Noble website or through the e-book creation tool that you use.

3. **Prepare and upload your e-book file (and cover) to B&N Press.**

4. **Agree to publish your book by clicking, which adds a virtual checkmark to the appropriate box.**

    After you complete this step, Barnes & Noble can accept presales or actual sales of your e-book.

You can find this process outlined in more detail at http://press.barnesand noble.com/how-it-works.

If you need help with any step during the writing, editing, design, file creation, file conversion, cover design, or file uploading to BN.com, you can hire an independent consultant who has teamed up with B&N Press to assist you. You can find and hire these experts by visiting http://press.barnesandnoble.com/self-publishing-services.

Draft2Digital (Smashwords)

Founded in 2008, Smashwords was created as an independent e-bookstore that caters mainly to small publishers and self-published authors. Over the years, the service has grown considerably and has established a loyal base of avid readers. In 2022, Smashwords joined forces with Draft2Digital (an e-book design, formatting, and distribution service). As of 2023, as a self-published author, if you want to make your e-book available for sale on Smashwords, you need to set up a publisher account with Draft2Digital to format and submit your content.

To set up a publisher account with Draft2Digital and submit e-books to be sold through Smashwords, visit `http://draft2digital.com/sw`. Here's how payments and fees work with Draft2Digital and Smashwords:

» **Free services:** Like most of the popular e-bookstores, Draft2Digital has no upfront charges for any of its services, which include e-book formatting, file conversion, distribution, and sales tracking.

» **Draft2Digital fees:** Draft2Digital charges a percentage of each book's sales and gets paid only when authors make a sale. Draft2Digital charges just 10 percent of the price that you set for your book.

» **Smashwords fees:** Smashwords charges per-sale fees (about 30 percent), in addition to Draft2Digital's fees.

So as a self-published author selling your book through Smashwords, you wind up keeping about 60 percent of your e-book's sale price.

TIP

One thing that sets Draft2Digital apart is that it can make your e-book available for sale on as many of the major e-bookstore platforms as you want, not just Smashwords. It can format e-books to be sold through

» Amazon (www.amazon.com)

» Apple Books (www.apple.com/applebooks)

» Barnes & Noble (www.bn.com)

» Kobo (www.kobo.com)

» OverDrive (www.overdrive.com)

» BorrowBox (www.borrowbox.com)

So, instead of creating individual publisher accounts with each major e-bookstore and then uploading your e-book to make it available for sale on each of them, for the extra 10 percent fee per sale that Draft2Digital charges, you can make your book available through multiple major e-booksellers and manage everything from one account. To find out more about how this process works, visit `http://draft2digital.com/steps`.

Google Books

When it comes to online (cloud-based) services, Google is typically a leader — the Google search engine, YouTube, Gmail, Google Photos, the company's Google Workspace apps, Google Maps, or the Google Play Store for Android apps are among its popular services and apps. Unsurprisingly, Google also offers its own e-bookstore, called Google Play Books, and it supports self-published authors.

You can sell e-books published through this service worldwide, and readers can access your e-book on the more than 3 billion active Android-based mobile devices and Chromebooks.

To get started, create your free Google account (or use your existing account), and then create a publisher account for Google Play Books (go to `http://play.google.com/books/publish`). Like most other e-bookstore services, Google Play Books offers several potential revenue splits for self-published authors. The most common revenue split sees 70 percent of the book's sale price go to the author and 30 percent go to Google.

REMEMBER

Android-based tablet users and Chromebook laptop users might consider purchasing e-books to read on their devices, but most Android-based smartphone users may be less likely to do so. Smartphone users have discovered that, although you can read an e-book on the small screen of a phone, it doesn't provide the most conducive reading experience. For that reason, although several billion Android-based mobile devices are active in the world, most smartphone users probably won't purchase e-books to be read on their device's smaller-size screen. So, when it comes to selling e-books on Google Play Books to users who have Android-based devices, target tablet and Chromebook users (you probably won't have success targeting readers with just a smartphone).

Kobo Writing Life

Rakuten (`www.rakuten.com`) offers its own lineup of Kobo e-readers (`www.kobo.com`) in the United States and in many other countries around the world. It also operates its own e-bookstore that offers an ever-growing selection of e-books and audiobooks for sale — many of which self-published authors and independent publishers have created. As a result of Rakuten's dedication to the e-book industry, Kobo e-readers have gotten very popular amongst readers. Thus, offering your e-book through Kobo's e-bookstore provides yet another viable option for reaching potential readers and selling your e-book to them.

REMEMBER

Rakuten also offers a free Kobo e-reader app for the Apple iPhone and iPad, and Android-based mobile devices, as well as Windows PC and Mac computers (www.kobo.com/apps).

After you create your e-book in the appropriate file format, set up a free publisher account with Kobo Writing Life (www.kobo.com/writinglife) and submit your e-book for sale. The process is very similar to other popular e-bookstores, and you earn about 70 percent of the book's sale price on each sale.

TIP

To access Rakuten's e-book publishing guidelines and learn more about the publishing process, visit http://kobowritinglife.zendesk.com and, under the Popular Articles section, click the Publishing on KWL: A Step-By-Step Guide link.

IngramSpark

As of June 2023, for $49 per e-book title (plus other fees based on services needed), IngramSpark offers services like Draft2Digital does, as described in the section "Draft2Digital (Smashwords)," earlier in this chapter. IngramSpark formats your e-book in all of the popular e-book file formats, and then distributes your e-book to the various popular e-bookstores that you choose (including Amazon, Barnes & Noble, Apple Books, and Kobo) so that those e-bookstores can sell your book. If you use IngramSpark, you have to use only one platform and a single set of tools to sell your e-book on multiple platforms.

In addition to the fees that you pay to IngramSpark, you still need to pay the sales commission associated with each e-bookseller. To find out more about this service and set up an IngramSpark publisher account, visit www.ingramspark.com/plan-your-book/ebooks.

TIP

IngramSpark offers online-based tutorials and tools that explain all aspects of e-book publishing, distribution, and sales through this platform. You can access these resources at www.ingramspark.com/self-publishing-courses.

Chapter **12**

Trying Out Short Run Printing

This chapter focuses on short run printing; so this chapter is for you if you're a self-publisher who plans to establish your own small publishing company (see Chapter 7 for details on this process) or who wants to handle many of the tasks associated with publishing a book yourself, without using a turnkey publishing solution such as a print-on-demand (POD; see Chapter 13) option.

Back in the day, to make the *offset printing process* (widely used in commercial printing) affordable, each print run needed to produce thousands of copies of a book. Not only did such a large print batch require a huge financial investment (and a high level of risk, in the event the books didn't sell), it also required the publisher to warehouse a tremendous number of books.

Today, thanks to technological advances, short run printers can affordably print small batches of your book per print run — starting with as few as 50 to 100 copies at a time. However, the more copies of the book you print per run, the lower your cost per book becomes.

In this chapter, I cover the basics of working with a short run printer, outline advantages (and disadvantages) of doing so, discuss features that you can choose for your book, and offer tips for hiring and cooperating with a printer.

The Basics of Working with a Short Run Printer

REMEMBER

If you choose to work with a short run printing option for your book, having your book printed and bound is one of the costliest aspects of the whole publishing project. You want your investment to result in the most professional-looking and highest quality book possible. Poor printing and/or binding impacts the look of your book, which can also dramatically damage your credibility. So go with a professional printer to make sure that your book looks its best.

A short run printer capable of printing and binding books is very different from your local print shop that specializes in printing business cards and stationery. In the following sections, I explain the pros and cons of using a short run printer for your book and give you hints on finding a pool of reliable printers to work with. (You can find out how to select the ideal printer for your publishing project in the section "Hiring the Right Short Run Printer for Your Needs," later in this chapter.)

The pros and cons of short run printing

The advantages of short run digital printing include

>> A consistently high image/print quality

>> Fast and easy production (typically within five to ten business days)

>> Lower per-copy printing costs than other printing methods, such as print-on-demand (POD; see Chapter 13)

>> Greater control over the final printed books when compared to using a POD service that typically offers fewer options

REMEMBER

If you're super confident that you're going to sell more than 1,000 or 2,000 copies of your book, consider working with a traditional offset book printer, rather than a short run digital printer. In this situation, an offset book printer can lower your per copy printing costs, but they require a significantly larger initial financial investment for the printing, shipping, and warehousing of the books until you can sell them. To find potential offset book printers to work with, launch your favorite Internet search engine and enter "offset book printer" in the Search field.

The disadvantages of using short run printing include

>> **Greater initial outlay:** Short run printing requires a larger upfront invest-ment than POD because you must pay for the printing of dozens, hundreds, or thousands of books in one run (before any book is sold). If you plan to print fewer than 100 copies of your book initially, using a short run printer probably doesn't make financial sense, unless you plan to use the book as a marketing tool for other aspects of your pre-existing business (and you're not planning to earn a profit from individual book sales).

>> **Minimum print runs and inventory storage:** To make the most out of short run printing, you must have a print run of at least 100 copies of your book. (The more copies the better, in terms of lowering per-copy costs, which means you also need to maintain an inventory until you can sell the books.) You also run the risk of not selling all of your books if demand doesn't meet expectations.

>> **More book-related obligations:** With a short run printer, you're responsible for handling many more of the book publishing–related tasks that a POD company might otherwise handle — unless you pay for a turnkey publishing package from a short run printer. A printer that offers a *turnkey package* typically handles a wider range of pre-publishing tasks on your behalf — such as page layout, cover design, and perhaps even the editing of your manuscript — all for a flat rate price.

Finding reputable short run printers

You can find a reliable book printer in many ways:

>> *Writer's Digest:* www.writersdigest.com

>> *The Writer:* www.writermag.com

>> **Referral databases:** These databases are available to members of writing and publishing organizations. For example, if you're a member of The Independent Book Publishers Association (IBPA), go to www.ibpa-online.org, then choose Resources ⇨ Industry Directories ⇨ IBPA Supplier & Services Discovery Database. You can search for the supplier and services database found under the Resources section of the website to see many full-service book printers, along with contact information and a short description of each company's specialties.

>> **Online searches:** Of course, you can also find a book printer by doing a search online (use the search phrase *short run book printing*) to discover well-established and reputable companies, such as

- *48 Hour Books:* www.48hrbooks.com

- *BookBaby:* www.bookbaby.com

- *Lightning Press:* www.lightning-press.com

>> **Social media:** Ask for printer referrals from self-published authors who are active on various Facebook groups, such as The Self-Publishing Support Group or Self-Published Authors Community (just search for either group's name from your Facebook account to access that group).

TIP

Don't choose a short run printer by location only. The printer you choose doesn't need to be in your immediate geographic area because they expect you to submit your book's galleys electronically (as a PDF file), and you can negotiate with the printer by phone or e-mail. After they print your books, they can ship those books anywhere.

Getting a quote for your print job

After you find one or more short run printers that you might want to work with (see the preceding section for tips on finding one), each printer's website should have a free online quote system that asks you specific questions about your book and then provides a ballpark per-copy printing cost based on the number of books that you want to print.

SHORT RUN PRINTERS USE DIGITAL PRINTING TECHNOLOGY

For printing thousands of copies of your book during a single print run, traditional offset printing still makes financial sense. However, to print fewer than 1,000 copies of your book, going with a short run printer can likely save you money. Short run printing relies on digital printing technology, not the offset printing process. Thus, short run printers don't have to use the pre-press operations regularly associated with offset printing (used by major publishing houses to publish thousands of copies of a book at a time). Instead, short run printers digitally print the books directly onto a paper stock by using toner or ink. Because digital printing requires minimal set-up, related costs for a production run are much lower. One of the biggest perks to short run printing (besides a lower cost) is the very quick potential turnaround time to print and bind books.

TIP

You get a significant price drop when you opt to print a greater quantity of books in one printing. Try getting quotes at various intervals — for example, for more than 200, 500, or 1,000 copies of your book.

If you head over to the BookBaby website (www.bookbaby.com) and choose Book Printing⇨ Paperback Book Printing, you can use the service's online-based quote tool by clicking Start Your Paperback Book.

Table 12-1 shows an example of a BookBaby quote generated for printing a 250-page, 6-x-9-inch trade paperback book that uses perfect binding, 60-pound natural paper stock, a gloss cover finish, and black interior printing.

As the table indicates, the more copies you publish in one run, the lower the per-copy price. If you set your book's cover price to $24.95, you can see how your per-copy profit potential increases while your per-copy cost goes down with a larger print run. (I'm using this pricing structure for demonstration purposes only, based on a quote generated in early 2023.)

TABLE 12-1   **Online Generated Pricing from BookBaby**

Number of Copies	Price Per Copy	Total Printing Cost	Potential Profit Based on a $24.95 Cover Price*
50	$12.33	$616.50	$12.62
100	$9.95	$995.00	$15.00
250	$9.41	$2,351.50	$15.54
500	$8.62	$4,309.00	$16.33
1,000	$8.11	$8,109.00	$16.84

*Potential profit doesn't consider other expenses related to the operation of your publishing business or the advertising, marketing, and promotional costs associated with the book's sales.

REMEMBER

Chapter 13 focuses on print-on-demand (POD), an entirely different process that allows you to print one copy of your book at a time and then drop-ship that copy to the individual buyer. Services such as Amazon Kindle Direct and IngramSpark rely on the latest print-on-demand technologies. If you want to offer printed books (as opposed to e-books) to your readers, POD requires the lowest initial financial investment. But because of its higher per-copy printing costs (compared to short run printing or offset printing), POD cuts into your profit margins. For example, a POD printer takes upwards of 60 percent of the book's cover price to print, bind, and ship individual copies of your books to people who have ordered it.

Choosing the Features of Your Short Run Printed Book

The interior of most trade paperback books uses 50-pound white or natural-colored paper and black ink. If you choose to use a fancier paper stock or a different color paper, or if you use two or more ink colors within the book's interior, you may improve the book's look, but your printing costs increase. Likewise, if you choose to do something fancy with your cover (such as embossed or raised printing), that decision impacts your per-copy printing costs.

By using standard paper stock and basic printing options, you can still create and publish a book that's very professional-looking and visually appealing. For most books, with the exception of high-end coffee table books or photo books, aim to publish a book that, in terms of quality of paper, looks just like any other book that you can purchase at a bookstore — or better. With professional layout (see Chapter 9) and a good cover design (see Chapter 10), your printer can produce books that meet or exceed your expectations without charging you for a wide range of extras. For a coffee table or photo book, you'll want to use higher-quality, potentially glossy paper, for example.

To ensure that you're happy with the result, try some of these suggestions:

>> Visit a bookstore and find books that you want your book to imitate in terms of trim size, paper stock, and overall design.

>> Work closely with the printer to communicate exactly what you envision.

>> Be open to advice and creative suggestions.

The following sections can help you decide what you want your book to look like. After you select your book's features, gather price quotes from potential printers and narrow your choices until you decide on one (see the section "Hiring the Right Short Run Printer for Your Needs," later in this chapter).

TIP

Visit the Printing Industry Exchange's Glossary page (www.printindustry.com/glossary.aspx) to get familiar with common printing terminology. Understanding the terminology that printers use can help you better determine and communicate your needs to the printer and understand the price quotes that you get.

Selecting trim size

The trim size of your book refers to its dimensions. A book's trim size impacts its page count. With a smaller trim size, fewer words fit on the page. Therefore, the book has a higher page count and appears thicker. That same manuscript printed in a book that has a larger trim size has a smaller page count and potentially cuts printing costs. The drawback, however, is that the book appears shorter because it contains fewer pages. Decide your book's trim size before you begin page layout to save yourself (and your book designer) a lot of extra work. If you don't nail down your trim size at the start, reworking your page layout and design to match different book dimensions will most likely cost you more money. See Chapter 9 for details about page layout and design.

TIP

The font size that you choose for the interior text in your book also impacts how many words fit on a page, and therefore the trim size that you choose. A larger font size (such as 12-point type) decreases the number of words on a page and increases your book's page count. Conversely, using a smaller font size (such as 10 points) allows more words to fit on the page, which decreases overall page count. However, using a too-small font size can make your book more difficult to read. *Note:* If your book is targeted to people with a visual impairment, using a larger font size may be necessary.

For a trade paperback (the most common type of self-published book; see the following section for a discussion of the decisions you need to make before printing your book), common trim sizes include

>> 6 x 9 inches

>> 8.5 x 11 inches

>> 5.5 x 8.5 inches

>> 7 x 10 inches

Depending on the print run, most printers can produce books of any trim size that's 8.5 x 11 inches or smaller. Again, the book's trim size and its total number of pages both directly impact your per-copy printing costs.

Deciding on hard covers versus soft covers

Printing softcover *trade paperbacks* (which are paperback books that use a thicker interior paper stock than newsprint and come in a variety of trim sizes) or *mass market paperbacks* (which are the size of paperback novels that use newsprint paper for the internal pages) is significantly less expensive than printing hardcover books. However, hardcover books look more formal and typically command higher cover prices. Although a mass market paperback book, such as a novel with a trim size of 4 x 6.75 inches, almost always sells for under $10, a trade paperback book can have a larger trim size and have a cover price from $9.95 to $39.99 (or more). Readers expect to pay at least $20 for a hardcover fiction book or much more for a non-fiction book.

TIP

Most self-published books or books published by small publishers are published as trade paperbacks. This type of book comes in a variety of trim sizes, offers full-color covers, and can be almost any length. They're also suitable for both fiction and nonfiction books and are the most economical to print, especially in small to medium size print runs (under 2,500 copies).

Selecting cover stock and coatings

The quality of the cover and the cover jacket (of a hardcover book) can get a potential reader's attention and give your book instant credibility. Covers come in different thicknesses (point sizes) and with certain coatings. For example, a trade paperback book commonly uses a 10-point or 12-point paper stock. You can then opt to add special coatings — glossy or matte finishes — to the cover. You can also add UV protection to prevent discoloration from sunlight.

A hardcover book must have a quality cover and cover jacket because the cover price of the book is significantly higher than for a paperback, and people expect to receive a high-quality product. For a hardcover, you have a wide range of options in terms of cover stock, as well as the stock used for the book's jacket. Your options vary by printer. Typically, the thicker the paper stock you use, the more expensive the printing is. You also increase your costs if you add coatings or laminates to the cover.

TIP

As you can find out in Chapter 10, people do judge a book by its cover! In addition to having a catchy title and a well-designed cover, you want your cover to look professional and convey quality. Before making decisions about printing your book's cover, look at some other published books (especially your book's competing titles) and examine the quality of their covers. Choose some samples that you like, and then have your printer offer you quotes to create a similar cover, from a printing-specifications standpoint.

Making a binding decision

You can have a book bound in a variety of ways. The *binding* refers to how the pages are held together; Figure 12-1 shows some binding methods. The most common types of binding are

>> **Perfect binding:** Most self-publishers opt for perfect binding, which uses glue to attach the pages to the book's cover. This binding type is most commonly seen among books sold through bookstores. *Self-Publishing For Dummies* is an example of a perfect-bound book. One benefit of perfect binding is that readers can clearly see the book's spine when the book sits sideways on a bookshelf.

- **Comb binding:** Plastic comb binding uses a piece of plastic that has teeth that fit into rectangular holes cut into each sheet of paper. Comb binding is mainly used for books printed at a local print shop in very small quantities. Keep in mind that bookstores and retail stores typically don't sell books with this type of binding, and the plastic binding itself could crack or break. This type of binding also doesn't look very professional.

- **Coil, wire, or wire-O binding:** This binding (also called *spiral binding*) refers to one piece of plastic (coil) or wire that forms a continuous coil that holds pages together by weaving in and out of many small holes cut into the book's pages. This type of binding is ideal for cookbooks and other types of books that need to lie flat without being held.

REMEMBER

Spiral binding is ideal for manuals, workbooks, or reports, for example, that readers refer to often. The plastic or wire coil allows the pages to turn 360 degrees, which makes it easier to keep a book open to a specific page without damaging the binding or pages. Meanwhile, wire-o binding works very much like spiral binding. However, it uses a looped metal wire. This type of binding looks more formal (so it's ideal for a business topic), but it's far less durable than a wire coil binding.

- **Thermal binding:** A cloth tape or plastic strip is heat-fused along the side of the pages to seal them together. This binding is an option for small print runs, typically when you don't plan to sell the book at retail.

- **Case binding:** Hardcover books use this binding method, which involves using thread to sew the pages together. If you're creating a hardcover book, you use this sturdy, classic-looking binding.

FIGURE 12-1:
Three methods of book binding: perfect, comb, and spiral.

Picking paper weight and color

The *weight* of the paper used for the interior of your book refers to its thickness. Using a thicker paper stock improves the feel of the book from a quality standpoint and makes the spine of the book thicker; but remember that by using a thicker (heavier) paper, your printing costs may increase. Because the book physically weighs more, it also costs more to ship.

Certain book types usually use a certain kind of paper. For example

>> **Full-color books:** Often use a brighter white paper with a glossy finish

>> **Hardcover books:** Might use a slightly heavier paper (60- or 100- pound) than do trade paperbacks (which usually use 24-pound; see the note in the last bullet)

>> **Mass market paperback books:** Typically printed on a less expensive, newsprint-like paper

>> **Trade paperbacks:** Often use a 24-pound white or off-white paper (but you have options). *Note:* 60-pound paper has the same thickness, same texture, and same weight as the 24-pound paper. The technical names for these papers are *24-pound bond* and *60-pound uncoated text*. They have different names because the paper producers use different manufacturing techniques to make them.

To find out more about choosing paper stock for your book, check out the information from Gorham Printing *Buy the Book* at `https://gorhamprinting.wordpress.com/2019/04/17/how-to-choose-the-best-paper-stock-for-your-book/`.

Opting for the use of interior color

Adding color gives you creative freedom and adds a tremendous amount of visual appeal to your book, if you use it correctly. For example, printers create the interior of most books on white paper by using black ink, but you can use two-, three-, or even full-color spreads in your book to add visual appeal, highlight important information, or categorize information.

Four-color printing is the same as full-color printing. The four colors used (cyan, magenta, black, and yellow) are combined during the printing process to create any other color. This system is also referred to as CMYK printing.

WARNING

Incorporating four-color (full-color) printing into your book's interior design dramatically boosts your printing costs. You probably can't dramatically increase the cover price of the book so that you can fully recoup this additional cost and still earn a respectable profit.

Including interior art, photos, and illustrations

Depending on the type of book that you're publishing, incorporating artwork, photographs, illustrations, charts, diagrams, or figures of any kind adds to the visual design of the book and allows you to convey certain types of information more easily. Although a novel typically doesn't incorporate any artwork, a how-to book on plumbing, for example, may use photographs or other graphic elements to help the reader identify certain parts of a plumbing project.

REMEMBER

When you start to include more types of artwork in your book, your printing costs may start to climb. These costs vary based on the technology used to layout and design your book, as well as the process that you use to print the books. However, you can usually add black-and-white graphics to your book (such as photos and illustrations) without impacting your printing costs too much.

TIP

To keep costs down, make sure that you supply artwork to the printer in a format of at least 300 dots per inch (dpi), in true photographic quality. Printers supply guidelines for submitting artwork of various types. Stick to these guidelines. If the printer needs to reformat your artwork, change its file type, or do editing to make it suitable for printing, they charge you extra for each image that they fix.

Adding inserts

Depending on the type of book that you're publishing, you may want to bind some type of insert into the book, such as a perforated coupon, checklist, page of stickers, or fold-out poster. Printers that can handle inserts charge extra for this service, based on the type of insert. Prices vary by printer. You also have to provide the insert in a format that the printer can bind into the printed books without having to make any changes. Details of these formats vary based on the printer that you're working with.

Hiring the Right Short Run Printer for Your Needs

Various printers use different equipment and specialize in different types of print jobs. In the following sections, I give you a few issues to consider upfront, explain the importance of customer service and proper pricing, and clue you in on what happens after you hire the printer of your choice.

What are a few upfront considerations?

To start with, you want to choose a printer based on the following:

>> **The company's experience in publishing books similar to yours:** Ask to see sample books that have similar printing specifications to what you anticipate needing.

>> **The professional quality of the output:** When you initially contact a printer, ask to see actual printed samples of the company's work. Upon request, a professional book printer can send you a handful of sample books that it has printed so that you can evaluate the quality of the work. If you're paying for a large print run, for a small additional fee, the printer may be able to provide you with a printed sample of your book before they create all the copies you ordered. Not all printers offer this service, however.

>> **Scheduling issues:** After you decide exactly how you want your book printed and begin gathering price quotes (see the section "Is the price right?" later in this chapter), determine the time needed for the initial printing and how long the publisher requires for subsequent print runs.

WARNING

Making special demands relating to your print job often requires additional time, which can delay the overall printing process. If the printer is extremely busy or overbooked, delays in your publishing schedule can occur, resulting in lost sales or money spent on ineffective advertising, marketing, and public relations.

>> **Payment terms:** For first-time orders, many printers require at least a 50 percent down payment with the balance due on shipment. For any order, make sure that you agree on the terms upfront and that you have the terms in writing.

>> **Warehousing and order fulfillment services:** Some printers warehouse your books and handle order fulfillment on your behalf (for a fee, of course). Having the printer store your books can ultimately save you money because you don't need to have the books shipped from the printer to your own warehouse (at your expense), and then have those same books shipped from your warehouse to your customers. You can also save time and money by having your orders fulfilled directly by the printer, assuming the printer offers competitive rates for these services.

REMEMBER

Unless you find a printer through a referral from a reputable organization or someone you know, do a bit of research about the company before making a hiring decision. Printers are often family-owned or have been in business for 50 or more years, so look for a well-established and reputable company to work with.

Is the customer service top-notch?

After making contact with a printer, you may be assigned an account representative. This person is your primary contact at the printing company. Make sure that they'll be readily available to answer your questions, negotiate pricing with you, and guide you and your book through each stage of the printing process.

TIP

Interview the rep assigned to you so that you can tell whether you can have a solid working relationship. Ideally, you want to work with a representative who understands your needs and who's willing to invest the time in working closely with you. You need to have faith in this person's knowledge and feel comfortable working with them. You want someone who's readily available to answer all your questions, address your concerns, and make sure that every phase of the printing process goes according to plan and stays within your budget (especially if you're working with a book printer for the first time).

Is the price right?

The printing business is highly competitive. Have printers detail the specifications for your job and offer a price quote, and then shop around for at least two or three other quotes to ensure that you get a good deal. The specifications provided by the printer as part of their price quote should include complete details about your printing project, including the pricing associated with it. For example, it should describe the type of paper to be used, the trim size, the binding type, and the number of pages in the book. It should also provide a description of the cover and how it will be printed. You always have room to negotiate!

Providing crucial information

Although you can begin contacting printers at any time, you can't begin soliciting bids for your print job or gathering price estimates until you determine exactly what you need. Each of these considerations impacts your costs and what your printed books will look like.

Printers typically have an online form that you fill out for quote requests, but in order to obtain an accurate quote, be prepared to provide the following information about what you want for your book:

>> **Trim size:** The dimensions of your book.

>> **Book length:** The total number of pages.

WARNING

You base the book's length on the PDF file that contains the laid-out and designed pages of your book. Don't use the number of pages of your manuscript in the form of a text-based Word document because that page count has no relevance to the printed book.

- **Book format:** Whether you plan to publish a hardcover, trade paperback, or mass-market paperback.

- **Paper stock for the cover:** And any special finishes that you want to add.

- **Number of colors on the book's front and back cover:** Full-color printing is the norm.

- **Type of binding:** This is how the interior pages of the book and the cover will all be held together.

- **Paper stock for the interior:** The paper stock (thickness and color) will help determine the physical quality of the book and its appearance.

- **Ink color(s):** Will your book contain exclusively black interior text? You also have the option of using two or three colors within the interior pages, or using full-color printing if your book's interior includes photos, charts, or graphics, for example. A cookbook or children's book is typically printed in full-color, but a mass-market paperback novel uses only black ink in the book's interior.

- **Inserts:** If you want the book to contain any add-ins.

In addition, be prepared to provide information about the following items:

- **Contact information:** Including your name, address, e-mail address, and so on.

- **Book-specific items:** Your book's title; whether you already have your own ISBN, barcode, copyright, and other book-specific items (see Chapter 8 for details) or whether the printer needs to do these tasks on your behalf (they typically offer these services for an additional fee).

- **Format:** Include the format of the content of your book, the book's front and back cover art, and how you plan to supply all of the laid-out pages and cover artwork to the printer. In most cases, you will be asked to provide a PDF file that's created in a specific resolution.

- **Initial print run:** The quantity of books you want printed. Some printers accept orders for as few as 100 books. However, to dramatically reduce the printing cost per book, obtain quotes for 250, 500, and 1,000 (or more) copies, assuming that you think you can sell this quantity of books over the long term and don't mind having to store them until you can sell them.

    For small print runs (100 books or less), seriously consider using print-on-demand (POD) technology instead (which I cover in Chapter 13). If you're considering a print run of more than 1,000 copies of your book, investigate traditional offset printing to save money.

- **>> Timeline:** How quickly you need the printing job done. Most printers charge extra for *rush jobs*. Figure out your overall publishing schedule and find a printer that can work within that schedule. Depending on the printer, a rush job might mean that they print and ship your book within 24 to 96 hours after receiving your order.

- **>> Packaging:** Whether the printer needs to shrink-wrap the book and box it in a specific way. Special requests typically cost extra.

- **>> Shipping:** How and where you want the printed books shipped. You have to pay for shipping charges, so decide how you want the books shipped and how quickly you need them to arrive. The faster the shipping method, the more you pay — especially for heavy boxes of books.

- **>> Additional services:** Additional fee-based services that a short run printer may offer include copy editing, proofreading, layout and design, cover design, preparation or editing of artwork content, creating multiple proofs, obtaining an ISBN and barcode, and rush printing services.

For the most accurate quote, provide the printer with a copy of your book's *galleys* (the laid-out and designed pages), typically in a PDF file format.

Reviewing quotes carefully

After you provide all the information in the preceding section to your printer, they then can provide you with an accurate written (or e-mailed) price quote. This quote should list all the print job's specifications exactly. If you notice that any elements of the job agreement don't appear in this list, discuss that with the printer and ask them to issue a new quote before you accept it. The quote you accept needs to list all of the prices associated with the print job, including the total price.

REMEMBER

Many book printers have websites that calculate instant quotes. You may find this service useful when estimating a budget, but use these quotes for estimate purposes only, and be prepared for a higher final quote.

After receiving a price quote that looks reasonable, contact the printer and go over every line of the quote to ensure that you understand what everything means. Ideally, the printer should also provide you with a sample of another book that they have already printed that looks similar to how yours will look so that you can see firsthand what to expect.

If you decide to move forward after receiving a final price quote, you need to formally accept it and pay a non-refundable down payment (or the full amount) before the printing process begins.

WARNING

Beware of hidden and unexpected charges when calculating your printing budget and evaluating quotes. When you get a quote, the printer bases that quote exactly on the printing specifications that you initially provided. Any deviation from the specifications that appear on the price quote may result in additional charges, depending on who makes the changes. If the printer needs to take the time to make changes to your book files on your behalf, you will typically pay extra for their time or for each change that you request. Make sure that you understand exactly what services the quote includes and exactly what the final printed books will look like.

REMEMBER

Shop around for the best prices and services based on your needs. If you receive two vastly different price quotes, determine why before you choose the company that provided the lowest quote. One printer may give you a quote for the job based on less expensive paper, for example.

Partnering with the Printer You Hire

After you agree to a price and officially hire a printer, determine exactly how that printer needs you to submit your galleys and cover artwork and in what format. You also need to sign a contract or work order with the printer to establish a formal relationship. To avoid delays and extra fees, adhere to the guidelines provided by the printer, especially when you prepare photographs and illustrations that you want printed in the interior of the book, and when you create the book's front and back cover.

WARNING

Providing interior pages, cover artwork, or digital photographs in the wrong resolution or in the wrong file format can negatively impact their appearance when printed.

The printer you choose becomes one of your publishing company's most important service suppliers. If your book sells well, you want to be able to quickly reorder books or use the same printer for future publishing projects. Aim to build a long-term relationship with the printer of your choice. To do so, follow these tips:

>> Develop a basic understanding early on about costs and scheduling.

>> Openly communicate with the printer throughout the process.

>> Make sure that the printer addresses all your needs, questions, and concerns.

>> Convey to your printer how you envision your final printed books looking.

IN THIS CHAPTER

» Understanding the basics of print-
on-demand technology

» Recognizing the benefits and
drawbacks of print-on-demand

» Following the print-on-demand
process

» Finding a print-on-demand company
that meets your needs

» Meeting some big names in the
print-on-demand world

Chapter **13**

Print-on-Demand for Demanding Self-Publishers

One of the most cost-effective ways to self-publish a printed book and have many of the often-confusing steps in the publishing process handled on your behalf is to pursue print-on-demand (POD) self-publishing. POD is fast and inexpensive. Using this technology, authors can make their book(s) available to potential readers through online distribution channels, such as Amazon and Barnes & Noble (www.bn.com). In fact, POD utilizes the latest printing and publishing technologies and offers a wide range of options for authors. For many people interested in pursuing self-publishing and selling printed books, POD provides an extremely viable option because you can order just one book at a time to be printed and typically have it drop shipped directly to the person who purchased it.

This chapter explains what POD is, tells you how it works, and offers the information that you need to take advantage of this technology so that you can publish your book through turnkey POD solutions. These turnkey solutions — including BookBaby (www.bookbaby.com), Amazon Direct Publishing (http://kdp.amazon.com) and Barnes & Noble Press (http://press.barnesandnoble.com) — take much of the guesswork and busywork out of publishing and distributing any type of printed book. The printer that you choose handles virtually all publishing and order-processing tasks on your behalf as the author.

Taking a Quick Tour of Print-On-Demand (POD) Technology

REMEMBER

Although an author still needs to write and edit their own manuscript, POD publishers typically handle everything else, from layout and design to online sales and order fulfillment. Self-published authors pay for a publishing package based on their needs, but they don't have to worry about things such as obtaining an ISBN, getting their book listed with online booksellers, or filling orders from customers.

A POD publisher operates very differently than traditional offset or short run book printers (which I cover in Chapter 12), although you end up with basically the same final product. When a printer creates POD books, they typically use high-end, 600 dots-per-inch (dpi) laser printers. These industrial-quality laser printers usually print on 20-pound white bond paper, using black toner to print the pages of the book, one copy at a time, as needed. They use a separate, full-color printing process to print each book's cover (reproduced at 300 dpi). The POD books then use proprietary binding technology, allowing for the creation of either a perfect-bound or coil-bound book (see the description of these bindings in Chapter 12).

The POD printer then arranges to have your book sold through one or more online booksellers and handles order fulfillment for each order. You simply need to write the book, and then promote it as being for sale on the online booksellers that list it.

Some POD publishers offer additional customization options for final printed books, allowing authors to request (for an extra per-copy fee) higher-quality, 24-pound white paper for their book's inside pages. They can also incorporate full-color pages within the book.

REMEMBER

Because the POD printer handles the printing, binding, sales, and order fulfillment, they typically charge anywhere from 40 to 60 percent of the book's cover price. Thus, your income per book is significantly less than if you use a short run printer to print your books, and then handle sales and order fulfillment yourself (or through your own publishing company).

Looking at the Pros and Cons of POD

Self-publishers commonly choose POD printing for a variety of reasons. The following sections cover the major benefits of POD, as well as some of the potential drawbacks.

Focusing on the benefits

POD offers many benefits, especially to first-time self-publishers and people looking for complete publishing solutions that don't cost too much. Check out the benefits discussed in the following sections.

Avoiding a lot of hassle

POD makes getting published easy for any author. Plus, using POD takes much of the hassle associated with publishing a book out of the process for you; it offers a huge benefit because you don't have to maintain an inventory and the POD printer typically drop ships your book to the people who purchase it. In many cases, POD printers offer a complete turnkey solution, so you don't have to mess with tasks such as printing and online sales. But you still need to write the book and then heavily promote it. (See "Surveying the POD Process," later in this chapter, for more details about ways to sell a book you've used POD to publish.)

TIP

Make sure that the POD company you choose gives your book project the one-on-one attention needed and that they don't use pre-created templates when designing your book's cover. Using a template makes the cover design process much faster, but it limits the designer's creativity and takes away the opportunity to create a unique-looking book cover. Chapter 10 goes into cover design details.

Potentially saving money

Back in 1995, the world of publishing changed dramatically with the introduction of POD technology. For decades, if an author wanted to have their book published, their options included working with a major publishing house or publishing their own book by using offset printing. Because short run book printing wasn't an option at that time, printing and publishing your own book was an extremely costly endeavor. Even today, most authors don't have $10,000 to $20,000 to invest in the offset printing of their own book (to print hundreds or thousands of copies), and have funds left over to properly market, promote, and distribute that book.

Now, in a matter of weeks and for an investment of under $1,000, anyone can have books printed and made available to the public via one or more well-known online booksellers, such as Amazon or Barnes & Noble.

TIP

If you know you want to self-publish your book, crunch some numbers to determine what makes sense based on your budget, sales expectations, and ability to market and distribute your own book. Do a cost comparison between POD, short run book printing (which you can read about in Chapter 12), or even e-book publishing (discussed in Chapter 11; you can publish e-books even more easily and cheaply than using a POD printer).

Table 13-1 offers a quick-look comparison between the short run and POD printing processes.

TABLE 13-1   POD versus Short Run Printing

Characteristic	POD	Short Run Printing
Initial outlay	Small initial investment, under $1,000	Potentially several thousands of dollars upfront (before any sales)
Inventory and shipping costs	Author typically pays shipping fees but no inventory storage cost	Author pays both inventory storage and shipping costs
Marketing and promotion costs	Assumed by the self-published author	Assumed by the self-published author
Per-book profit	40 to 60 percent of the cover price (before marketing and promotion costs)	Up to 70 percent of the cover price (before marketing and promotion costs, based on how your books are sold)
Potential tasks included	Design, printing, distribution	Design, printing, distribution, warehousing
Print run demands	One book at a time	At least 100 books (up to thousands) per print run
Timing	Books printed after someone submits an order	Books printed before the printer receives orders
Who benefits from the process	Self-published authors who don't want to handle direct sales	Self-published authors who have an e-commerce website or other direct-sales method

REMEMBER

To determine whether POD makes sense for your book publishing project, perform a simple cost-benefit analysis to compare POD with other printing options:

>> **Printing and order fulfillment costs:** The printing/order fulfillment costs per copy are significantly higher than with more traditional book printing methods; this situation takes away from your per-copy profit potential.

>> **Financial and time investments:** You have a significantly lower initial financial investment, and as the writer/publisher, you have far fewer responsibilities. The printer handles virtually all the major steps involved with bringing your book to print (after you write and fully edit the manuscript). You typically pay for these services as part of the publishing package that you purchase, but you can save significant time and money in the long run.

Also, you take on much less of a financial risk (where you can potentially lose your upfront investment) when you publish your book by using POD. There are POD services, such as KDP and Ingram, which don't charge the author anything upfront. But they do take a percentage of each sale that the service handles.

TIP

If you opt to use POD printing, set aside money in your overall budget to purchase at least 25 to 50 copies of your own book so that you have printed copies on hand for purposes such as in-person sales, or generating publicity and potential reviews by sending printed review copies to select media outlets. In many cases, the POD printer offers a discount if you ask for larger quantities of books in one order, but you still have to pay more per copy than you do using a short run printer.

Enjoying speed and versatility

After you write and edit your manuscript, POD allows you to have your book published in a matter of weeks, not months. You can choose from a wide range of printing specifications, including the book's trim size and paper stock. Then print books if and when you sell them — even if you print only one copy at a time.

REMEMBER

As you can discover in Chapter 12, the technologies used by short run printers have improved dramatically in recent years, and you can now have your book printed in small quantities in just a few days (plus shipping time). So, for example, you can initially order 100 to 250 copies of your book, wait until you sell almost all of them, and then initiate another print run, getting more books very quickly. If you use POD, however, you never have to worry about keeping inventory in stock or running out of books.

Noting the drawbacks of POD

Depending on how you plan to market and distribute your book, POD does have certain drawbacks. The following sections explore some of them.

Rejecting returns and standard credit

The biggest drawback of POD is that most of the POD printing companies don't accept returns. All the major publishing houses do accept returns (typically within 90 days) if the books don't sell. If a bookstore or retailer purchases books for resale — but nobody buys them — those books can be returned to the publisher. However, books published using POD or short run printers aren't typically returnable.

WARNING

Booksellers and retailers don't get industry-standard credit terms or bulk discounts through POD printers. All orders must be prepaid. Inability to buy on credit, combined with the no-returns policy, makes it extremely difficult for authors who use POD to sell their books through traditional booksellers and other retail stores. These outlets don't pay in advance, and they cycle their books for returns if those books don't sell. Therefore, individual people who want to purchase your book must make their purchase directly from the POD company, directly from the author, or from an online bookseller, such as Amazon or Barnes & Noble.

TIP

To get around these drawbacks, you, the author, can pre-purchase a large quantity of books and sell them directly to distributors or booksellers, offering industry-standard discounts and returns. This procedure, however, may greatly reduce your book's profit potential because you pay around 40 to 60 percent of the book's cover price to purchase copies of your own book for resale. In this situation, authors often find it more cost-effective to use more traditional book printing methods, as opposed to POD; see Chapter 12 for details about short run printing.

Noting issues with layout and design quality

When it comes to the layout and design of books, POD can also have drawbacks:

» The resolution and reproduction of photographs and artwork incorporated into the book may not look as good when you print through POD technology when compared to other book printing methods.

» You may have more limited options for the type and quality of paper used to print the internal pages when you use POD, rather than a short run printer or traditional offset printing, for example.

» The POD printer may offer only limited use of full-color within the inside pages.

Although you have many options when choosing the printing specifications of your book by using POD, this printing technology differs from what the major publishing houses use to print their books. Thus, print resolution is typically not as high for books printed by using POD. This high-end laser technology is quickly improving, but it has certain issues that relate to the quality of photographic images and the type of paper that you can use for a book's internal pages. Each POD publisher uses slightly different technology, so request actual samples of books from the POD company that you want to use and discuss printing limitations with them.

REMEMBER

If you don't have to worry about cost, short run or offset printing always gives you a better-quality end product, but you have to invest hundreds or thousands of dollars up front, depending on the quantity of books that you order for each print run.

>> **Short run printing:** The upfront investment for short run printing is lower than for offset printing, but you wind up with fewer books and the printing cost per copy is higher.

>> **Traditional offset printing:** The initial investment is significantly higher because you need to pay for the printing costs upfront. This method has a lower per-copy printing cost, and it allows you to order hundreds or thousands of copies of your book at one time. But you then must warehouse the books until they're sold and typically pay to have the books shipped to bookstores, wholesalers, or your individual customers (depending on how you sell your books).

Surveying the POD Process

Just like with traditional offset or short run book publishing (which I cover in Chapter 12), using POD to design, publish, distribute, and market your book is a multistep process. But many of the POD companies handle a lot of the confusing steps in the process on your behalf. In the following sections, I steer you through the major steps in the POD process and explain what a POD company needs from an author to start the printing process.

TIP

In most cases, as soon as you begin working with most POD companies, you get a project or account manager as your primary contact. This person walks you through the entire self-publishing process with POD and can answer your questions. With some of the larger services (such as Amazon's Kindle Direct Publishing, or KDP), however, you don't get a real, live project manager. Instead, you go through an automated process, but you can easily navigate through this process online.

Looking at the major steps

After you complete your manuscript, make sure that your text undergoes rigorous editing, as I discuss in Chapter 6. Many POD companies can help you hire an editor, for an additional fee, but most assume that the manuscript you send them is ready to be laid out and printed.

After you have your manuscript ready to begin the POD process, follow these major steps:

1. **Select a POD company.**

   I provide a list of several reputable POD companies in the section "Checking out a Few Prominent POD Companies," later in this chapter.

2. **Submit your manuscript and necessary account paperwork to the POD company.**

   You also turn in your artwork, the author's agreement (provided by the POD company), your payment (if applicable), and a variety of other materials (see the following section).

3. **Complete the layout and design process (including the scanning of artwork, as needed), along with your book's cover creation process.**

   This step can take between one and three weeks, depending on the POD company that you work with. But you have creative input during each stage of your book's development process.

4. **Review the author proof of your book that you receive from the POD company and make needed changes.**

   The *proof* is a mock-up showing exactly what each page of your book looks like; it's what your readers see when the book is ultimately printed. This stage gives you a final chance to make last-minute edits and ensure that the layout and design of the book is exactly how you envisioned it.

   Make edits, fix errors, or improve the content of your book before the POD company prints it and makes it available to the public. Proofread your book carefully! *And when you think it's ready to go, proofread it again at least one more time.* Between the times you do your final proofreading, perhaps wait at least 24 hours so you can view the pages with fresh eyes and with a clear mind for the final time.

5. **Begin promoting your book through advertising, marketing, and public relations.**

   Don't skip this step — you're solely responsible for it. Plan your public relations, marketing, and advertising carefully so that you can maximize your budget and reach the most potential readers. (See Part 5 of this book for details on marketing your book.) Before you announce a publication date for your book, consult with the POD printer to make sure that they'll have your book listed with the online-based booksellers prior to announcing the book's availability.

6. **Start selling and distributing your book.**

In most cases, your POD company ensures that your book appears on services such as Bowker's Books In Print (www.bowker.com/books-in-print; a comprehensive directory used by bookstores and libraries that lists all books currently in print), Amazon, and Barnes & Noble (www.bn.com). The POD company also notifies major book distributors about the publication and availability of your book.

REMEMBER

The POD company prints books and fulfills orders when they receive those orders. (These services are built into the fees and commissions that you pay to the POD company.)

WARNING

Many of the POD companies that offer turnkey solutions also offer a wide range of extra services to help you market and promote your book. In some cases, the publishing package that you purchase includes these services. You may, however, need to pay extra for them, based on your needs. Check out the section "Working with Companies to Manage Money Issues," later in this chapter, for more about fees that you may need to pay.

Knowing what a POD company needs to get rolling

To ensure that your book turns out exactly the way you envision it, provide the POD publisher with everything they need. Depending on the services that the POD company offers, you may need to provide the internal pages of your book in a PDF file format (after you or someone you hire fully edits, lays out, and designs it), as well as your book's cover artwork (which you also need to provide in a very specific file format and resolution). The following sections focus on preparing the materials that your POD publisher needs from you.

Materials for layout and cover design

When you finish writing and editing your manuscript, and after you collect all the photos, illustrations, and artwork that you want to include in the book, you can turn your work over to a POD company for the layout and design process — or you may opt to handle these tasks on your own (or hire your own graphic designer for an additional fee).

If the POD company handles your page layout and design, as well as your front and back cover design, plan on providing the following materials:

- » **A digital copy of your entire edited manuscript** (typically in Microsoft Word format). When the POD publisher handles your page layout and design for you, you can often offer ideas or even sketches of what you want your book's pages to look like.

- » **A sketch or draft of the book's front cover** and other information about the content of the cover that you want the POD company to design.

- » **Digital copies of any graphics, images, artwork, or photographs** that you want to include within the book, complete with figure reference numbers. Make sure that you label each piece of artwork with a proper filename (based on requirements provided by the person doing your book's layout and design and/or your printer). Each piece of artwork must also meet the technical specifications spelled out by the POD company that you're working with.

TIP

If your book includes many photos or a lot of artwork, seek out a POD company that doesn't limit the number of visuals that you can include nor charge extra to incorporate them into your book. The number of photographs or pieces of artwork generally allowed varies based on the publishing package that you purchase and the POD company that you work with. **Note:** By paying extra, however, you can typically incorporate an unlimited number of photographs or pieces of artwork in your book.

If you complete the page layout and design, as well as the cover creation, yourself, hand over these materials to the POD printer:

- » **PDF files of your page layout and design** that are ready to print. See Chapter 9 for details on how to get your book into the appropriate PDF file format.

- » **The final cover artwork in a digital file format** that meets the POD company's specifications. If you had your cover pre-designed by a professional graphic artist or completed the design work yourself (see Chapter 10 for details on cover art), you need to match your final files to the company's requirements.

TIP

You can ensure that your book's interior layout and design comes out the way you envision by looking at other books and providing your book's graphic designer with actual samples that you like. You can even take design elements from several different books to create something unique for your book.

Information about the book and its author

When you initially begin working with a POD company, you need to provide specific information about your book and your vision for it. Some of the details that the POD likely asks for include

>> Your book's final title and subtitle.

>> The category or genre that the book fits into, such as fiction, how-to, self-help, poetry, cookbook, and so on.

>> The main subject matter that your book covers.

>> The book's intended audience.

>> The desired trim size of your book (usually a minimum 5 x 5 inches and maximum 8.25 x 10.75 inches for perfect-bound books).

>> The type of book you want to print and bind — trade paperback or hardcover, for example — and whether you also want to create e-book files.

TIP

At the same time that your POD publisher creates the files for the printed version of your book, often for an additional fee, the company can simultaneously create e-book versions in all popular file formats. As you can find out in Chapter 11, however, you can also handle e-book publishing yourself.

>> The type of binding (perfect or spiral) that you prefer.

>> A short description of your book (one or two sentences).

>> A more in-depth description of your book (a paragraph or two).

>> Keywords or phrases that a potential customer might use when they're searching for your book or a book like yours (provide up to a dozen keywords or phrases).

>> Biographical information about the author.

>> A photograph of the author.

>> The completed author questionnaire provided by the POD company (if applicable).

>> The signed author's agreement provided by the POD company.

>> Your payment (if applicable) to the POD company.

REMEMBER

Some POD publishers charge authors an upfront fee to prepare their book for printing and sale. Others don't charge an upfront fee but charge a commission on each book sold.

>> The cover price. Depending on the POD printer you use, as the author, you'll likely be responsible for choosing your book's cover price. However, some POD publishers set the price for you based on their own criteria.

COMMONLY-OFFERED TRIM SIZES

While you envision what you want your printed book to look like, after you write it and know it's approximate length, choose a trim size. The *trim size* represents the book's overall height and length dimensions. (The width depends on the book's number of pages, the type of paper used in the book's interior, and the thickness of the cover.) Remember, you can tinker with page count during the layout and design process by adjusting the font size, character spacing, and page margins, for example. Some of the common book trim sizes that most POD companies support include: 5.5 x 8.5, 6 x 9, 8.5 x 11, 8.5 x 8.5, or 9 x 7 inches. But other trim size options may be available from the POD company that you choose. In addition to trim size, you can also likely choose between several paper stocks. Your choice of paper stock often impacts your printing costs, as well as the thickness, visual appearance, and weight of your book.

Picking a Great POD Company for Your Book

The POD business has grown dramatically in recent years, and many companies now offer these services to self-published authors. The following sections focus on a few of the more established and better-known POD publishers that offer complete turnkey publishing solutions.

As an author, you pay the POD company a predetermined fee for a specific publishing package, and then you can possibly purchase copies of your own published book at a discount. Remember, unlike when you work with a major publishing house, when you use POD to publish your book, you retain all rights to your book, including the copyright. See Chapter 8 for the full scoop on copyright.

When it comes to choosing a POD printing solution for your book, you have many options. I cover several prominent POD companies in the section "Checking out a Few Prominent POD Companies," later in this chapter, but you can find additional companies online by entering the search phrase "print-on-demand book publishing" in any Internet search engine.

REMEMBER

Not all POD companies are alike. Each has slight differences in the services offered and prices charged, based on what comes included in the respective POD publishing packages or offerings. Some POD companies may offer authors à la carte services, such as layout and design, POD printing, distribution, and promotions, rather than a complete turnkey solution. Depending on how much of the self-publishing process you want to handle yourself, you may want to use the a la carte option to save yourself a little money in printing costs.

Focusing on quality and cost

To find the right POD company capable of meeting your needs, first focus on what your needs are, in terms of your book's design, printing, publishing, distribution, and marketing. After you pin down those points, follow these guidelines:

>> **Find a POD company that you can afford.** Keep in mind, most of the POD companies offer several publishing packages for authors at different price points. Each package includes specific services.

>> **Research the company's history and reputation.** Make sure that the company you choose has experience publishing books like yours and is well-established. Interview a representative from the company and request to see actual samples of their work.

>> **Look for quality.** The print quality of POD books can vary, and that quality often doesn't quite meet the consistent standards of offset printing. Whenever possible, view samples of POD books from a particular company that you don't get directly from that company. (You can order them online, for example, just like a regular reader would.) Many POD companies tend to select their very best print runs for samples. Even with a single print run, the print quality can vary, just the way the quality of laser copies can vary with the amount of toner in the machine, its age, if it's well maintained, and so on.

>> **Choose a company that offers the specific services that you need and can benefit from the most.** Some POD companies focus more on book design and printing, while others focus on assisting you in marketing, promoting, and distributing your book.

Knowing what you should expect from a POD company

While you prepare to have your book published through a POD company, consider these important factors of POD publishing:

>> The initial cost of the publishing package (if applicable). Again, some POD printers, like Amazon's KDP, charge a percentage of each book's sale, but don't charge an upfront fee.

>> The services included with the publishing package

>> How and when the POD company calculates and pays out royalties to the author

>> The discount at which you can purchase copies of your own book from the POD company

>> The amount of time from the point when the POD company receives your manuscript to initial publication of your book

>> How much control, if any, you have over the book's cover price

>> How long it takes for the POD printer to process, print, and ship each order after they receive that order

>> How much marketing, advertising, and public relations support you hope to receive from the POD company and what form that support will take. For example, Amazon's KDP service and Barnes & Noble Press allow you (the author/publisher) to create a free author page to promote yourself and your book. You also get a detailed book listing on Amazon or BN.com that you can customize to help sell your book online.

REMEMBER

Before choosing a POD company, always read the company's author agreement and other contracts carefully. These legal documents outline the services that the POD company offers you and the fees related to those services. After you have that information, calculate your overall budget. Determine approximately how many copies of your book you need to sell in order to break even on your investment, then determine whether you can reasonably hit that sales figure, based on the distribution, sales, marketing, advertising, and publicity opportunities that you anticipate having available to you (see the following section for money matters).

Working with Companies to Manage Money Issues

The POD company that you choose can help you make important decisions about your book's cover price, while ultimately impacting your profit margin. The following sections deal with some of the financial issues and decisions that you need to contend with as a self-publisher (or self-published author) who uses POD.

Watching out for hidden costs

Many first-time authors don't calculate all the anticipated costs associated with publishing their book. Using a *turnkey POD solution* (that handles most or all of the book printing and distribution steps for you) helps control costs, but you can still incur many expenses, in addition to the POD publishing package that you purchase. These expenses include editing services, acquiring artwork, graphic design, advertising, marketing, and public relations efforts.

Determine exactly what services the POD publishing package that you plan to purchase includes, and what additional services you need and have to pay for separately.

WARNING

POD companies typically specialize in publishing and distributing books — not marketing and promoting them. Thus, unless you pre-purchase a package in which the printer helps promote and advertise your book, as the author, you have the sole responsibility of getting word out about your book. You can, of course, hire professional salespeople, online advertising specialists, and public relations people to help you. If you don't properly promote your book, no matter how good the book actually is, it won't sell. It's that simple. See Part 5 for the lowdown on publicity, marketing, and advertising.

Pricing your book

Every book has a cost-per-copy to print, based on the number of pages and the type of binding. Most POD companies provide you with the exact printing cost per copy and require that your book's cover price be at least 2.5 times the printing cost per book.

This pricing model ensures that you, as the author, as well as the POD company, can make a profit on each copy of the book sold. As the author, you also want to be able to purchase copies of your book from the POD company at between 40 to 60 percent off the book's cover price, plus have the option to resell books directly to customers for the book's cover price. Most POD companies initially supply you with a predetermined number of copies of your book (specified in the publishing package that you buy), but not all of them do.

The POD company bases the royalty that you earn from each book sale on several factors, including the number of pages in the book, its binding, the ink color(s) used, and the type of paper used. As of 2023, if you purchase a print-on-demand publishing package from BookBaby (www.bookbaby.com/book-printing/print-on-demand) for $399, they make your printed book available through Amazon, Barnes & Noble, BookBaby, and more than 50 other online-based booksellers. Of course, you also have the option of setting up accounts with each of these booksellers separately and making your book available on Amazon, BN, and other services yourself (which can get time consuming).

This mini-table shows a rundown of your profit per book, assuming these factors: Your book has a 6-x-9-inch trim size, 200 pages, perfect binding, and the interior uses only black ink on 60-pound paper.

Retail Cover Price	Per-Book Royalty Amount	Royalty Percentage
$10.99	$1.23	11%
$12.99	$2.03	16%
$13.99	$2.44	17%
$14.99	$2.84	19%
$15.99	$3.25	20%

These figures vary if you alter any of the book's specifications or choose a different publishing package from BookBaby, so use these numbers for estimation purposes only. Also, remember that other POD companies offer different pricing structures.

REMEMBER

Some POD companies give authors input into their book's cover price. Others don't. Your book's cover price can have a tremendous impact on its profit potential. Pricing it correctly can mean the difference between earning a profit and losing money on your publishing venture over the life of your book.

Calculating your royalties

TIP

The POD companies typically pay royalties to the author on a monthly or quarterly basis. This timeline varies, however, depending on the POD company that you work with. Ask your contact person about royalty payments before you sign a contract so that you know what to expect.

Every POD company uses a different formula to calculate an author's royalties:

>> **Percentage of gross profit:** When the POD company sells copies of your book, you receive a royalty based on a predetermined percentage of the gross profit earned per book. Some POD companies offer up to a 60 percent royalty on gross profit from each copy sold.

>> **Type of sale:** Another part of this formula relates to the method of sale — either directly by the author, via the POD company's online-based bookstore, or through an online bookseller (such as Amazon or Barnes & Noble).

Make sure that you understand the formula that your POD company uses to calculate your royalties.

To calculate how much of a royalty you earn per book, determine whether the customer pays the full cover price or purchases the book at a discount. Here are some scenarios:

Direct sales

If the POD company sells one copy of your book (cover price $29.95) directly to an individual for the full cover price, here's how to calculate your royalty:

1. **Take the cover price and subtract the printing costs to find the gross profit.**

   For this example, the cover price is $29.95, and the printing cost is $9.03.

   $29.95 – $9.03 = $20.92

   This leaves $20.92 in gross profit.

2. **Calculate the value that you, as the author, receive as royalty from the POD company.**

   For this example, say you get 60 percent of the gross profit.

   $20.92 x 0.6 = $12.55

   So you make $12.55 on the sale of that book.

Retail booksellers

If you sell your book through an online bookseller or a traditional bookstore or distributor, you calculate your profit by factoring in the percentage discount that you give to the seller. Here's how to calculate your royalty:

1. **Determine how much money you initially get from selling your book to the reseller.**

   Say that you sold your $29.95 book at a wholesale price of 50 percent off of the book's cover price.

   $29.95 x 0.5 = $14.98

   So you have $14.98 in profit.

2. **Subtract the printing costs from the discounted book price to find the gross profit.**

   In this example, the printing costs are $9.03.

   $14.98 – $9.03 = $5.95

   Which leaves a gross profit of $5.95.

3. **Calculate your royalty by multiplying the gross profit by the percentage of that profit you receive.**

   As the author, say you earn a 60 percent royalty on $5.95.

   $5.95 x 0.6 = $3.57

   So your royalty is $3.57 per copy sold.

With such low royalties, you obviously want to make money by selling hundreds or thousands of copies of your book.

Author sales

You can purchase copies of your book directly from the POD company as the author, and you probably receive a 40 to 60 percent discount off the book's cover price (depending on the quantity of books ordered at the same time). Follow these steps to calculate how much you can make from using this sales approach:

1. **Purchase the book from the POD company at the discount that the company offers you.**

   Say that you purchase a $29.95 book for 40 percent off (so you pay 60 percent of the cover price).

   $29.95 x 0.6 = $17.97

   You pay $17.97 per book to the POD company.

2. **Resell that book directly to customers at the cover price, and then subtract the price that you paid to determine your gross profit.**

   $29.95 – $17.97 = $11.98

   You make a profit of $11.98 when you sell your POD book yourself.

You can sell copies of your book to your existing customers and clients when you make author appearances, give lectures, or sell books directly from your website. Using this POD sales scenario, however, you have to fulfill orders and potentially maintain an inventory of books. Fear not, though; I give you details on order fulfillment, inventory, and shipping in Chapter 16.

Checking out a Few Prominent POD Companies

The following POD companies offer comprehensive solutions for authors interested in self-publishing and selling printed books:

- » **Amazon Direct Publishing:** http://kdp.amazon.com
- » **Barnes & Noble Press:** http://press.barnesandnoble.com
- » **BookBaby:** www.bookbaby.com/book-printing/print-on-demand
- » **IngramSpark:** www.ingramspark.com
- » **iUniverse:** www.iuniverse.com
- » **Mixam:** http://mixam.com/books
- » **Trafford:** www.trafford.com
- » **Wheatmark:** www.wheatmark.com

Keep in mind that the preceding list gives you just a sampling of the many printing and publishing companies that offer turnkey POD solutions. I mention these companies because they're prominent in the industry.

DISCOVER BookBaby

BookBaby Print On Demand Distribution (www.bookbaby.com/book-printing/print-on-demand) is a well-established and reputable POD company that also does short run printing, plus offers many other services to authors and small publishing companies. According to the company's website, "Print on demand is a revolutionary process where authors can conveniently and affordable print and distribute their books as needed. Your books will be marketed and sold across the globe, without you having the hassle of storing or shipping them. And you'll never have to worry about having enough books in stock! Print on demand services offer you the flexibility to distribute your book on an as-needed basis. That way, you won't have to put out larger costs up front, only to have tons of books that need to get onto bookstore shelves."

The printing and distribution process takes just a few steps when you use BookBaby's POD services (and many other POD companies work very much the same way). When a customer orders your book online, through a site such as Amazon or Barnes & Noble, the order goes directly to BookBaby. No matter what the size of that order, BookBaby promptly prints, binds, and packages your books and ships them to the buyer. After BookBaby collects payment, the company deducts its predefined printing and selling costs, and you then get paid the net sales.

Just like with many other POD companies, BookBaby gives you (the author) the option of whether you want to offer hardcover or paperback books. You can also choose the trim size and binding of your book and select from a few paper stock options. One thing helps to set BookBaby apart from other POD companies: In addition to offering several comprehensive POD publishing packages for self-published authors, the company also offers just about every service you might need (on an à la carte basis), such as editing, cover design services, e-book creation services, book printing, and order fulfillment/distribution.

4

Making Your Book a Bestseller: Distribution Methods

Find out about the pros and cons of selling your book through the popular online booksellers (such as Amazon and Barnes & Noble) and how to do so.

Get distribution for your book through traditional retail bookstores and specialty stores.

Figure out how to efficiently handle warehousing, order fulfillment, and shipping for your book.

Chapter **14**

Selling Your Book through Popular Online Booksellers

or a self-published author, your book's listing on online booksellers, such as Amazon (www.amazon.com) and Barnes & Noble (www.bn.com), may offer your primary outlet for nationwide distribution of your traditionally printed books. Because your book probably lacks national retail distribution, you need to make it available on Amazon and Barnes & Noble online to generate sales. You can also sell your book online through your own e-commerce website; see Chapter 17 for details.

And when you do an interview with the media or tell people about where to buy a copy of your printed book, you can easily say, "It's now available on Amazon, Barnes & Noble's website, or my own website, www.[*booktitle.com*].com."

This chapter tells you all about how to generate sales and positive reviews by having your short run or traditionally printed book listed with popular online booksellers. I focus on how to create the best possible listings for your book to capture the attention of potential readers; I also describe other ways to promote your book through online booksellers.

Creating an Effective Listing

Use the listing for your book on Amazon, Barnes & Noble, or any other online bookseller as an opportunity for you to sell your book to potential readers. In essence, you create a digital brochure. The more informative and sales-oriented your listing is, the better chance you have of getting someone to click the Buy button to purchase your book.

REMEMBER

If you want to publish and sell e-book versions of your book, refer to Chapter 11; e-books require a separate distribution strategy that may involve working with e-booksellers, such as Amazon, Barnes & Noble, Apple Books, Google Play Books, Kobo, and Smashwords, for example. You can also sell your e-book directly through your own website or through shoppable posts on social media, such as Instagram (http://business.instagram.com/shopping).

The major online booksellers contain millions of book listings. Although all of these listings contain basic bibliographic data, you can expand on your book's listing information and greatly improve your chances of getting your book noticed.

Elements to include in an online listing

When you create your book's listing for Amazon, Barnes & Noble, or another online-based bookseller, you have to include basic information, such as

>> The book's full title

>> The author's name

>> Publisher information (if applicable). (As a self-published author, if you haven't established your own publishing company, you can simply use your full name as both the author and publisher.)

>> The price

>> The ISBN

>> The page count

>> The book's trim size

You also want to provide a detailed, sales-oriented description of the book, along with some information about the author that helps to give the book added credibility.

Your listing should provide all the information a potential reader needs to convince them to purchase your book online, right on the spot. The book's listing should read and appear just like a listing that you can find for a book published from a major publishing house. Make your listing short and well-written, and incorporate keywords that people (and the search engines) recognize as relating to your book.

TIP

Before you start writing your own book's listing, head over to Amazon or another major online bookseller, and seek out books that you believe will be your book's competition. Study those books' respective listings. And while you're at it, check out the listings for current bestsellers. Pay attention to the language, approach, writing style, format, and content that captures your attention.

Delivering essential details about the book

In order to create an effective listing for your book, you must write it in a way that quickly generates the reader's interest. Here's some of the information that you should incorporate into your book's listing:

» **A detailed description of your book:** Make this info engaging and include all the information that someone wants to know about the book. Adapt the material that you create as part of your book's back cover copy (see Chapter 10) and press materials (see Chapter 18). Start the listing or book description with a strong, attention-grabbing headline and first sentence.

» **An author bio:** Providing information about the author helps establish the book's credibility (especially for non-fiction titles) and promotes you, the author, as an expert in your field. If the bookseller allows you to, also include an author photo within the listing. See Chapter 18 for more about author bios and photos. And if the online bookseller gives you the opportunity to create a separate author profile, be sure to take that opportunity, as well.

» **The book's front and back cover image:** You create the book cover as a marketing and sales tool for your book (see Chapter 10). Your book cover art should help entice potential readers to buy your book when they see it as part of the book's listing.

» **Additional images from the book (if possible):** Providing additional images or graphics from within your book can help you offer a better preview of what the reader can expect.

» **Your book's Table of Contents:** Providing a Table of Contents allows you to convey exactly what information your book contains and the order in which you present that info.

» **A sample chapter from your book (or at least six to ten pages):** Providing a sample chapter can capture a potential reader's attention and draw them into what your book offers.

- **Excerpts of published reviews about your book:** You, as the author, think that your book is fantastic. But potential readers are more apt to trust the opinions of professional and well-known book reviewers, journalists, and reporters — not to mention other readers.

  After your book begins receiving positive publicity, include excerpts from the most positive reviews and editorial coverage. Also, if an expert in your field or a high-profile person that potential readers would relate to has positive things to say about your book, try to get quotes from them to include within your book's online listings. Proof that other people love your book gives you a powerful sales tool, and it can help you quickly build trust with potential readers.

- **Add a message from the author:** Some popular online booksellers allow the author and/or publisher to post information targeted directly to potential readers within the listing.

- **End with a call to action:** A *call to action* is a polite command that creates a sense of urgency and tells the reader exactly what to do next. For example, you might write, "Click the Buy Now button to order your copy of [*insert book title*]." Take advantage of strong verbs and persuasive language when you compose your call to action. Because you know your book's target audience (check out Chapter 3 for help identifying these people), you can compose a directive that resonates with them.

TIP

If you plan to sell your book through multiple online-based booksellers, including Amazon, Barnes & Noble, and a few others, feel free to duplicate the content from one book listing to the next. Figure out what wording works best to draw attention to your book, and then over time, tweak each listing, as needed. You know when your wording works well because you'll be generating book sales. For inspiration, you can review the descriptions for competing book titles, but never plagiarize someone else's work.

Reaching the readers with keywords and metadata

Many potential readers can find your book on Amazon or Barnes & Noble's website by doing a search based on subject matter, topic, keyword, category, or the author's name. Therefore, categorize your book correctly with online booksellers and create a description and related content that makes it easy for someone to find your book.

Choose the words that you use in your book's title, subtitle, description, and other elements of a book's listing carefully. By including the right information about your book, readers can find it faster and easier. Barnes & Noble offers tips for providing book *metadata* — the details you provide in your book listing that allow search tools to categorize and display your book to the appropriate audience. Visit `http://press.barnesandnoble.com`, and then choose Author Resources⇨ Author Tools & Tips. In the page that opens, scroll down and click Book Metadata Basics.

Terrific tactics for writing a listing

While you write your book's listing, keep its target audience in mind. Include information that those readers are interested in. And most importantly, be concise. You might have a potential reader's attention for only a few seconds or brief minutes. Focus on what's new or innovative about your book. What sets your book apart from the competition? Why should someone read it? The following sections offer detailed advice on how to write a creative, high-impact, and sales-oriented listing for your book.

Barnes & Noble offers tips for creating marketing copy for a self-published book that applies to creating book listings for online-based booksellers. Find these tips by going to `http://press.barnesandnoble.com`, then choosing Author Resources⇨ Author Tools & Tips; scroll down and click How to Write Sales Copy for Your Books.

Target all types of readers and online shoppers

Create a listing that caters to your core audience, but don't alienate the masses. People who browse for books via an online bookseller fall into one of several categories:

>> **People who know what they want:** These folks go online, and within the Search field of an online bookseller, they type in the exact book title or ISBN that they want to find. Then they order that specific book. (These people don't bother to read the listing because they already know what they want.) It's your job to ensure the book's title, ISBN, author, and book cover image is correct and up to date so that you don't confuse the reader.

>> **People who browse by subject matter:** When someone enters a subject or topic as a search phrase while shopping on Amazon or Barnes & Noble's website, many book titles and descriptions probably appear as part of their search results. Browsers typically know that they want a book on a specific

topic, but they haven't yet selected a specific title. In this moment, you have a great chance to sell your book to this potential reader, so by creating a well-written and informative listing, you can make your book stand out from the competition.

>> **People who have heard about your book:** If someone has heard about your book, possibly through a social media post or ad, and it piques their interest, they want to know more. Your listing should transform their casual interest into a sale.

>> **People who look for new or trending topics:** These people know that they want to order a book, but they don't necessarily have a topic or specific book title in mind. They're true browsers. When they find a book that they want, they order it. Your book listing should engage these people and get them interested in *your* book.

Keep in mind, this type of buyer may be looking to purchase a book as a gift for someone else. Thus, if your book would make a good gift for a graduation, baby shower, engagement, or birthday, for example, make this fact obvious to the person reading your book listing.

TIP

Fee-based tools, such as Publisher Rocket ($97; www.publisherrocket.com) can help you compose your book listing(s) by offering choices for the best keywords and the most appropriate categories for your book. These choices are all based on real-time research related to what readers are actually entering into Amazon search (and other online-based booksellers) to find the books related to your subject matter. This tool works for fiction or non-fiction books.

Avoid babbling

Create an informative, comprehensive, and well-written listing for your book, but remember that the attention span of online shoppers is extremely short. Keep your listing as concise as possible, and make sure it appeals to your book's target audience.

Within the description of your book, not only should you focus on what the book includes and whom you wrote it for, but also describe what makes it unique and how the reader can benefit from reading it. Why should someone read your book, rather than another book covering the same topic?

Use a creative, upbeat writing style when writing the listing for your book. Offer the reader a preview of what to expect and get them excited about the prospect of buying and reading it. This type of content should also appear on your book's back cover. (Chapter 10 has cover crafting details).

TIP

Consider how your listing will look on a full-size computer screen, e-reader display, tablet screen, and smaller smartphone screen. People most likely use these devices when shopping for books online. For example, if someone is using their smartphone to shop for books on Amazon or Barnes & Noble's website, and they need to engage in excessive scrolling to get through your book's entire description, eventually they may get bored and move on to something else without tapping that all-important Buy button. To help with brevity, consider using bulleted lists, as well as bold or italic text to make key ideas stand out quickly.

Submitting Your Listing to Popular Online Booksellers

In many cases, after you get your book an ISBN, register it with the *Bowker's Books In Print* directory (`www.bowker.com/books-in-print`), and make it available through one or more of the major book distributors (such as Ingram or Baker & Taylor, both of which I talk about in Chapter 15), you can obtain a basic listing on Amazon and Barnes & Noble easily — and, in some cases, automatically. (See Chapter 8 for more about obtaining an ISBN and registering with Bowker's.)

However, you can also manually list your book with each of the popular online booksellers. Or sign up with a publishing turnkey solution to handle dispersing listings for you, such as those from

>> **BookBaby:** www.bookbaby.com

>> **Draft2Digital:** www.draft2digital.com

>> **IngramSpark:** www.ingramspark.com

Depending on the self-publishing method you use, the printer or POD service may consider you the author, but not the publisher. For example, if you use one of the popular print-on-demand (POD) publishers (see Chapter 13), those companies may consider themselves the book's publisher. Therefore, the company should obtain a listing for your book with the major online booksellers on your behalf. After the company creates the listing, however, as the author, you can fully customize that listing. See "Creating an Effective Listing," earlier in this chapter, for ideas on how to create a listing that can make the most impact.

If you're both the author and the publisher (because you used a short run printer or traditional offset printer; see Chapter 12), you probably have to establish the listing for your book, unless your printer handles this service on your behalf. In the following sections, I explain how to submit a listing to Amazon, Barnes & Noble online, and other online booksellers.

TIP

If you plan to use print-on-demand, you can guarantee that your book appears on both Amazon and Barnes & Noble. Set up POD publishing through Amazon's Kindle Direct Publishing (http://kdp.amazon.com) to sell both a paperback and e-book edition of your book. Also register with Barnes & Noble Press (http://press.barnesandnoble.com) separately to simultaneously sell a paperback and e-book edition of your book through Barnes & Noble's website (www.bn.com).

Listing your book on Amazon

You can get your book listed on Amazon in several ways, including

>> **Taking advantage of Amazon's Kindle Direct Publishing program** (http://kdp.amazon.com): Create and sell an e-book version of your book, and also use Amazon as a print-on-demand (POD) service to sell a paperback edition of your book.

>> **Working with a POD publishing turnkey solution:** These services, such as BookBaby (www.bookbaby.com), Draft2Digital (www.draft2digital.com), or IngramSpark (www.ingramspark.com), use print on demand, but also can handle listing your book with the major online booksellers. Each service charges an additional fee (above Amazon's commission) to handle the various tasks involved with bringing your book to market.

>> **Joining the Amazon Sellers program** (http://sell.amazon.com): This service allows publishers to utilize the Amazon service to sell and distribute products, including physical books, as well as audiobook CDs and DVDs. To participate in this service, you pay a monthly fee (around $40), plus a per-sale fee (a percentage of the sale).

Listing your book with Barnes & Noble

Many turnkey self-publishing solutions include having your book listed with Barnes & Noble online (www.bn.com), which you, as the author, can then customize. If you become your own publisher, however, you need to register your publishing company and list your individual book titles with Barnes & Noble directly.

At the bottom of the BN.com main webpage, click Publisher and Author Guidelines under the B&N Services heading to access information about getting your book listed on Barnes and Noble's website. The process involves first becoming a *vendor of record* (which, in this case, makes you a publishing company wanting to sell books), and then submitting content about your book electronically.

TIP

As a self-published author, you can utilize Barnes & Noble's POD service, called Barnes & Noble Press (`http://press.barnesandnoble.com/self-publishing-services`) to sell both an e-book and paperback version of your book.

Generating Excellent Online Reviews

Although you can generate interest and sales for your book by having your book reviewed in *The New York Times* — or in any other newspaper, magazine, or well-established website — or featured on a blog or popular podcast, many readers rely on other readers to help them make their book selections.

Many popular online booksellers allow people to write their own reviews of any book and give the book a rating (between one and five stars). In addition to displaying all reviews written about each title, the bookseller displays a cumulative average score within each book listing. So, even if a potential reader doesn't spend the time reading all the posted text-based reviews written by other consumers, in a matter of seconds, anyone can glance at a book's average rating and determine how other people liked that book. Would you buy a book that's received an average rating of two stars, when a competing book has an average rating of five stars?

REMEMBER

Having a handful of good reviews attached to your book's listing on Amazon and Barnes & Noble's website instantly helps establish your book's credibility. Positive reviews work as a very powerful sales tool. After all, many people rely on what other readers have to say, in addition to reading the promotional description and hype that you include about your book as part of its listing.

In the following sections, I give you the scoop on having folks you know post reviews and why you should review other books yourself so that you can get noticed as an author.

Asking others to post reviews

As soon as your listing appears with Amazon and Barnes & Noble, for example, have a few close friends, relatives, or coworkers who read your book post a positive review through both online booksellers. The more positive reviews you generate, the better. Just make sure that the reviews posted by people you know are believable and not too over-the-top. (Oh, and while you're at it, please feel free to post a five-star and incredibly positive review for this second edition of *Self-Publishing For Dummies* on both Amazon and BN.com).

Relying on strangers to post positive reviews about your book is an honorable thing to do, but most readers invest their time in writing negative reviews about books that they feel somehow ripped them off or that they didn't enjoy reading, rather than posting positive reviews of books that they enjoyed.

Becoming a book reviewer

While people are busy reviewing your book and hopefully making your book's listings on Amazon and Barnes & Noble appear more credible, as an author, post reviews of other books that your target audience may also be interested in. In other words, review your competition and utilize their book listings to promote your book. Readers who visit your competitions' listings may feel compelled to visit your book's listing also, and they might wind up choosing your book over others.

The best book reviews capture a reader's attention and provide useful information. As a book reviewer, make sure to follow these guidelines while you create your review:

>> **Start with a hook** — a sentence or two that grabs the reader's attention.

>> **Provide basic information** about the book and a brief plot summary. However, never reveal any plot spoilers if you're writing a review of a fictional work.

>> **Incorporate your own thoughts and opinions.** Tell other potential readers why you like or dislike the book. Be specific and back up what you say with examples. Don't just state, "I loved this book." Expand this idea with statements that contain specific examples or an explanation. For example, "I loved the plot and characters because . . ."

>> **Provide your recommendation.** Towards the end of your review, whether it's a few sentences or a few paragraphs long, explain why you do or don't recommend the book. Again, share your rationale and use examples.

Because you want to showcase your own personality and writing style, and perhaps get people interested in the book that you've written, never be unkind or include wording that the book's author or the review's readers might find insulting or downright mean. Remember, any reviews that you publish online or elsewhere provide a reflection of you and your reputation as an author.

TIP

Be sure to proofread your work before publishing it. If you need help writing a compelling book review, Grammarly (a tool used by writers to correct grammar and spelling), offers a blog post that can help you through this process. You can find this article at www.grammarly.com/blog/how-to-write-book-review.

REMEMBER

Within your reviews for other books, position yourself as an expert in your field and as an author. Mention the title of your book. For example, say, "As the author of [*insert book title*], I've read and reviewed many books on this topic. This one provides . . ." Also, make sure that you include information that's accurate, honest, and not too promotional (when discussing your own book within a review for another book). Always maintain your professionalism and be courteous to your fellow authors and the community of readers who see your review.

Exploiting the Goodreads platform

Goodreads (www.goodreads.com) is a free online community that encourages avid readers to post and share reviews of books, as well as recommendations to other readers. This is the world's largest book reviews site. The service also generates personal book recommendations for readers. As an author, you can take advantage of Goodreads to promote your book for free. For example, you can establish an author page on the service by visiting www.goodreads.com/author/program. In addition, Goodreads has an online advertising program (www.goodreads.com/advertisers) that self-published authors and small publishers can utilize for a fee to reach a targeted group of the service's more than 125 million members (as of early 2023).

Resources from Online Booksellers

In addition to creating a well-written and comprehensive listing for your book, consider utilizing the other tools and resources available to authors and publishers on the popular online booksellers' respective websites.

>> **Author Profile Pages (aka Author Central on Amazon):** Authors who have books being sold on Amazon can create one of these pages. Using the service's online tools, you can create an author profile that offers information about yourself, messages to readers, links to your book (or books), a link to your personal website, details about your social media accounts, and other information of interest to readers. This service is free; you simply need to complete an online registration. For more information, visit: https://kdp.amazon.com/en_US/help/topic/G200644310.

>> **Amazon Associate:** By becoming an Amazon Associate, you can create your own online bookstore to sell your books and generate commissions from sales. Everyone can access this opportunity to sell products through Amazon, but for authors, the service offers yet another way to promote your book and generate revenue. You also earn a commission on book sales for titles that you didn't write or publish. Visit http://affiliate-program.amazon.com/home for details.

>> **In-person author events at Barnes & Noble stores:** To find out about these opportunities and how to put yourself in the running to appear, contact your local store manager. You can also visit www.barnesandnobleinc.com, and then, from the top menu, choose Publishers & Authors ⇨ How to Be Considered for an Author Event.

>> **An author page that includes your photo:** Like Amazon, Barnes & Noble's website enables you to create your own author page on its service that you can use to promote yourself and your books. To find out more about this free marketing tool, visit http://help-press.barnesandnoble.com, and in the Search text box, enter "Creating an Author Page." When you hit Search, a result titled "Creating an Author Page on BN.com" appears. Select that link to access the article.

IN THIS CHAPTER

» Understanding the challenges of major retail distribution

» Selling through wholesalers and distributors

» Partnering with independent booksellers and specialty retail outlets

» Targeting trade associations and other niche groups

» Trying your luck with mass-market retailers and bookstore chains

Chapter **15**

Distributing Your Book through Traditional Channels

This chapter focuses on how to obtain traditional distribution for your self-published book. It describes some of the hurdles that you may face and ways to potentially overcome them. I wish I could say that self-publishing offers all the benefits and profit potential as having your book published by a major publishing house, and that self-publishing has no drawbacks whatsoever. But, unfortunately, that's not the case. Although you can potentially make self-publishing a viable and lucrative option, you do have to face a lot of challenges while you try to obtain traditional retail distribution for your book.

I do have some good news, though, so don't lose heart. In this chapter, I help you understand that — with a bit of work and salesmanship — you can get your book into some independently owned bookstores and specialty retail stores. You can also try your hand at getting niche groups (trade associations, for example) interested in buying large quantities of your book. Plus, by working through a major wholesaler or distributor, any bookstore could potentially order your book for a customer, even if the store doesn't normally stock it on its shelves.

Securing Major Retail Distribution for Your Book

Self-publishers can face a variety of challenges when attempting to obtain distribution through retail bookstores — especially a major chain, such as Barnes & Noble. Here are a few of those hurdles:

>> **Buying on credit:** Major publishing houses, distributors, and wholesalers offer bookstores credit terms (up to 90 days) when those bookstores place orders. When you use most self-publishing solutions, the printer you use requires that you pay for orders in advance. To overcome this obstacle, you need to inventory (store) your own printed books at your expense until they're sold. So you have to lay out the money needed, ship the books to the bookseller with industry-standard credit terms, and then wait to be paid.

Unfortunately, as the author, if you're buying your books at 40 to 50 percent off their cover price, you need to offer this same discount to booksellers. Therefore, at best, you break even on the sale or earn just a small profit, while tying up your money for months in the process.

>> **Accepting returns:** Major publishing houses accept returns on unsold books. But companies that offer self-publishing solutions or print-on-demand (POD) services usually don't accept returns. Unless you plan to establish your own publishing company (see Chapter 7 for more about this task) and handle your own printing, warehousing, and distribution, you don't have the option of allowing bookseller returns. Again, as a self-published author, you can inventory your own books, and then take on the risk that you might receive returns 30, 60, or 90 days later. *Note:* In many cases, the booksellers may return books in used or damaged condition. Thus, you probably can't resell returned books as new.

>> **Lacking a sales team:** Major publishers have sales teams that establish relationships with key buyers at the major distributors, wholesalers, and bookstore chains. As a self-publisher, you can overcome this obstacle by hiring an independent trade salesperson who has industry connections (see the section "Going After Mass-Market Retailers," later in this chapter, for details on this approach). However, for your outside salesperson to effectively sell you book, you also need to overcome the preceding two obstacles in this list.

A few independent trade sales reps work with self-published authors who have only one or two titles, but you can have significant difficulty finding such a rep who can sell your book, especially if you have a niche-oriented topic.

>> **Having a single title to sell:** Major publishers offer multiple titles at the same time. Most buyers are extremely busy and can't focus their time on evaluating and purchasing just one book title (or a small series of books) from a small and independent publisher. You can get around this obstacle by hiring an independent trade salesperson who sells a handful of titles simultaneously, from several small publishers. But you first need to overcome all the preceding obstacles described in this list.

Brick-and-mortar bookstores — whether part of a chain, such as Barnes & Noble, or independent booksellers — are becoming far less popular amongst consumers than ever before when it comes to consumers purchasing books. More and more people shop online for printed books, and the number of people who use an e-reader to read e-books (as opposed to a printed book) continues to increase rapidly. For this reason, if you have limited resources, you can likely have more success relying on online sales to move your book.

Don't count on retail distribution only to achieve sales success for your book. You need to use a variety of sales and distribution methods, beyond the methods discussed in this chapter, to sell large quantities of your book.

Working with Wholesalers and Distributors

As far as the self-publishing world is concerned, wholesalers and distributors are pretty much the same thing. (Self-publishers tend to use the two terms interchangeably.) You can most easily get your book into retail stores by making it available through one or more of the major wholesalers or distributors that already have established relationships with key retailers. Each distributor, however, has different criteria for choosing publishers to work with and which actual book titles they inventory and sell.

If you're working with a well-established print-on-demand (POD) publisher (see Chapter 13 for POD details), that company may already have an established relationship with one or more of the major distributors. If not, you need to contact the distributors yourself. In the following sections, I introduce the major distributors that you can work with. *Note:* A distributor might be able to get your book into mass-market retailers, such as Walmart and Target, as well as Barnes & Noble. But realistically, you, as a self-published author, have a slim chance of getting this exposure.

TIP

For help obtaining retail distribution and getting the attention of a major distributor, consider joining The Independent Book Publishers Association (www.ibpa-online.org). This organization offers a wide range of educational programs and resources for self-published authors and small publishing houses. Through the organization's targeted publications, you can advertise your book to booksellers nationwide.

Banking on Baker & Taylor

Founded in 1828, Baker & Taylor has been a pioneer in the book publishing industry. It's now one of the largest book distributors in the nation and a supplier to virtually all of the United States' leading booksellers and libraries.

The key benefit to working with Baker & Taylor (www.baker-taylor.com) is that virtually all bookstores, libraries, and other retail outlets that sell books have an established relationship with them. After you get your book listed with Baker & Taylor, booksellers can easily order it.

Investigating Ingram Content Group

Ingram is the industry's other major book distributor (besides Baker & Taylor, discussed in the preceding section). Typically, Ingram works directly only with publishers that offer more than ten book titles, so self-published authors need to work through IngramSpark (www.ingramspark.com), a division of Ingram set up to help independent authors sell books.

However, if you establish a publishing company with multiple book titles for sale, the Ingram Content Group (www.ingramcontent.com) offers a comprehensive collection of services, including content preparation, book printing, inventory management, distribution, marketing, and analytics.

Looking into other major distributors

Even if you can't get the attention of Baker & Taylor or Ingram, many smaller book distributors can handle getting your book into bookstores and other retailers. Some of the other well-established book distributors include those in this mini-table.

Distributor	Web Address
The Alliance Company	`https://alliancepublishingpress.com/index.html`
Book Clearing House	`www.bookch.com`
Bookazine	`www.bookazine.com`
Consortium Book Sales & Distribution	`www.cbsd.com`
Independent Publishers Group	`www.ipgbook.com`
National Book Network	`www.nbnbooks.com`
Publishers Group West	`www.pgw.com`
SCB Distributors	`www.scbdistributors.com`

For more information, contact any of the distributors in the preceding table, and be prepared to submit a complete package that includes

- » A published copy of your book
- » A detailed description of the book, as well as your marketing materials (see Part 5 for more about marketing and advertising)
- » Copies of published reviews and media coverage
- » A description of your marketing, advertising, and public relations plans
- » Information about yourself, the author
- » Retail and potential wholesale pricing

Approaching Independent Booksellers

Independent booksellers typically have their own in-house buyers (often the owner or manager of the store) and welcome the opportunity to work with small and independent publishers to offer a selection of books that their competitors don't. Working with independent booksellers offers the self-publisher an opportunity to break into traditional retail stores, especially if you can support the independent booksellers by making author appearances or participating in book signings.

Trade associations and industry publications can help you reach many independent bookstores at the same time by renting a database, through paid advertising, or by participating with other small publishers in a group mailing that goes to buyers. You typically have to pay a fee for this service. Contacting these booksellers individually is a time-consuming process that generates relatively few book sales. You have to approach each independent bookstore separately, from a sales standpoint, and each store that agrees to carry your book typically orders only a small number of books at a time.

Many self-publishers discover that they can better utilize their time and financial resources by selling books directly to consumers or by selling their books through online booksellers (refer to Chapter 14 for details on online booksellers).

Creating a sell sheet

You can most effectively sell to independent booksellers by offering them credit terms and accepting returns, and then target them with a one-page marketing sheet that advertises your book. This piece, called a *sell sheet*, is a sales tool for your book. Major publishing companies create one-page sell sheets (in digital or paper-based form) for each of their titles, so you should do the same if you plan to sell directly to booksellers. Make your sell sheet easy to read, professional looking, and designed to convince bookstore buyers and other retailers to purchase, inventory, and sell your book.

To create an outstanding sell sheet, check out the following tips:

>> **Highlight your book's features.** Prominently display your book's title, cover image, and bibliographic information, which includes its

- ISBN

- Cover price

- Page count

- Trim size

- Author

- Publisher

- BISAC Subject/Audience information

>> **Fine-tune your book's description.** Include a short but detailed description of your book, along with an explanation of its target audience, in addition to the bibliographic information. You can use the same description that appears on your book's back cover. See Chapter 10 for details on back cover descriptions.

>> **Outline your book's availability.** Mention whether a major distributor offers the book so that booksellers know whether they can easily place an order for the book through a distributor it already has a relationship with. (See the section "Working with Wholesalers and Distributors," earlier in this chapter, for more information.)

>> **Promote your book's marketability.** Include any useful facts or statistics (using a bulleted format) that may help the sale of your book to booksellers. The list can include info such as the size of the potential audience or the industry that your book targets.

>> **Portray the author (yourself) as an expert and/or accomplished writer.** Include a short author bio and author photo (see Chapter 19 for more about author bios and photos).

>> **Hire a professional designer to help you create your sell sheet.** Consider hiring a professional graphic designer so that the sheet has a high-end look and feel.

Making contact through bookseller directories

You have a variety of ways to contact independent booksellers across the country, including by telephone, using a traditional mailing, or via email. Using one of the following directories may save you considerable time while you build your mailing list and pinpoint the booksellers that you want to target with your sales efforts:

>> **The American Booksellers Association (ABA):** Offers tools to market your book to independent bookstores nationwide. Visit www.bookweb.org and select For Publishers from the top menu.

>> **The Independent Publishers Group (IPG):** An organization that has an established book sales and marketing team that works with self-published authors and small publishers to help them establish distribution through retail booksellers. This organization does more than simply act as a distributor; it also helps the self-published author market and promote a title. Check it out by going to www.ipgbook.com and choosing Publishers from the top menu.

Scoping Out Specialty Retail Stores

Specialty retail outlets can include any retail store that sells books but isn't a traditional bookstore. For example, independently-owned gift shops and boutiques often sell books, and retail chains such as Urban Outfitters sell novelty books that cater to its young and hip demographic.

REMEMBER

This type of distribution strategy works well for books that focus on a niche-oriented topic. The advantage to pursuing specialty retail shops as a distribution outlet is that you can potentially increase awareness and sales opportunities for your book. But as a self-published author working alone, you may find getting through to the appropriate buyer and getting their attention a challenge.

The process of selling your books through specialty retail stores is very much the same as selling to independent booksellers (see the section "Approaching Independent Booksellers," earlier in this chapter). You need to contact the appropriate buyer at the retail store or chain. Hiring an experienced salesperson can help you establish connections and get some assistance in the sales process. See the section "Going After Mass-Market Retailers," later in this chapter, for the scoop on finding such a person.

Hooking Up with Trade Associations, Special Interest Groups, and Conferences

Many professional trade associations, special interest groups, and trade show/conference planners sell books and educational materials to their members. As part of your market research (see Chapter 3 for more info on doing your research), pinpoint groups and associations whose membership may be interested in selling your book (or buying large numbers of books to give away to its members), and then contact those groups directly. Consider offering a special discount to members or allowing the organization to publish excerpts from your book (for free) on their website to generate interest and sales.

Any company, organization, or group that sells books (or that's set up to sell products in person or online) to customers, clients, or members could potentially sell your book. You just have to help the decision makers at these organizations realize how selling your book can potentially benefit everyone involved and generate a profit, too. Provide your book's press documents and marketing materials to key decision makers (such as the buyer for the organization). And make direct contact with these same people. You can entice organizations, special-interest clubs, or trade associations by offering a significant discount (up to 60 percent off the cover price) on high-quantity orders.

NOW SHOWING . . .

You can find industry-oriented and consumer trade shows held throughout the world. They focus on many different industries and interests. These gatherings bring together professionals working in an industry or who have a similar interest from all over the world. They allow for the exchange of information and provide valuable learning and networking opportunities. When attending a trade show, bring plenty of marketing materials for your book so that you can hand them out when you network.

For example, if you wrote a book related to sci-fi, superheroes, or pop culture–oriented TV shows or movies, selling your book at the various Comic-Con conventions held around the U.S. can offer great exposure.

The biggest book-related trade shows are BookExpo and BookCon. Booksellers, buyers, major publishing houses, authors, distributors, wholesalers, the media, and a wide range of other people working in the book publishing industry attend these shows. If you're looking to sell your book directly to readers or seek out distribution, attending these shows and perhaps renting a small booth to showcase your book can help you get your book noticed by publishing industry professionals, distribution outlets, and consumers alike. After the COVID-19 pandemic, the show's producers are trying to reimagine and relaunch BookCon and BookExpo.

TIP

If your book caters to people working in a specific industry or who gather for an industry or consumer-oriented trade show, consider renting booth space at these trade shows or conferences and selling your book directly to attendees and participants. Offering attendees a special discount and providing an autographed copy of your book give you excellent sales incentives. For a listing of events that cater to specific industries, visit Ten Times Online (www.10times.com).

Going After Mass-Market Retailers

Self-published authors and small publishers can find breaking into mass-market retailers or into a major bookstore chain, such as Barnes & Noble, extremely challenging. Realistically, don't expect to obtain this type of distribution for your self-published book. Getting the attention of a buyer who represents a mass-market retailer requires a lot more than your being a good writer. Major publishing houses have entire sales departments whose job involves cultivating relationships with these buyers. Keep in mind, the chances of getting your independently published (self-published) book into a chain of retail stores in slim, but here are a few things to get you to the plate:

>> **Hire an experienced sales representative who has established connections with buyers associated with mass-market retailers.** Many sales representatives work with a handful of authors and small publishers simultaneously. Even though you have to pay for the services of a sales representative, your chance of important buyers seeing and evaluating your book improves greatly if you hire the right person.

The sales rep you hire should have experience working with the key buyers that you want to target and have a good understanding of your book and who will want to read it. A successful sales rep has pre-established relationships with buyers that you can benefit from.

>> **Team up with the manufacturer or distributor of an established product that already has mass-market distribution and bundle your book with that product.** This maneuver requires approaching and negotiating with a company that offers a product of interest to the same target audience as your book. Contact the sales or marketing department of the company whose product you want to bundle your book with. You need to pitch the idea — and probably need to follow up with a detailed written proposal.

Chapter **16**

Getting a Grip on Warehousing, Order Fulfillment, and Shipping

I n many cases, authors can reap financial rewards for selling their own books directly — either online or in the physical world. These sales allow authors to increase earning potential on each copy sold. But this potential does come with a little bit of work and higher upfront costs. For example, you need to use a short run or offset printer (see Chapter 12) to print copies of your book, and then warehouse them until they're sold. You must also set up your own operation for warehousing, order taking, fulfillment, and shipping. Many self-published authors do these processes from their homes.

When you begin selling your own books, you need to establish some type of formal business (mainly for tax purposes). Chapter 7 helps you set up your publishing business. In this chapter, you can find ideas for easing into the warehousing, fulfillment, and shipping processes, and how to establish your operational procedures.

Warehousing Your Books and Managing Inventory

Selling your own books requires maintaining an inventory (meaning warehousing books) to fill orders. In the following sections, I explain the importance of safely storing your books and carefully monitoring your inventory.

WARNING

If you plan to store books in your home or in a storage unit, you need to acquire business insurance to cover your inventory and any office-related equipment that you have. Homeowner's or renter's insurance doesn't cover operating a home business (and maintaining inventory, and so on).

Storing your books safely

If you use short run or offset printing (see Chapter 12 for details) to publish a large quantity of books, you wind up with a bunch of large cartons filled with books that you need to warehouse somewhere. If you use print-on-demand (POD), which I talk about in Chapter 13, you can keep a much smaller quantity of books on-hand, and then reorder more as needed.

Many self-published authors use their basement, garage, or attic to store book inventory. You may find this storage method convenient if you plan to sell books directly to readers, booksellers, or retailers and want to work from home.

Check out these important tips for keeping books in excellent condition:

>> Keep the books in a climate-controlled, clean, and dry environment.

>> Store cartons on pallets (a few inches above the ground), especially if you're storing boxes in your basement and have flooding issues.

>> Pack the books in large, sealable plastic containers to ensure that they stay clean and dry until you sell them and prepare to ship them out.

Taking stock of your inventory

A wise business operator regularly maintains a good grasp of their inventory levels. You need to establish a simple way to handle inventory control so that you always know how many books you have on hand. Monitoring inventory also involves being able to anticipate demand and pre-ordering additional inventory at the appropriate time so that you have it available when you need it. If you're selling just one product — your book — you can calculate inventory levels by hand. Keeping detailed invoices also helps with this process.

After you begin selling a significant number of books, consider investing in some basic inventory management software. Some turnkey e-commerce website solutions, such as those available from Shopify (www.shopify.com), have backend inventory management tools. Intuit offers QuickBooks (http://quickbooks.intuit.com), an excellent software package that allows you to manage many aspects of your small business operations, inventory, and finances.

Taking and Fulfilling Orders

Depending on how you plan to sell your books, your order-taking and fulfillment operations vary:

>> **In-person:** You may sell your books in person at a variety of events, such as author appearances or trade shows. In this case, you take the orders, as well as payment for them, and then hand the customers their books or arrange shipping on the spot.

>> **Online:** You may want to create an e-commerce website to accept orders online. You can find out how to set up an e-commerce site in Chapter 17, as well as how to sell books directly through social media platforms. Delivery varies depending on whether you fulfill the orders yourself (see the section "Shipping Your Books to Customers," later in this chapter) or have a service provider (such as Amazon) that fulfills the orders for you.

When you receive orders or make sales, document them promptly and fulfill the orders ASAP. Make sure to process payments, manage a database of customers, and print invoices. I cover all these processes and more in the following sections.

REMEMBER

Whatever methods you use to accept orders and interact with customers, you need to offer top-notch customer service to those people. When you begin selling books directly to customers, whether those customers are booksellers or individual readers, those people expect to do business with a professionally-run company. You can seamlessly run this company from your home on a part-time basis if customers can easily place orders and you (or the drop-shipping service you hire) promptly process and ship those orders. Achieving this level of service requires you to establish carefully thought-out procedures for all aspects of the order-fulfillment process.

Handling different order options

You can sell your books in person, through an 800-number, through your own website, or via social media. The following sections offer some additional details about these various options.

When taking orders in person

If you sell books in person at author appearances, seminars, trade shows, and other events, prepare for the events. Bring a generous supply of books (so that you don't run out) and a small table or trade show display where you can sell the books (if the show's management doesn't supply a table). Be ready to accept cash, debit card, credit card, and electronic payments (such as Apple Pay or Google Pay). Have a method to generate receipts for customers and keep a duplicate copy of each receipt for your own records. Many companies allow you to accept credit card, debit card, and electronic payments when selling books online or in-person, including

>> **Square:** www.squareup.com/payments

>> **PayPal:** www.paypal.com/business/accept-payments

>> **Authorize.net:** www.authorize.net

>> **Stripe:** www.stripe.com

TIP

Do you need an inexpensive but professional-looking display to showcase your books at bookfairs, trade shows, and author appearances? Check out the offerings from

>> **Post Up Stand:** www.postupstand.com

>> **Fantastic Displays:** www.fantasticdisplays.com/products

REMEMBER

Selling books in person allows people to meet you and purchase the book right on the spot, without having to place an order and wait for delivery. You can even offer to sign and personalize each copy. People often prefer the instant gratification of obtaining what they purchase right away. You always have the option of giving people the appropriate Amazon or Barnes & Noble URL where they can order your book, but you run the risk that potential customers won't follow through with placing their order later.

Establishing a toll-free phone number

You can easily establish an incoming toll-free number to accept orders. The service you use to acquire the toll-free number can program the toll-free number to ring on your existing home, cell, or office phone. The following list gives you a small sampling of companies that offer inexpensive, incoming, toll-free phone number services:

>> **800.com:** www.800.com

>> **Dialpad:** www.dialpad.com

>> **FreedomVoice:** www.freedomvoice.com

>> **Grasshopper:** www.grasshopper.com

>> **RingCentral:** www.ringcentral.com

>> **Vonage:** www.vonage.com

REMEMBER

Having a toll-free number often means that you pay by the minute for each incoming call (although some services offer a flat monthly fee with no per-minute charges). After you have a toll-free phone number set up for people to call and place their orders, have someone well trained on hand to answer the phone during business hours. This can be yourself or a family member, as long as they know what to say, how to answer questions, and understand the importance of acting professionally during each call. Of course, you can also hire a professional answering service to answer your incoming calls, but this can be expensive.

Launching an e-commerce website

An e-commerce website is slightly different than a regular website because it comes equipped with a shopping cart module that allows someone to place a secure order online by using a major credit card, debit card, or an electronic payment service (for example, PayPal, Google Pay, or Apple Pay). You can add a shopping cart to a website or create a simple e-commerce website for your book relatively easily and inexpensively. Chapter 17 goes over the details.

TIP

Many turnkey website hosting services offer easy-to-use e-commerce website creation tools that require zero programming skills. These companies include

>> **GoDaddy:** www.godaddy.com

>> **Shopify:** www.shopify.com

>> **Squarespace:** www.squarespace.com

>> **Wix:** www.wix.com

>> **WordPress:** www.wordpress.org

These turnkey e-commerce solutions can also help you set up a merchant account so that you can accept credit card payments (and other payment methods) online via your website. With these solutions, you can access all the tools online, and you need absolutely no programming knowledge to create and operate the website.

If you don't want to set up and operate a full website, Chapter 17 also explains how to sell books directly through social media platforms, such as Facebook and Instagram.

Accepting payments

Selling books, whether in person or online, requires you to accept different forms of payment to generate the most possible sales and offer convenience to your customers. To accept credit card payments, you must establish a merchant account with a bank or merchant account provider. You also can accept payments via PayPal, Apple Pay, Google Pay, or cash.

REMEMBER

Although you can always accept cash, many people prefer the convenience of making purchases by using their credit or debit card, or an electronic payment service directly via their smartphone. When selling online, you don't have the option to accept cash, so you need a merchant account with the ability to process credit card payments automatically as orders are placed on your website.

Many companies allow small businesses to set up a merchant account quickly and easily. These companies include Square, PayPal, Authorize.net, and Stripe. However, if you process a lot of credit card payments per month, you might want to contact your bank or financial institution and shop around for the best merchant account deal for your small business.

Keeping the right records

Every business requires its operators to handle many types of paperwork (and digital records) to track customers, record orders, process those orders, maintain inventory, and manage finances. You absolutely need proper recordkeeping to keep track of your finances and tax information. Refer to Chapter 7 for information on popular accounting and bookkeeping applications, including QuickBooks (http://quickbooks.intuit.com). Many e-commerce turnkey solutions also integrate bookkeeping, invoicing, inventory management, and label-printing tools into the backend of their applications.

Here's a rundown of the types of information that you likely need to handle when selling books and operating your small business:

>> **Orders:** Maintain a detailed list of all incoming book orders. You can use a database program, spreadsheet, or hard-copy files.

- >> **Customer database:** Maintain a database of your customers, especially if you plan to publish additional books in the future or want to sell these same customers additional products or services. Having order information at your fingertips can also help you provide top-notch customer service to repeat callers or existing customers. For each customer, make sure that you have their full name, address, phone number, ordering details, method of payment (and payment details), and the preferred shipping method.

- >> **Sales receipts:** You issue a sales receipt to the customer when they buy from you, typically in a retail or in-person environment. Keep a copy of your sales receipts for recordkeeping purposes and so that you can track orders. And regarding order tracking, make sure that you ship all books by using a method that provides you with a tracking number.

- >> **Invoices:** You can use an invoice as a sales receipt, or you can create an invoice if you're shipping books to customers and receiving payment later. Whether you use invoices or sales receipts depends on how and where you plan to sell your books.

- >> **Returns:** Keeping track of returns helps you maintain accurate inventory records and manage your finances.

REMEMBER

Because you're running a business, doing the appropriate paperwork and filing tax returns as needed keeps you out of trouble with the IRS and helps you better manage your finances, track profits and expenditures, and generate the most revenue possible from your publishing venture. You may want to hire a bookkeeper to manage your day-to-day paperwork if you're not comfortable doing your own bookkeeping and financial paperwork. An accountant can also help you set up procedures for handling this paperwork. But having these people do all of the bookkeeping for you can get costly, so maybe take a class or two on financial management for small business.

Shipping Your Books to Customers

Setting your publishing company up to accept orders and sell books also includes having the ability to ship orders to customers, whether a distributor wants 100 books, a bookseller wants ten books, or individual customers want one book at a time.

Surveying shipping options

When it comes to shipping books to customers, you have a variety of options. The service that you use depends on your budget and how quickly you need your books to arrive at their destinations. Plan to investigate shipping options to figure out cost-effective and convenient ways to ship your books.

Checking out the United States Postal Service (USPS)

The USPS offers a variety of services that merchants can use to ship their goods. You can order stamps and shipping supplies online (www.usps.com), or purchase and create shipping labels (with postage) from your computer. Check out the following shipping methods:

>> **Priority Mail:** The USPS offers envelopes for free when you use their flat-rate Priority Mail. This service typically takes two to three business days (including Saturday) for delivery, and it includes package tracking.

>> **First-Class Mail:** First-Class Mail is often (but not always) a bit cheaper than Priority Mail, but you must pay for the envelope. First Class mail typically delivers in one to five business days within the U.S., and the cost of shipping doesn't include package tracking (that service costs extra).

Looking at major shipping companies

For larger shipments or overnight, two-day, three-day, or ground shipments, consider establishing an account with a major shipping company:

>> **DHL:** www.dhl-usa.com

>> **FedEx:** www.fedex.com

>> **UPS:** www.ups.com

You can set up accounts with these companies by visiting any of these couriers' websites and using a major credit card. After you set up an account, you can print shipping labels and schedule pickups from your computer.

Opting for other shipping services

TIP

If you know you need to ship quantities of books to many individual addresses, investigate companies such as Pirate Ship (http://ship.pirateship.com), which offers significant discounts on USPS and UPS shipping fees. You can set up an account for free, and you don't need to ship a minimum number of packages per month to get the discounts.

You can also find other services that cater to small businesses and offer significant discounts on domestic and international shipping rates, such as

>> **ShippingEasy:** www.shippingeasy.com

>> **Stamps.com:** www.stamps.com

>> **Shippo:** www.shippo.com

>> **ShipStation:** www.shipstation.com

>> **EasyPost:** www.easypost.com

Expanding the service scope with drop-shipping

You can consider hiring a drop-shipping company to handle everything for you. This type of company takes care of not only shipping, but also accepting online orders, warehousing your books, processing orders, and handling the necessary accounting and customer management. For example, Amazon does these tasks for self-published authors and its other Amazon Sellers. Check with your printer to see whether it offers drop-shipping services, or find other companies to help you out by searching online for "order processing" or "order fulfillment."

REMEMBER

Hiring a drop-shipping company can get expensive and quickly eat away your profits. If, however, you begin to receive too many book orders and don't have the time to fulfill them yourself, a drop-shipping service could be the perfect answer.

Setting up your shipping department

To save time and money, stock up on shipping supplies and have everything on hand so that you can promptly fill orders. Necessary supplies may include

>> Bubble wrap or packing peanuts

>> Invoices or packing slips

>> Packing tape

>> Padded envelopes and other packaging, such as small boxes

>> Scissors

>> Shipping labels

>> Stamps or postage; mailing labels and a label printer

You can save money by purchasing shipping supplies in bulk. Anticipate your needs on a monthly, quarterly, or semi-annual basis, and then stock up. You can also save time if you invest in a small and dedicated shipping-label printer. You can find these printers for less than $200 on Amazon, for example. In the Search field, simply type "shipping label printer." Most of these printers work with Windows PCs or Macs. The most convenient label printers are wireless and utilize Bluetooth to communicate with your computer. When you register with the appropriate shipping services, this same printer can create and print postage.

Take measures to make sure that your packages don't arrive damaged. Use an appropriate-size envelope, and either make it a padded envelope or wrap the book in bubble wrap before placing it in the envelope. By protecting your book during shipment, you make your customers happy. And you don't have to worry about your business suffering because of goods damaged during shipping that unhappy customers return.

Creating an unboxing experience for your readers

Take pride in how you package and ship each book so that when the reader receives and opens your package, it becomes an experience that gets them excited to start reading your book right away. Don't just throw your book in a padded envelope, slap on a shipping label and postage, and then send it off. Consider adding these personal touches to your packaging:

>> **Custom-printed packaging and inserts:** For example, get envelopes, invoices/receipts, and shipping labels that showcase your company name and logo.

>> **A thank you card:** You can use a notecard that has a pre-printed message, but as the book's author, hand-sign each note. And for a small investment, you can have custom thank you cards printed with your own message and company logo.

VistaPrint (www.vistaprint.com) or Moo (www.moo.com) are two of the many printing companies that can create these professional-looking notecards for you.

Simply by creating an all-around positive experience related to ordering, receiving, opening, and then reading your book, your readers are more likely to share positive reviews in person (amongst their friends, coworkers, and family), online (through their own social media accounts), and by posting positive ratings and reviews on the major online bookseller sites or your own e-commerce website. Positive word-of-mouth related to your book gives you an extremely powerful and inexpensive sales tool.

5

Creating a Buzz: Publicity and Marketing

Find out why you, as a self-publisher, need to create a website for your book (and yourself as an author) and become active on social media.

Create publicity materials for your book that get attention from mainstream media, as well as niche-oriented podcasters, bloggers, vloggers, and social media influencers.

Discover the power of public relations and how it can help you sell more books.

Take advantage of paid advertising — online and in the real world — to quickly build awareness for your book and cost effectively sell it to your target audience.

Generate more reveneue from your book by developing and selling spin-off products that cater to your book's intended readers.

IN THIS CHAPTER

» Making an author-centric or book-focused website

» Crafting an (e-commerce) website for your book

» Determining what to include in your website

» Driving traffic to your site to boost your sales

» Developing a community around your book through social media

Chapter **17**

Creating a Website and Social Media Accounts for Your Book

You have many ways to sell a self-published book, both in the physical world and on the Internet. Many authors rely mainly on the product pages for their book that appear on Amazon, Barnes & Noble's website (www.bn.com), Apple Books (www.apple.com/apple-books), and other online booksellers to sell printed or e-book versions. They then use paid advertising, social media, in-person appearances, and other grassroots efforts to drive traffic to their book's page on one or more online-based booksellers.

Using the services of an online bookseller probably offers you the easiest method for selling books because after you write and publish the book, you rely on those booksellers to handle many of the tasks associated with processing and fulfilling orders (for a print book) or distributing the e-book version of your book. Your job mainly becomes marketing your book and driving traffic to the online bookstores that sell it.

If you opt to have your books printed by using a short run or offset printer (see Chapter 12), or you plan to sell various e-book editions (see Chapter 11) of your book, you have a few other online-based options for selling those books. For example, you can create and manage a customized e-commerce website for your book, or you can sell books by using *shoppable ads* (paid ads that appear on popular social media platforms). See Chapter 20 for info on shoppable ads.

This chapter focuses on creating and managing a stand-alone e-commerce website for your book, establishing and using social media as a marketing and promotional tool for your book, and creating an online community based on your book and its subject matter.

Choosing Between an Author or Book Website

Depending on your goals, you can choose between creating a website for yourself as an author, for your publishing company (if applicable), or for e-commerce dedicated to your book. Any of these options can ultimately serve the same purpose (to sell your book), but how you present information on each type of site is typically different.

REMEMBER

A website can consist of a single webpage or a collection of webpages accessible by using an onscreen menu or hyperlinks incorporated into a webpage's content.

Consider these nuances when deciding what type of website to create:

>> **An author website:** Focuses on the author and has a separate section (or webpage) that showcases their book(s) and enables people to purchase those books from the site. Or the page can direct the potential customer to links on Amazon and other online booksellers. Go with this website option if you want to

   • Establish yourself, the author, as a leader in your field

   • Promote yourself as a consultant available for clients to hire

   • Showcase your body of work

>> **A website for your publishing company:** Brand the site with the company's logo. You can use this site to promote and sell multiple books and potentially other products — either from just yourself as the author, or possibly a stable of authors that your publishing company works with.

>> **An e-commerce website:** Probably what you want to create if you aim to promote and sell a single, self-published book. A dedicated e-commerce site has a primary focus of showcasing, promoting, and selling just that book. But the website can also include other elements, such as an About the Author section.

TIP

When you create a website focused on selling a single book, make sure that you brand the site heavily around that book by prominently showcasing the book's cover and catering content specifically to the book's target audience.

Monetizing the Web: Opting for an E-Commerce Website

Until recently, if you wanted to create and manage an e-commerce website to promote and sell one or more physical products (such as printed books) or downloadable content (such as e-books), you either needed to design and program that website from scratch yourself or spend thousands of dollars to hire professional website designers, programmers, and graphic designers to do it for you. And the website often took at least several months to get online. You then needed to develop a relationship with a merchant account provider to accept online payments.

Today, you can sign up with one of many *e-commerce turnkey solutions* (which include an online-based e-commerce web hosting service and a collection of easy-to-use tools and professionally designed templates) to create your own e-commerce website in days — not weeks or months. Best of all, the creation process is extremely inexpensive and doesn't require any programming know-how whatsoever. *Note:* If you already know how to use a web browser to wander the Internet and you can use a word processor, you have the skills needed to create and manage an e-commerce website that's capable of promoting and selling your book online.

Checking out e-commerce turnkey solutions

Many e-commerce turnkey solutions can cater to the needs of self-published authors. The trick, however, involves first determining the desired functionality that you want for your website. For example, you may want to showcase yourself as an expert in your field, sell just your book, or be able to sell a selection of products in conjunction with your book. Next, through research, choose a service that offers the benefits shown in Table 17-1. Part of your research should involve visiting the websites of e-commerce turnkey solution providers to see sample sites that they can create.

TABLE 17-1   **E-Commerce Turnkey Service Benefits**

Reputation and Service	Usability	Full Features	Flexibility
Well-established	Has powerful, easy-to-use design and publishing tools	Offers suitable, professional-looking templates (also called *themes*)	Displays the website on any size screen (computer or mobile)
Has reliability with a 99.9% uptime operation guarantee	Offers a simple shopping cart that facilitates ordering	Includes pre-created apps (integrations or plug-ins) to add special functionality	Allows customization with original programming or widgets
Affordable, with straightforward rates (no hidden fees)	Accepts debit or credit cards and electronic payment services (Apple Pay, Google Pay, or PayPal)	Provides backend tools for bookkeeping, sales tracking, and inventory management	Allows you to provide customers with multiple shipping and delivery options (including digital)
Provides telephone or e-mail–based technical support 24/7	Allows use of their company's merchant accounts for payment processing	Provides integrated order tracking for customers	Is compatible with your merchant account service or other institution for payment processing
Requires no long-term contracts		Offers seamless social media integrations	

REMEMBER

Don't invest the time and money working with an e-commerce turnkey solution that goes offline often (making it unreliable), that's run by a small company that could shut down with no notice, or that charges outrageous fees to host your website and process electronic payments.

Picking your turnkey solution

You have many e-commerce turnkey solutions to choose from, and you can use almost any of them to create a website that's capable of promoting and selling printed books and/or e-books. Find these companies by entering the search term "e-commerce turnkey solution" into your favorite web browser, such as Google.

TIP

Ideally, work with an e-commerce turnkey solution that's based entirely online — meaning that you have no software to download and install when it comes to creating, publishing, and managing your website. With these solutions, you can do everything by using any Internet-connected computer and your favorite web browser. And, in some cases, you can even handle certain upkeep and management tasks from anywhere by using an Internet-connected smartphone or tablet.

Some of the more well-established and reputable services that you can set up to help you sell printed books or e-books online include

- » **GoDaddy:** Go to www.godaddy.com, and then choose Commerce ➪ Online Store from the top menu.

- » **OpenCart:** Open www.opencart.com and choose Features from the top menu.

- » **Shopify:** From www.shopify.com, choose Solutions ➪ Sell Online from the top menu.

- » **SamCart:** www.samcart.com.

- » **SquareSpace:** From the top menu of www.squarespace.com, select Products ➪ Ecommerce Overview.

- » **ThriveCart:** https://thrivecart.com.

- » **Weebly:** On www.weebly.com, choose Online Stores from the top menu.

- » **Wix eCommerce:** Go to www.wix.com and choose Start ➪ eCommerce Website from the top menu.

- » **WordPress:** On www.wordpress.com's top menu, choose Products ➪ Store.

THE DIFFERENCE BETWEEN A TRADITIONAL AND AN E-COMMERCE WEBSITE

You create a *traditional website* primarily to disseminate information to online readers, in the form of text, photos, graphics, animations, video, music, audio, or other types of multimedia content. You can also find interactive websites that allow users to interact with each other — to play games, for example.

An *e-commerce website* starts off working just like a traditional website, but it includes individual product pages that display (usually prominently) a Buy button. After someone clicks or taps on that button, they're automatically transferred to an online shopping cart. That cart collects payment and shipping information so that the customer's order and payment can be processed online and then immediately fulfilled by the merchant who ships the ordered product to the buyer. Or, in cases when a buyer purchases downloadable content (such as an e-book), the website allows for the buyer to instantly download that content after their payment processes.

Well-designed e-commerce websites look professional, and the customer can easily navigate them. These sites showcase products by using text, photos, video clips, or other content that encourages the online shopper to become a paying customer and press the Buy button to make a purchase. The customer gets their order tracking information and happily awaits delivery, and the merchant gets the information and functionality needed to manage their website and other key aspects of their business (including bookkeeping, inventory management, order fulfillment, and a customer database, for example).

The best e-commerce turnkey solutions are easy to use — both for the business operator and the online shoppers who visit the website — and require no programming skill whatsoever. To create a website through one of these solutions, just fill in company and product information into a template and use the tools provided that walk you through every step of the website creation, publishing, and management process.

Exploring the Anatomy of a Book-Selling Website

When creating anything that you want everyday consumers to use, you've probably heard of the KISS strategy, which stands for *Keep It Simple, Stupid.* So when you want to sell books, create a professional-looking e-commerce website that an online shopper can easily use without a bunch of distractions. The site should allow a customer to quickly locate your book, find out about that book, and then place an online order for it in the quickest and easiest way possible.

While you work with the tools offered by the e-commerce turnkey solution that you select, you can choose a website template, customize it, and then add all sorts of fancy bells and whistles by using plug-ins or integrations. But just because you *can* load up your e-commerce website with all sorts of flashy features (such popup windows and games people can play to earn a discount) doesn't mean that you *should*. In fact, you shouldn't. While you develop the design and choose the functionality of the website that you plan to use to promote and sell your book, focus on three things:

>> Your target audience (see Chapter 3)

>> The sales message that you deliver to your potential buyers

>> Making the customer's online shopping experience as quick, straightforward, and as easy as possible

If you look at e-commerce websites operated by major companies, such as Amazon, Apple, Nike, Walmart, Target, and countless others, they all allow the customer to find exactly what they're looking for easily and quickly. They all include a ready search feature and then offer concise and accurate product descriptions crafted to sell their products. (For a website designed to sell your book, you can use your carefully crafted book description from your book's back cover or perhaps from your publicity materials.) From a design standpoint, the webpages contain a lot of whitespaces, an easy-to-read font, and professional-quality (and extremely detailed) product photos.

REMEMBER

Very few e-commerce websites operated by major retailers include any bells and whistles — pop-up windows, distracting music, or animations that don't directly help the selling process, for example. Customers can find these extras distracting or confusing, so avoid them.

Designing a website to sell your book

With every website design and creation decision that you make, take your target audience into account and strive to accomplish one core objective — sell your book! However, that same website can have secondary objectives, such as to collect e-mail addresses, encourage an online shopper to follow your social media accounts, or provide details about any in-person appearances that you plan to make as an author.

After choosing the e-commerce turnkey solution that you plan to work with (see the section "Picking your turnkey solution," earlier in this chapter), set up an account and start by browsing the library of website templates (also called *themes*) that your solution offers. The template that you choose plays a major role in determining the overall look and functionality of your website. However, you have the opportunity to customize that template by incorporating your own publishing company logo, book cover graphics, text that promotes and sells your book, and other content about your book and its author.

TIP

The Design for Authors website (www.designforauthors.com) offers a collection of website templates created specifically for authors. These templates work with many of the popular e-commerce turnkey solutions. You do have to pay to use these professionally designed templates. Each e-commerce turnkey solution also offers a library of free and paid templates to choose from.

Including essential elements in your e-commerce website

Using the KISS design principle for simplicity, the most important elements of an e-commerce website that you design specifically to sell books include

>> **A book description and sales-oriented section:** This section prominently displays the book's front cover, includes back-cover copy, and offers additional sales-oriented content designed to sell your book to its target audience.

>> **A shopping cart module:** To handle online sales. After someone clicks or taps the Buy icon, the shopping cart should walk the customer through placing the order and the payment process, making this purchase a quick and simple procedure — with zero distractions.

>> **A page or section for reviews:** Showcase a collection of media reviews or reader reviews to give your book instant credibility.

>> **An About the Author section:** This section — you guessed it — focuses on the author. In addition to an author photo, include a brief author bio so that the potential customer can quickly get to know you in a way that resonates with the target audience.

>> **An author contact form:** Include links to your social media accounts (or the book's own Facebook page or group, prominently displayed) and a form that an online shopper can use to contact the author or publishing company via e-mail. Using an author contact form — rather than displaying the author's or publisher's phone number or e-mail address — makes an immediate, faster, and easier process for the person trying to make contact.

>> **A press/media section:** Make available all the press materials that you create for your book (refer to Chapter 18), including press releases, the author bio, and an author photo, in electronic form for members of the media to download. This section should also include a form or e-mail address that a

member of the media can use to request a review copy of the book and/or an interview with the author.

>> **A blog (optional):** Many authors choose to create and publish a weekly or monthly blog (or free electronic newsletter) for readers and potential readers. You don't have to write a blog, but if you choose to add one to your website, you must maintain it with regularly published updates (called *blog entries*).

TIP

Depending on the website template that you choose, you may incorporate each of these sections into a single webpage or spread them out onto multiple webpages. Make sure that users can easily access multiple pages via a prominently displayed menu that appears on each page of your website. If your website focuses on selling one book, plan to use fewer webpages in the website to avoid a potential customer losing interest through click-fatigue or being distracted by too much information.

Offering the customers ongoing contact

REMEMBER

Chapter 21 presents the concept of establishing a paid, subscription-based, electronic newsletter as part of your online presence. Doing so allows you to provide ongoing information that you think your readers may perceive as valuable or insightful, and which they're willing to pay for. You have the option to publish a free digital newsletter or blog, and then use it as a promotional tool, or create a subscription-based digital publication that generates an ongoing revenue source. Base this decision on the type of content that you plan to provide and the audience that content appeals to.

Whether free or paid for, offering ongoing content and contact helps you with

>> **Email collection:** People wandering the Internet (who are potential customers) can sign up for your e-mail list so that you can keep them up to date on new books, appearances, or products that you offer. You can use an e-mail list comprised of people in your target audience as a valuable tool for further promoting your original book, but also for selling future books and/or products to your target audience.

REMEMBER

If you focus on selling books only through popular online bookstores, such as Amazon, Barnes & Noble, or Apple Books, you can never obtain any information about the people who purchase your book. With an e-commerce website that has a hook by offering ongoing content, you can build a loyal following as an author and an e-mail list that you can use for your future marketing efforts.

>> **Promoting author appearances:** You can also display a schedule of upcoming author appearances (if you have them), book signings, or other events that you, the author, plan to attend — places where readers or fans can meet you in person. If you choose to include this type of information on your website, make sure you keep it up to date.

You can get some online advice from the experts on how to best set up your author website:

>> **IngramSpark:** From the main web page (www.ingramspark.com), enter "creating an author website" into the Search text box and select the entry that appears titled "The Complete Guide to Creating an Author Website." This free blog entry goes into great detail about the key elements every author website should include.

>> **Rocket Expansion:** This digital marketing company caters to authors. On its website (www.rocketexpansion.com), click Author Websites in the top menu to see useful strategies for creating an author website or a website designed specifically to sell books.

Acquiring a memorable .com domain name

When you establish your website by using an e-commerce turnkey publishing solution — or any website-hosting service, for that matter — your website receives a unique *URL*, another name for a website address, that can be long and likely convoluted. Using such a hard-to-remember URL makes promoting your website location difficult.

As soon as you get a website URL from the hosting service, head over to a website domain name registrar and obtain a domain name that's better suited to your website, such as www.[*Author'sFullName*].com or www.[*BookTitle*].com. Consider using one of these popular registrars:

>> **GoDaddy:** www.godaddy.com

>> **Google Domains:** http://domains.google

>> **Register.com:** www.register.com

Make the domain name(s) that you register unique. Also make each name easy to remember, easy to spell, and related directly to your book's title, your name (as the author), or the publishing company's name. A domain name should never violate another person or company's copyrights or trademarks.

Although you can find many domain name extensions besides .com, your primary website domain name needs to end with the .com extension because people browsing the Internet tend to assume web addresses end in .com and, out of habit, type that ending into their web browser. You can register multiple domain names for the same website, using any other extensions that you deem appropriate, but ultimately, you want to control the .com URL for your domain name because that's what web surfers are most familiar with and are most apt to remember. Registering each domain name should cost you less than $20 per year.

TIP

At the same time that you register your website's domain name, for an additional fee, you can acquire e-mail addresses that end with that domain name, and then create e-mail addresses such as *Author'sFirstName*@*BookTitle.com*, *BookTitle* @*Author'sName*.com, Press@*BookTitle.com*, and any other e-mail addresses that you think can help you promote yourself and your book. In some cases, the domain name registrar can help you establish the appropriate e-mail addresses. You can also set up domain name e-mail addresses through Microsoft or Google (http:// workspace.google.com/lp/gmail), for example.

GETTING THE HELP YOU NEED TO CREATE AND PUBLISH YOUR WEBSITE

E-commerce turnkey solutions make designing, publishing, and managing an e-commerce website as simple as possible, even if you have no programming or design experience. However, you can still work with freelance professionals who can help transform your selected website template into a website that truly stands out from the competition and that does an excellent job catering to your target audience.

Based on the functionality and design requirements that you establish for your website, you always have the option of working with a freelance website designer, programmer, graphic artist, professional photographer, online sales expert, or web marketing agency so that you can tap the expertise or skills of others that can benefit your website's operation starting from day one. Upwork (www.upwork.com) is just one online service that you can use to find freelancers to help design, publish, and manage your e-commerce website. However, the e-commerce turnkey solution that you choose likely maintains a directory of freelance experts that have experience using its platform and that have already been vetted.

Forwarding traffic from your registered domain

After you register your custom and unique domain name, use the registrar's free forwarding service to automatically forward traffic from your new domain name to the URL assigned to your website by the e-commerce turnkey solution or website hosting service that you're using.

TIP

Immediately after registering your website's domain name and associated e-mail addresses, create social media accounts on services such as Facebook, Instagram, Twitter, YouTube, TikTok, and LinkedIn, using the same username for each service so that you have continuity between all the online-based promotional and sales activities that you do as an author and for your book. Even if you aren't active or later choose not to be active on one or more of these social media platforms, you want to control the same username on each platform, if possible.

If You Build It, Will They Come? Generating Traffic to Your Website

After you publish a website (see the section "Caught in the Web: Opting for an E-Commerce Website," earlier in this chapter), you then need to drive a steady flow of traffic to it. You can start by continuously promoting your website through your advertising, marketing, and PR efforts — both online and in the physical world. For example

- » Design your social media posts to promote your website's URL.

- » When you do an interview as an author, mention your website address at least two or three times.

- » Include your website address within all your press and marketing materials, as well as paid advertising for your book.

Applying your upfront research

Before you choose a website template, take the time to browse the Internet, checking out other author or book websites as part of your research. Figure out what design and feature elements you like (such as easy ordering and a well-designed page to promote the author's credentials, for example), and then determine what content you want to incorporate into your own website and how to present it.

REMEMBER

Choose a website template that caters to your book's target audience, is easy to navigate, looks professional, and offers the features and functions that you want to incorporate into your site — while always staying focused on the website's primary objective, to sell books.

However, even if you design and publish an amazing e-commerce website that you believe can do an incredible job showcasing and selling your book and promoting its author, simply publishing the website online doesn't mean visitors will immediately come flocking to your site. They won't!

Promoting your e-commerce website

REMEMBER

Only by continuously marketing and promoting your website, taking a multi-faceted approach, can you drive a steady flow of traffic to your website. You have to discover the best and most cost-effective approaches to take, based on the target audience that you're trying to reach. As soon as you stop promoting your e-commerce website, traffic to it quickly dwindles. This reduction in traffic, in turn, leads to fewer book sales.

You've probably heard that focusing on search engine optimization (SEO) also helps drive traffic to your website, and this is true to some extent. However, focus on simply getting your website listed with the most popular Internet search engines (Google, Bing, Yahoo, Yandex, DuckDuckGo., and then focus your efforts on directly marketing your website to its target audience.

Focusing on SEO can easily become an expensive and time-consuming process. You can find other ways — such as paid advertising or becoming (more) active on social media — to generate potentially better results. That said, free and paid online services can help quickly get your website listed with the search engines and get you started with best practices for your website's SEO. Check out

>> **Semrush's Become an SEO Rockstar:** www.semrush.com/lp/seo-challenges.

>> **GoDaddy's SEO Services:** www.godaddy.com/online-marketing/seo-services.

Promoting Your Book Online by Using Social Media

These days, social media is the most powerful, cost effective, and easiest way to reach a niche audience. After all, billions of people around the world are active on social media platforms, such as Facebook, Instagram, Twitter, YouTube, TikTok,

LinkedIn, and others. Based on your target audience and which social media platform(s) you determine that audience actively frequents, set up free accounts on each of those platforms.

Use your (the author's) name, your publishing company's name, or your book's title as the username for each account. (For example, if you have www.*YourBookTitle*.com as your website address, set up @*YourBookTitle* as your account username on each social media platform). Each username that you choose must be unique on that platform. (If someone already has your book's title as their username, try a similar alternative or something else that's memorable and related to your book's subject/topic. For example, the book's title, followed by the word *novel* or *book* and then the .com extension.) Focus the username on your primary objective, based on whether you want to focus on promoting an individual book title, yourself (the book's author), or your publishing company.

REMEMBER

Nothing prevents you from creating multiple usernames on each social media platform — but keep in mind that maintaining each account, building a following, and publishing a steady flow of content on each account that caters to its target audience can be a time-consuming task.

Advantages to social media interaction with your audience

Use social media to directly communicate with your target audience, promote your book, promote your website, establish your credibility as an author and topic expert, and potentially sell books directly to your followers through specific social media platforms (a topic that I cover in Chapter 20). With social media, you can take an informal and soft-sell communication approach. You can also target a very niche audience and build a following comprised of people in that target group.

You accomplish direct book sales through social media by including *shoppable ads*. Instead of driving traffic directly to your e-commerce website, to your feed on that social media platform, or to your book's listing on a popular online-based bookseller, these ads include a Buy button. That service (or an integrated e-commerce service) then handles the e-commerce aspect of taking the order and provides you with payment and the shipping address for the order. When someone purchases a book through a shoppable ad, you typically have the job of shipping orders for printed books directly to those customers. However, in some cases, the customer can purchase and download an e-book immediately after you receive their online payment.

Becoming active on social media is time consuming, but it's basically free. Social media therefore gives you a powerful tool for promoting and selling your book to a targeted audience at little cost. However, although you want to publish a steady flow of content on your social media accounts, keep your key marketing and sales message related to your book consistent. In other words, the content you publish on social media should synergize with your website, press materials, paid advertising, and other marketing materials. This continuity helps you establish a brand around your book and/or its author, and it also helps you better communicate with your intended audience.

DON'T FORGET TO USE HASHTAGS

A *hashtag* (a word preceded by the # symbol) is a keyword that relates directly to a post. At the end of a post, include between one and five hashtags that people might be searching for on that social media platform that's of direct interest to them. In other words, hashtags can attract a larger audience for your published content and help your posts stand out from the more than 95 million other posts (according to Semrush, a company that offers tools for online marketing) published on any given day.

Hashtags help content creators broaden their reach with each new post. Research conducted by Semrush indicates that using hashtags properly can increase user engagement by 21 percent or more. To create a hashtag, at the end of a post, simply use a pound sign (#) and immediately follow it with a single keyword or relevant phrase (without adding spaces). For example: #NewBook or #*YourBookTitle*.

You can find tools to help you compile a list of relevant and popular keywords for each of your posts. To find these free and fee-based resources, enter "hashtag tool" or "hashtag generator" into your favorite Internet search engine. Here are some examples of these tools:

- **Semrush Keyword Research Tools page:** www.semrush.com/lp/keyword-magic-tool-1

- **Keyword Tool for Instagram Hashtags:** www.keywordtool.io/instagram

- **Hashtagify:** www.hashtagify.me

- **Instasize's Hashtag Generator:** www.instasize.com/hashtag-generator

- **Jasper's Instagram Hashtag Generator:** www.jasper.ai/tools/instagram-hashtag-generator

Choosing and connecting the right social media platform(s)

Yes, you can become active on all the popular social media platforms, but maintaining an active presence takes up an extraordinary amount of time, even if you choose to repurpose the same content on each platform. You still need to invest the time to respond to all questions and comments that you receive, for example. Based on your research and knowledge of your readers' preferences, initially focus on just one or two social media platforms that you determine your target audience is most active on. But keep in mind that trends change — sometimes very quickly.

TIP

New social media platforms are constantly being launched. For example, in July 2023, Threads went online and within weeks, gained 100 million active users. While you can jump on the latest social media trends, sticking with social media platforms that are well established and used by your target audience is often be a better use of your time and resources.

After you activate your website and social media accounts and start creating other advertising and promotional materials for your book (including press materials), promote and cross promote your website URL and social media accounts wherever and whenever you can. For example

>> Prominently display links to your social media feeds on your website and include a link to your website on each social media account profile

>> List your website and social media usernames in your press releases, on your business cards, and on any promotional materials (such as printed bookmarks) that you distribute during events or tradeshows to promote your book.

REMEMBER

You can use the size of your social media following to indicate your legitimacy among potential readers and the media. In the long term, aim to build up your social media following on each platform to at least 10,000 followers/subscribers. In cases where you can purchase *verification* (a label that you receive after proving your authenticity) on a social media platform, having that label — for example, the infamous blue checkmark next to your username — immediately gives the account an added level of credibility.

While you explore each of the social media platforms, not only determine which ones to focus your efforts on, but also pinpoint the very best way to use the format, features, and functions of those services to your utmost advantage. And keep in mind that every social media platform works slightly differently and appeals to its users for different reasons.

ESTABLISHING A FACEBOOK GROUP AND BUILDING AN ONLINE COMMUNITY

Anytime you publish a post on a social media platform, you disseminate information to an audience. However, in addition to your traditional Facebook account, you can create a free Facebook Group, which you use to establish an interactive online community. In this group, followers can interact informally with you (the book's author) and each other — they have a moderated place to virtually gather and discuss topics related to your book. You can make a Facebook Group public so that any Facebook user can join and interact, or you can set it up as a private (invitation-only) online community. The Facebook Group that you create is directly linked to your Facebook account, so create a separate author or book-oriented Facebook account, separate from your personal account, to tie to this Group. To find out more about how to create and manage a Facebook Group, visit www.facebook.com/help and choose Using Facebook ⇨ Groups from the menu on the left of the page.

Social media content creation tips and strategies

The sole purpose of creating and managing book-related social media accounts is to pursue engagement with people who are active on each platform and may potentially want to purchase and read your book. Every day, people are literally bombarded by social media content created and shared by family, friends, coworkers, businesses, and others trying to get their attention. For this reason, direct all your content to your audience, make it relevant and valuable to that audience, and create it in a way that looks (and sounds) professional.

REMEMBER

Social media posts can contain text, photos, video clips, animations, music, and audio. Make each post attention-getting but short enough that a viewer can consume it in only seconds. In other words, get your point across quickly and in an interesting way.

Posting goal-oriented content with the right frequency

After you create accounts and become active on social media, you have to post new content on a regular schedule — whether several times per day, once a day, three times a week, or at whatever interval you think makes sense based on your audience and your available resources (including your time). You want each post to have a goal — to get someone to click on a link to purchase your book, visit your website, post a comment, click on the Like button, or share your content with their followers (which is how content goes viral).

CREATE A VIDEO-BASED TRAILER FOR YOUR BOOK

If you have the budget and resources, create a 15-second video-based trailer for your book that you can showcase on your website and through your social media accounts. Just like a movie trailer, a book trailer should capture the viewers' attention, preview what the book offers, create an immediate desire to read the book, and encourage someone to purchase the book immediately. Video-production experts can create a short video-based trailer for your book (often without charging you a fortune), but if you choose to use this type of promotional and sales tool, don't skimp on the budget — you don't want the video to look amateurish. Use graphics, video, text-based headlines, music, and a professional voiceover announcer — just like you see and hear in movie trailers.

For helpful tools, advice, and resources, check out these websites:

- **Animoto Blog's How to Make a Book Trailer in Minutes:** http://animoto.com/blog/guides/how-to-make-a-book-trailer

- **Biteable's Make a Jaw-Dropping Book Trailer:** www.biteable.com/trailer/book

- **Motion Array Adobe After Effects Templates:** www.motionarray.com/browse/after-effects-templates

- **The Book Designer's How to Make a Book Trailer: 4 Must Haves:** www.thebookdesigner.com/how-to-make-a-book-trailer

- **Upwork's How to Make a Book Trailer for Promotion:** www.upwork.com/resources/how-to-make-a-book-trailer

- **Veed.io's Book Trailer Maker:** www.veed.io/create/trailer-maker/book-trailer-maker

WARNING

You have to walk a fine line between posting new content regularly and posting too much content in a way that annoys your audience. If you post too much, people may unfollow or block your account. But, if you post too infrequently, your audience can't properly engage with your content. Based on your audience, find the ideal publishing frequency by studying your audience's engagement over a several-week or several-month period, but never post more than once or twice per day.

Taking a professional approach to social media

To accomplish your goals with social media, take a well-thought-out and organized approach. Create a posting calendar and pre-plan your posts days or weeks in advance. Mix and match different types of content within your posts to get your message across and build a following on each platform. How to manage social media content and a content publishing schedule effectively is a skillset unto itself. You can figure out how to do it yourself, or you can hire expert content creators to help you (for a fee, of course).

Make everything that you post on social media look and sound professional because those posts are a direct reflection on you and your book. Keeping in mind that people who use social media have very short attention spans, quickly establish credibility with your audience when you create original content by following these guidelines:

>> **Make your content focused and consistent.** Always focusing on your target audience.

- Stay on message and synergize with your other marketing, promotional, and advertising efforts.

- Share reviews and testimonials related to your book. Research from Semrush shows that 67 percent of customers make their buying decisions based on reviews and testimonials. When you share this information, try to make the content visually interesting.

- Add a call to action within each post. Make it clear what you want the person seeing your post to do and when.

- Offer quick tips or very short excerpts from your book.

- Use social media to periodically run online-only sales or giveaways. For example, once per month, you can give away an autographed copy of your book.

>> **Maintain content quality and variety.** Discover ways to communicate your core messaging differently by using both text and visuals.

- Proofread everything before it gets published!

- Post only crystal-clear and well-lit photos.

- Post in-focus, great-looking, short video clips that have clear sound. (Make them less than 15 seconds long.)

- Take advantage of relevant hashtags within your posts and use them correctly.

- Repackage already-created content and showcase it in different ways.

- Make sure that none of your content violates someone else's copyrights or trademarks. You can share posts from other people, companies, or organizations, but always give them proper credit and obtain permission, when necessary.

- Whatever you do, keep each post short and to the point.

>> **Direct your always-upbeat content to your current and potential readers.**

- Make your content directly relevant to your target audience. Give them information that they find entertaining, informative, and relevant. If you can, answer questions that people pose, solve a problem that people face, or provide information that your followers perceive as valuable.

- Never publish anything that could offend someone or that could turn your target audience against you.

- Encourage interaction with your audience. Invite people to like, subscribe, and comment on your posts, as well as share your posts with their own online following. You can also ask questions or post simple surveys that encourage followers to respond.

- Be creative! Make your content stand out in a positive way. Try to tell short stories through your content that the audience can relate to.

- Refrain from using an overly promotional approach (no begging) or hard-sell language in your posts. Instead of commanding people to purchase your book, showcase reasons why your book will appeal to them, so that it's their idea that they should purchase and read your book.

WARNING

Avoid artificially inflating your following. Many services (for a fee) guarantee a dramatic increase in your social media subscriber base. Most of the time, these services are scams. You pay a fee, and the company follows your account with hundreds (or thousands) of fake accounts that do nothing to generate more book sales. Instead, these fake accounts detract from your credibility. Any of your real or potential followers who look at one of these generated account profiles can easily determine that it's fake. Creating a legitimate social media following takes time and persistence. Aside from paid advertising or paying to boost/promote your posts, you get (almost) no shortcuts.

TIP

One of the only legitimate shortcuts that you can use on some social media platforms (for example, Instagram) to increase views and engagements with your posts is to boost them. *Boosting* means you spend anywhere from $30 to several hundred dollars for the social media service to ensure that many people in your target demographic see that post. I've personally used this strategy to quickly promote posts that include information about my self-published e-books and have achieved decent sales results if the post included a link directly to the web-page where someone can purchase them.

Chapter **18**

Crafting and Distributing Publicity Materials

A dvertising and publicity have one important difference: the impact on your wallet. Advertising (covered in Chapter 20) can cost a pretty penny, but generating publicity can be much less expensive. Even if you hire a public relations (PR) firm or freelance PR consultant, the cost can be less than you might spend on advertising. Alternatively, you can act as your own publicist and begin making contacts within the media world yourself.

When I discuss getting your book promoted and reviewed in the media, I'm talking about in magazines, newspapers, on the radio, and on TV. This kind of exposure requires getting attention from members of the mainstream media. A much easier approach to obtaining media contacts involves first targeting well-known and respected bloggers, YouTubers, podcasters, and social media influencers who create online content that caters to the same target audience as your book. In some cases, these content creators have much larger and more dedicated audiences than traditional media, such as network TV morning shows, cable news programs or local newspapers.

This chapter helps you prepare the publicity tools that you need to begin working with the media in a professional way. For example, you can find out how to create a well-written press release and prepare engaging author biographical materials. You can discover how to supply reporters, journalists, editors, producers, bloggers, YouTubers, podcasters, and social media influencers with the information that they need, in the format that they want, within a timeframe that works well to meet their deadlines. Check out Chapter 19 for details on how to handle yourself with the media.

Going Over the Basics of Press Materials

The quality of the press materials that you create directly affects your success in generating publicity for your book. A well-written and informative press release may pique the interest of a journalist or content creator and result in a positive article and/or review. The media likely ignores a poorly written press release, so your book doesn't get any publicity. Use the press materials that you create as a tool when you execute your pre-planned publicity campaign.

The objective of a successful PR campaign for your book is to

>> Generate positive reviews of your book.

>> Convince specific media outlets to feature an article or segment about you as the author of your new book. (The campaign should include profiling you, the author, as an expert on the topic that you write about in your book.)

>> Get you on radio and television talk shows, as well as on podcasts, as a guest.

>> Book in-person author appearances, speaking engagements, and book signings (which I cover in Chapter 19).

REMEMBER

Print media refers to printed and distributed newspapers and magazines, as well as industry or special-interest newsletters. *Electronic media* coverage includes radio and TV. *Online media* coverage includes getting you and your book featured on websites, within digital publications, in special interest blogs, on podcasts, on YouTube videos, and in online content created by social media influencers. Keep in mind, when it comes to media outlets such as national TV shows and magazines, they often have online counterparts: Submit your press-related materials to those counterparts separately.

Knowing why your book needs press materials

Press materials are tools that you create, in printed or digital form, to educate the media about you and your book. The items that you create should all work together to communicate information quickly and efficiently. In a nutshell, your press materials should help you to do the following:

>> **Generate positive attention.** You want to create professional-looking press materials (which give you the easiest and least expensive way to tell the media about your book). After you get the media's attention, your press materials need to convince those people to feature your book in their editorial print, electronic, or online coverage.

REMEMBER

Most people working in the media are extremely busy, so the squeaky wheel gets the grease. Reporters and the like receive dozens of press releases and story pitches each day from people looking for publicity. It's your job to create an attention-grabbing headline and intro sentence that will make the reporter, journalist, producer, or talent booker want to learn more.

>> **Clearly define your message.** Avoiding ambiguity may send your story to the top of the pile. Pitch your book in a unique way that tells an engaging story that the media wants to share with the public. Try to incorporate something that's timely or that piggybacks off of a major news event that's happening. If you can't piggyback, focus on conveying a really compelling human-interest story that fits within the journalist's beat.

>> **Describe unique features of your book.** Clearly describe what's interesting, newsworthy, timely, or exciting about your book and position yourself as an expert who can speak with authority on the topic of your book. For fiction writers, focus your message on the plot of your book, as well as any relevance or timeliness it has to real-world issues, and the target audience.

TIP

If you can connect your book to an upcoming (and timely) holiday, trend, or event, you may capture the media's attention. For example, if you have a book about raising children, promote it in advance of Mother's Day or Father's Day, or as a holiday gift for current or expecting mothers and fathers. Doing so can help get your book included within holiday coverage that's already planned by the media outlet you're approaching.

TEAM UP WITH A MAJOR BRAND

While you brainstorm ways to promote your book, consider tracking down and teaming up with a national brand that may be looking for a spokesperson. If you have a company in mind that you want to approach and that you feel would be a good fit, either initiate contact with the company's VP or Director of Marketing, or the account representative at the company's PR firm. You, as the author of a book that covers a specific topic, can lend credibility to the promotional message of a company by serving as a paid spokesperson for media appearances and consumer or trade show events the company is hosting.

Surveying press material elements

Every item that comprises your printed or digital press materials should complement the others in terms of content, without being too repetitive. Get right to the point — and keep it brief! Continuity across all your printed and digital press materials has as much to do with appearance and design as it does with content. Remember, the media wants and needs exact information for their stories or content, so if you don't present your information properly within your press materials, the journalists you send your materials to will likely just ignore them. Traditionally, press materials include the following items:

» A one- or two-page press release about your book (discussed in the section "Writing an Attention-Getting Press Release," later in this chapter)

» An author bio and the author's photo (see the sections "Writing a Compelling Author Bio" and "Putting Your Best Face Forward with a Publicity Photo," later in this chapter)

» Copies of previous articles and reviews about your book

» A review copy of the book or an online form that a reporter, journalist, or content creator can use to quickly request a free review copy of your book

Customizing your message to specific media outlets

While you develop the PR campaign for your book, focus on customizing your message to the specific media outlets that you target. After you define who you're trying to reach (your niche target audience, which you can define with the help of Chapter 3), focus on the best ways to reach those people. The following sections cover some ways that you can target specific media outlets.

Media categorized by geography and audience

Being the publicist for your own book requires you to write a customized marketing message and pitch it to specific media outlets. These outlets need to have an interest in covering your book and its topic. Professional publicists categorize media outlets in a variety of different ways:

>> **Regional and national media:** Describes the geographic coverage a media outlet reaches.

>> **Consumer-oriented media:** Comprises newspapers, magazines, radio, TV, websites, blogs, podcasts, and content created by social media influencers that caters to a broad audience or mass-market consumer.

>> **Niche media:** Includes special interest media outlets that cater to small — but highly focused — audiences. This type of media can include blogs, podcasts, content created by YouTubers, social media influencers, and people who run popular (but niche-oriented) Facebook Groups. If you write a book about golf, examples of niche-oriented magazines include *Golf Digest, Golf* magazine, *Golf Business,* and *Golf Aficionado.*

>> **Industry-oriented media:** Target people working in a specific industry.

While you create your message, consider specific story ideas that the various media outlets may want to pursue. A lot of PR has to do with timing. You want your press materials to get in front of the right journalist or content creator at the time that they're putting together articles or coverage pertaining to a topic that somehow relates to your book. Create a PR message that journalists want to share with their audience. Your PR message should quickly explain to a journalist how and why your book appeals to the audience that they reach and convey why your book is relevant to their audience.

TIP

Always personalize and customize your pitch letter specifically to the journalist, reporter, editor, producer, content creator, blogger, YouTuber, or podcaster you send it to. Demonstrate that what you're pitching is relevant, timely, and of interest to their audience. And make sure that you approach the right people. If your book deals with how to succeed in business, don't contact the political, entertainment, or sports reporters, producers, writers, or editors at a media outlet.

Special tips for electronic media

When you target electronic media outlets, you typically pitch yourself to be a guest on a specific show or podcast, or to have your book featured or reviewed within a website, podcast, or blog, for example. If you pitch yourself to be a guest that the host will interview, the producer or content creator/interviewer needs to know that you're knowledgeable, well-spoken, appropriately groomed, professional, and media savvy enough to be an entertaining guest.

You can most easily prove your demeanor by providing an electronic press kit (EPK). In addition to the items included with your traditional press materials, an EPK contains either audio or video clips of you appearing on other radio or television programs, other podcasts, or on related YouTube channels, for example. This content allows the show's producers, booking agents, host, or interviewer to determine whether you qualify as a good guest for their audience.

TIP

After you generate a handful of publicity opportunities about your book and yourself, create a list of what media or online outlets you and your book have appeared in, and include this list within your press materials. An impressive list of past media coverage showcases your credibility to other media outlets.

A *micro-influencer* is active on social media and has a loyal following, but their total number of followers or subscribers is typically between 10,000 and 100,000. A full-fledged *social media influencer*, however, might have a loyal following comprised of hundreds of thousands or even millions of subscribers and followers. When you're starting out, you can much more easily (and cost effectively) work with micro-influencers whose audience is comprised of people who fall into your target audience. When a micro-influencer or social media influencer promotes your book, offers their audience a review of it, or does a book giveaway, for example, this exposure likely leads to more sales.

REMEMBER

All the major (national) media outlets pay close attention to what the popular blogs, podcasts, content creators, social media influencers, and YouTubers are talking about. If those mainstream media outlets keep seeing you and your book pop up within various online outlets, they may contact you about covering your book or having you as a guest on their program. So, when it comes to kickstarting your PR efforts, focus on the smaller, online-based media outlets that are more approachable, and then build your way up to national radio and television shows.

Writing an Attention-Getting Press Release

The most important document within your press materials is the *press release* about your book. This one- or two-page document, written in a very specific format, provides the needed facts, but in a very concise way. A press release must answer the following questions: Who? What? Where? When? Why? How?

Your press release also needs to convince the reporter or journalist that your information is actually newsworthy, relevant, credible, timely, and of interest to their audience. Again, if the publication date of your book ties in to a specific event or holiday, make that information clear within the release.

REMEMBER

What you say in your press release and how you say it depends on the type of book that you publish and the PR message that you want to convey. Within each press release, include the following information:

>> **Who:**

The author's (your) name and bio

Your contact information (or the contact information of someone working with you, such as your publicist)

One or two short quotes from you, the author

>> **What:**

A catchy headline that announces the publication of your book

The book's title, cover price, publisher, page count, and release date

>> **Why:**

The target audience for the book and specifically why your book appeals to its readers

Specific content about what makes your book or its approach unique

>> **Where, when, and how:**

A dateline (the date and city where the press release was issued)

One or two sentences about how, where, and when someone can purchase the book

The anatomy of a press release

Before you start writing your press release, focus on the message that you want to convey and determine exactly to whom (the media outlet and target audience) you want to convey that message. You also have to figure out how to share the information about your book in a catchy, upbeat, and concise way — while keeping the press release down to just one or two pages. (One page is the ideal length; most people working in any aspect of the media are too busy to read long documents.)

TIP

Throughout the entire press release, use the same typeface. Choose one that's easy to read, such as New Times Roman. Although the font should remain consistent, you can use typestyles (bold or italic, for example) to emphasize key points. And in the headline, you can use a slightly larger point size for the text. For the main body of the press release, use 1.5 or double spacing.

The headline

The *headline* is the first line of your press release. In one or two lines (using as few words as possible), come up with a catchy way to attract the reader's attention — through puns, statistics, or statements about your book. The press release's headline should be

Centered at the very top of the press release

Presented in an easy-to-read, 14- to 16-point **bold typeface**

No more than two lines and fewer than ten words, if possible

The release date

Below the headline, type the words "For Immediate Release." Format this phrase as follows:

In all caps (FOR IMMEDIATE RELEASE)

Left-justified on the page

In an easy-to-read, 12-point **bold typeface**

Contact information

The contact information on your press release lists a person, phone number, and e-mail address directly below the headline so that journalists or reporters have the information to reach you (via your publicist, if you have one) quickly.

REMEMBER

Ideally, you don't want the contact person to be you, the author. You quickly earn more credibility with media professionals if you appear to have a publicist. If you haven't hired a publicist, consider listing your secretary, business partner, spouse, or someone else as the main contact person, as long as that person has a different last name.

Even if you already have contact information on your publishing company's letterhead, repeat it in the press release as part of the contact information section and then at the very end of the press release. Use the same typeface and point size as the main body of the press release, and format the contact information as follows:

Under the headline and right-justified on the page

In a 12-point, non-bold typeface

The dateline

Under the contact information and left-justified to match the For Immediate Release line, skip one line and then add a dateline. This line includes the issuing city and state, followed by the date of the release. For example

Boston, MA — July 7, 2023

After the date, include a dash (—), followed by the first sentence of the press release's lead paragraph. For the dateline segment only (not the sentence from the lead paragraph following the dash), use this specific format:

A 12-point, **bold typeface**

The lead paragraph

In the first sentence or two of the lead paragraph, you must grab the reader's attention, while providing key information about your book. This key info includes your book's title, the author's name, and the book's topic, publisher, audience, cover price, page count, and other related details (such as where people can find the book). Generally, don't write more than one to three sentences.

Format the lead paragraph as follows:

Fully justified on the page

In a 12-point, non-bold typeface

The press release's body text

Within the next one or two paragraphs of the press release, provide details about your new book: what sets it apart, whom it targets, and why people will be interested in it. If your first paragraph doesn't fully answer the W questions (who, what, where, when, why, and how), then convey that information in these paragraphs. Also, include at least one short quote from the author, and then detailed information about how to order the book.

The body text should contain all the information that you want the public to know about your book. Many journalists lift information directly from a release and place it verbatim within their articles, reviews, or content, so format your text as follows:

Fully justified on the page

In a 12-point, non-bold typeface

Information about the author

This separate paragraph, titled About the Author, describes your credentials (as the author) and establishes you as an expert in your field. The information can also include reasons why you can make an interesting guest if the media outlet interviews you. This paragraph can also list you and your book's website address and social media links.

Format the About the Author section of the press release as a separate paragraph within the body of the press release as follows:

Fully justified on the page

In a 12-point, non-bold typeface

The final sentence of the last paragraph should state:

For more information, or to schedule an interview with [*Your Name*], please call [*Phone Number*], visit [*Website URL*], or send an e-mail to [*E-mail Address*]. Review copies are available to the media upon request.

TIP

Also, display the contact person's full name, title, company name, mailing address, phone number, e-mail address, and website at the very bottom of the release, if room permits. This is particularly important if your press release runs two or more pages (although two pages should be the maximum length). You want to make it as easy as possible for the journalists to find your contact information within the release, and they know to look at the top of the first page and at the end of the last page for this information.

The ending

At the very end of the release, skip one or two lines, and then include three hashtags, each separated by two spaces (# # #). Center these hashtags on the page, at the bottom of the release.

Creating your press release

You can use any popular word-processing application to create and format your press release. Figure 18-1 shows how to format a typical one-page press release in your chosen word processor.

Press Release Headline

FOR IMMEDIATE RLEASE

Contact: Jason R. Rich, Publicist
Phone: (###) ###-####
Email: ####@####.com

Boston MA--July 7, 2023—[The first sentence of the press release.]

[Body Text Paragraph #1]

[Body Text Paragraph #2]

[Body Text Paragraph #2]

[About the Author Paragraph]

For more information, to schedule an interview with the author, or to request a review copy of the book, please contact: [Publicist's name], [Publicist's phone number], [Publicist's email address].

# # #

FIGURE 18-1: The proper format for a press release.

TIP

If you plan to distribute your press release via e-mail or make it accessible on your website, compose and format it by using your favorite word processor, but export and distribute it as a PDF file. Taking this step ensures that the press release remains formatted properly, no matter what type of screen the person reads it on or what type of printer they use to create a hard copy. As a PDF, all formatting and colors (if you include colors) remain intact. Using any popular word processor, you can create a PDF file from a text document by using the Save As command and then choosing the PDF file format. Be sure to name the file something straightforward, such as [*Book Title*] Press Release.

Tips for putting together a press release

The press release conveys your unique PR message in a standardized format. Although you definitely want to communicate the relevant facts, you can tap your creativity to make your releases stand out. Here are some tips to help you format and create your press releases so that they receive the attention they deserve from the media:

» **Print a press release on 8.5-x-11-inch white paper.** Use a standard 1-inch top and bottom margin and 1.25-inch left and right margin. Stick with a common, easy-to-read font, such as Times New Roman, Helvetica, or Arial. Ideally, double-space the main body of the release; but, if necessary, use 1.5 line spacing to ensure that all of the text fits on just one (preferably) or two pages.

» **Visit PR Newswire (`www.prnewswire.com`).** This website offers a press release distribution service. Read a handful of actual press releases issued by companies, study each release's formatting and content, and determine what elements of those releases you can use to help convey your own PR message.

» **Hire a freelance writer or PR professional to assist you with the writing and formatting of your press release.** One excellent resource for finding skilled freelance writers is Upwork (`www.upwork.com`). Plan on spending between $100 and $500 to have a press release professionally written, edited, and formatted.

TIP

For more help writing and properly formatting press releases, visit these websites:

» **Mailchimp's 10 Tips for Writing a Press Release:** `www.mailchimp.com/resources/writing-press-releases`

» **Shopify's Get Noticed: How To Write a Press Release in 7 Steps 2023:** `www.shopify.com/blog/how-to-write-a-press-release`

» **Grammarly's How to Write a Press Release: A Step-by-Step Guide:** `www.grammarly.com/blog/press-release`

Writing a Compelling Author Bio

The press release announces the publication of your book and describes to members of the media what it's all about. (I talk about the press release in the section "Writing an Attention-Getting Press Release," earlier in this chapter.) The author bio, however, needs to focus on the author. Describe yourself and your professional experience, and position yourself as an expert in your field. Format the author bio by using the following specs:

One 8.5-x-11-inch page

Single- or double-spacing

12-point type size

The author bio also gives you an opportunity to showcase your personality through the tone in which you write your bio. After reading your author bio, a media rep hopefully wants to meet, interview, and feature you in their coverage or content.

REMEMBER

Although you absolutely must follow a certain format for your press release, you can make your author bio a bit less structured (although, visually, the bio needs to complement your press release and the overall design of your other press materials).

The heading

Place your full name at the top of your author bio, formatted as follows:

Centered on the page

In a 16- to 18-point **bold typeface**

Directly under your full name, type your title or main credential. For example

Author, [*Book Title*]

President and CEO of [*Company Name*]

Format in a slightly smaller 14-point **bold typeface**

Beneath your name and title, skip a line or two, and then add your contact information, including your mailing address, phone number(s), e-mail address, and website URL. Format this section with a non-bold typeface, using a 10- or 12-point type size. *Note:* For added credibility, include the name of a contact person other than yourself within the author bio. Make it the author's (your) publicist or personal assistant, for example. If you don't have a publicist or personal assistant, include a friend or family member's name, as long as their last name is different from your own. Mainstream media outlets are accustomed to working with publicists, so you want to make it look like your book is represented by a publicist or PR firm.

Some authors and publicists incorporate a small photo of the author on the author bio page. You don't have to add a photo, but it helps people see who they're reading about and helps them better relate to that person. Research has proven that for radio, TV, and online video-based media appearances, press materials that contain an author photo generate more requests for interviews. See "Putting Your Best Face Forward with a Publicity Photo," later in this chapter, for more details.

The body text

Below the heading of your author bio (see the preceding section), create three or four well-written paragraphs that describe you — your credentials, your background, your education (if relevant) — and tell your story. Be sure to include your marketing message within this bio and use wording that helps to convey your personality.

Deciding on the author bio body content

Relate who you are and what you do to the topic your book covers and focus on the relevance between the two. What makes you the ideal person to write the book? Why should the media outlet that you're pitching to interview you? Some of the topics that you may want to address within your author bio include

>> **Facts about you:**

- Your professional and educational background

- How and why you became an expert in your field

- Interesting, newsworthy, or unusual facts about yourself

>> **Information about your book:**

- Why you wrote your book

- What readers can get out of reading your book: How they can benefit and what they can learn

>> **Personal information:**

One or two sentences that contain personal information about your family, hobbies, interests, and/or where you live. For example:

- John Doe is a graduate of Harvard University and currently lives in Boston, Massachusetts, with his wife and two children.

- When not writing, he enjoys traveling, sailing, and spending time with his dog, Lexi.

Not all of the information in the preceding list applies to every author. Keep the topic of your book and your target audience in mind. You can also reveal this information in whatever order you want to; however, the first paragraph needs to grab the reader's attention and quickly summarize who you are and why you're an expert (and also mention your book).

REMEMBER

If you want to be booked as a guest on a podcast, radio show, or television program, the author bio provides your best tool. The bio can persuade producers, talent bookers, and hosts that you're an ideal guest for their show. At the end of the author bio, many authors and publicists include a list of between five and ten sample interview questions for the show host to ask during an interview. By offering these questions, along with background information about yourself (the author) and your book, you provide the information that interviewers need, without making them do research or too much pre-interview preparation. Use the heading Sample Interview Questions, and then provide the questions as a bulleted list.

Displaying your author bio body text

For the body of an author bio, make sure that the text looks visually pleasing on the page. Use plenty of whitespace to avoid the text looking too cluttered and be consistent with formatting. Here are some suggestions:

- » Create the author bio on a standard 8.5-x-11-inch page
- » Choose a 12-point, non-bold typeface
- » Fully justify the text
- » Keep lines spaced at 1.5 or double spacing

If you plan to distribute the author bio in digital form (via e-mail or as a download via your website), export and send the document in the PDF file format — not as a Word document.

Putting Your Best Face Forward with a Publicity Photo

Many publications and websites run photos of a book's author in conjunction with reviews or articles, but they require the author or publisher to supply the high-resolution photo. In the following sections, I discuss the preferred look and potential cost of your publicity photo.

Following photo particulars

Media outlets typically request a professionally taken, digital color photo of the author presented in the JPG file format and with a resolution high enough to make an 8-x-10-inch print from that file. This professional headshot should also subtly showcase the author's personality.

Your best option for acquiring your photo involves finding a local photographer who can take a professional headshot by using a high-end camera. However, you can instead visit a photo studio such as Picture People (www.picturepeople.com) in a mall. If you have a collection of non-professional photos of yourself, you can upload these photos to a service that uses artificial intelligence to generate a professional-looking headshot that's a composite of the multiple images that you provide. Here are some examples of these online services:

>> **Headshots.com:** www.headshots.com

>> **HeadshotPro:** www.headshotpro.com

>> **StudioShot:** www.studioshot.ai

Taking and using your best shot

Here are some suggestions for creating an attention-getting author headshot:

>> **Have a professional photographer take your publicity photo.** If you work with any professional photographer, they know exactly what to shoot, if you specifically request a publicity headshot.

REMEMBER

A *traditional headshot* is a close-up photo showing your upper chest and head, as opposed to a full body shot. It shows what you (the author) look like. Although some authors opt to use a photo taken 10 years ago to make themselves appear younger, this dated picture creates false expectations for the people who ultimately see or meet you and can damage your credibility.

>> **Consider the tone.** The publicity photo that you use conveys a message about your personality and the tone of the book itself. If you're promoting a funny or upbeat book, for instance, make sure that the publicity photo showcases your fun and cheerful personality.

>> **Have the photographer take a handful of different shots.** You can showcase one of the headshots on your website and use another as your profile photo for your social media accounts. Distribute a third variation of the headshot to the media and use it as your publicity photo. If you plan to use different headshots for different purposes, consider changing your outfit during the photoshoot.

TIP

As a promotional tool, when you make in-person appearances as an author, consider having a two-sided photo business card or full-color bookmark created to give out. On one side of the card, you can put a full-color image of your book's cover with the website address for ordering the book prominently displayed. And on the opposite side of the business card or bookmark, put your photo and a few words about yourself or your book. The following two low-cost printers can print full-color bookmarks in any quantity, starting at just 100 (the more you print, however, the less each card or bookmark costs to print):

>> **VistaPrint:** Go to www.vistaprint.com and enter "bookmark" in the Search text box.

>> **PrintRunner:** On www.printrunner.com, choose Promotional Products ⇨ Bookmarks from the top menu.

Writing a Knockout Pitch Letter

A *pitch letter* accompanies your press materials when you submit this information to the media. This brief letter introduces the publicist who is writing the letter or e-mail, and briefly states why they're sending the press materials that contain information about the author's newly published (or about to be published) book.

Pitch your story in a way that perfectly addresses the audience of that media outlet. Focus on how their audience directly overlaps with the target audience for your book. To give yourself added credibility, you don't want to be pitching yourself to the media. It's better if the pitch letter comes from your publicist, assistant, or VP of marketing at your publishing company. While I won't come right out and suggest you make up a fake publicist, if necessary, self-published authors have been known to do this (and have achieved great success getting the media's attention).

Crafting the content of your pitch letter

TIP

Personalize each pitch letter to a specific person. While you write the letter (or e-mail), make sure that it addresses the needs of the media professional you plan to send it to and that the information you send relates to a topic that they typically cover (their *beat*). For example, if your book is about sports, don't send your press materials and pitch letter to the lifestyle editor, or even the managing editor, of a publication. Address your pitch letter or e-mail directly to the sports editor. See "Starting a target press list," later in this chapter, for more about how to carefully target the journalists you want to reach.

Write your pitch letter in a traditional business letter/e-mail style and keep the length under one page (around 250 to 300 words). Keep in mind, you can typically hold someone's attention for only the time it takes them to read one paragraph (at the most), so get right to the point. Here's how to structure your pitch letter:

>> **First paragraph:** Introduce the book and the author. If you have a specific story angle to pitch, mention it here.

>> **Second paragraph:** Talk about why you (the author) are an expert in your field.

>> **Third paragraph:** Showcase exactly why the recipient's audience will be interested in the book and what you have to say about the topic as the author. If you're pitching the author (yourself) as a guest on a radio or podcast talk show, for example, describe some of the reasons why you can make an entertaining and informative guest.

>> **Final paragraph:** Invite the reporter, journalist, editor, or producer to review the enclosed/attached press materials, give them an opportunity to request a review copy of your book in printed or e-book form, and encourage them to make contact if they want to book you for an interview or receive more information.

TIP

Use your pitch letter to direct its readers to all of your publicity materials. Some authors incorporate audio or video clips from past interviews within their website's Press or Media section. This section of their website also makes all press materials, including press releases, an author bio, and the author's publicity photo, available for download. Make sure to reference your website's URL within all of your press materials (including the pitch letter) so that members of the media can easily find it. See Chapter 17 for more innovative ways to use your website as a promotional tool.

Posing your pitch as professional

If you have a publicist, have them send the pitch letter on your behalf. If you have e-mail addresses set up with your book's title as the .com, consider using the email address Press@[BookTitle].com as the e-mail address that you use to send the pitch e-mail and press materials.

WARNING

When pitching your book to the media, never disclose that it's a self-published book. Whenever possible, use the name of an independent publishing company that you create. An actual company name gives you more credibility. Many major media outlets don't cover or review self-published books, so make it look like the book comes from a traditional publishing company.

Distributing Your Press Materials to the Media

After you create all the necessary the press materials for your book (see the section "Writing an Attention-Getting Press Release," earlier in this chapter) and its author (flip to the section "Using Successful Strategies for Writing Your Author Bio," in this chapter), the next step involves distributing these materials and contacting the media. You can most easily get your press materials to the media through e-mail.

TIP

Start to generate hype for your book at least 60 days before it hits the stores or becomes available for sale online. Remember, you can set up services such as Amazon and Barnes & Noble (www.bn.com), as well as your own e-commerce website, to accept pre-orders for your book. Create excitement by developing and launching a well-thought-out PR campaign. Although you may want to obtain a guest spot on *The Today Show, Live with Kelly and Mark,* or *The View,* and then sell thousands of books overnight, more realistically, to generate positive media attention for your soon-to-be published book, you need to contact a wide range of media outlets, starting with the smaller ones.

Creating a targeted press list

When kicking off any PR campaign, you need to carefully target the media and develop your press list. Follow these steps:

1. **Write down all the print, electronic, and online media outlets that you want to pitch your book to.**

   Create lists for two waves of PR efforts:

   - Start with a list of blogs, podcasts, YouTube channels, and social media content creators that target the same audience as your book.

   - In the second wave of your PR efforts, branch out and contact newspapers, magazines, trade journals, radio shows, and TV shows that have authors as guests.

2. **Track down the media representative directly responsible for covering the topic that you're pitching.**

   See the next section for more info on targeting the right media contact.

3. **Send your pitch e-mail, attaching the press materials, to each media person that you're targeting *just once.***

4. **If you don't get a response from the e-mail that you send in Step 3 within a week, send one (yes, *just one*) follow-up e-mail.**

WARNING

Whatever you do, don't start sending the same pitch repeatedly to the same media person (or to multiple people at the same publication). Not only does getting e-mail after e-mail from you annoy them, but it also virtually guarantees that you won't receive any publicity from that media outlet.

Zeroing in on the right media contact

Follow these tips for tracking down the right person to send your materials to:

>> Contact the main switchboard or receptionist at each media outlet and ask for the name and contact information for the journalist or editor you're trying to reach. If you wrote a cookbook, ask for the food editor or book reviews editor, for example.

>> Purchase an up-to-date media directory (see the section "Using media directories," later in the chapter).

>> When you contact electronic media, such as radio or television shows, pinpoint exact shows that you want to be a guest on. Call the production office for that show and ask for the name of a segment producer or talent booker who's responsible for booking authors as guests.

REMEMBER

Don't try to pitch your idea directly to the executive producer or host. Even though, at smaller shows (especially at local radio or TV stations), sometimes the person responsible for booking guests actually is the show's executive producer or even the host, don't assume that. Unless you know exactly who handles bookings, first contact a segment producer or talent booker at a show.

REMEMBER

Contacting the wrong media representative not only wastes your time and money, but also wastes the time of the media professionals you contact. The wrong person has absolutely no interest whatsoever in what you're pitching. Don't rely on a person within a media organization passing along your book and press materials to the appropriate person — this kind of sharing seldom, if ever, happens.

Research the right person — a specific journalist, reporter, editor, producer, talent booker, podcast producer, blogger, or social media content creator — to contact right from the start; for example

• If you want to obtain book reviews from newspapers, blogs, or online-based publications, target the book reviews editor.

• If you wrote a memoir or a book that has a strong human-interest element, contact the features editor of that media outlet.

Sending your pitch and publicity materials

One of the most convenient (and least expensive) ways to pitch a story idea to a media outlet is via e-mail. Based on the response that you receive from your initial e-mail pitch, you can then send a printed book and printed versions of your press materials. You can also direct the media professional to visit your website (where you have your press materials available to the media in a Press or Media section) for more information about the book and its author.

REMEMBER

Post-COVID-19, many media professionals now work remotely (not from a formal office). Unless they specifically instruct you to do so, don't just mail your book and media materials to the media outlet's primary mailing address. You likely have better luck sending your materials via e-mail and offering a free e-book edition for the journalist to review. Follow the journalist's lead on what to ship to them and where to send your materials.

Using media directories

A handful of directories, publications, and online databases that professional publicists use contain detailed contact information for every reporter, journalist, editor, producer, blogger, podcaster, YouTuber, and social media influencer who works in various aspects of the media. Any of these directories give you the perfect starting point for developing your targeted media list.

WARNING

Before investing in any media directory, determine whether that directory offers the information that need, based on the type of media and specific contacts that you want to find. Also, determine how often each directory is updated and verified for accuracy. Any information that's more than six months old probably contains outdated listings. If you hire a publicist, one of the things they bring to the table is established media contacts the publicist can contact on your behalf.

By using one or more media directories, along with your own research, you can develop a comprehensive media list that targets media outlets and individuals within those outlets to send your press materials and (e-mail) pitch letter to. Some of the more popular media directories include

>> **Cision:** www.cision.com

>> **Everyone's Internet News Presswire:** www.einpresswire.com

>> **The Handbook:** www.thehandbook.com

>> **Heepsy:** www.heepsy.com

>> **Influencer Marketing Hub:** https://influencermarketinghub.com

- » **Influencers.club:** https://influencers.club
- » **MatchMaker.fm:** www.matchmaker.fm
- » **PR Newswire:** www.prnewswire.com
- » **Press Hunt:** www.presshunt.co
- » **Prowly:** https://database.prowly.com
- » **Radio-TV Interview Report:** www.rtir.com
- » **RadioMall:** https://radiomall.com
- » **SRDS:** https://srds.com
- » **Writers Write Media Directory:** www.writerswrite.com/bookpromotion/resources/media

Paying attention to media lead times

Plan your PR efforts based around each media outlet's *lead time,* meaning the time between when their coverage is created or produced and when it's published/broadcast to the public. If you know that a magazine has a lead time of three months, begin contacting the appropriate writer or editor of that magazine four or five months before the publication of your book. Even web-based publications typically work on a lead time of at least several weeks, so plan accordingly.

REMEMBER

To help ensure that you get the media attention that you and your book deserve, kick off your PR efforts well in advance of your book's release date. After you release the book, many media outlets no longer consider the book newsworthy. Most media outlets want to coordinate their coverage with the actual release date of your book.

IN THIS CHAPTER

» **Presenting yourself to the media**

» **Putting on a polished appearance**

» **Pursuing book reviews**

» **Setting up author appearances and book signings**

» **Working with a professional publicist or PR firm**

Chapter **19**

Publicizing Your Book for Free with the Media's Help

A re you convinced that you wrote a bestseller? Do you want to see yourself on television, making radio appearances, being a guest on podcasts, and reading reviews of your book in your favorite printed and online publications? If so, focus on generating publicity by soliciting the help of the media.

Public relations (PR) is all about utilizing the media — print media, radio stations, TV stations, podcasts, blogs, and content created by YouTubers and social media influencers — to generate reviews, articles, feature stories, and interviews related to you and your book. As opposed to paid advertising (which I cover in Chapter 20), when any media outlet writes an article about your book, or when you appear as a guest on a TV program, radio show, or podcast, you don't have to pay that media outlet for the coverage. This free, extremely powerful tool lets you reach potential readers at all levels.

In Chapter 18, you can find out how to create and distribute press materials to help promote your book. But this chapter puts the fruits of your labor to work while you promote the publication of your new book. You can find out how to speak to (and look good in front of) the media, generate book reviews, and set up special appearances, including in-person author appearances and book signings. You can also find out about the costs and potential benefits of hiring a publicist to help you with your PR tasks.

Talk It Up: Saying the Right Thing to the Media

Contact key media outlets — including social media influencers and podcasters — to pitch your story. (See Chapter 18 for full details about how to create the right PR materials and contact the right media representatives.) If you get the right materials to the right people, you probably start getting invited to be a guest on podcasts, as well as radio and television shows. Time this publicity perfectly — before your book gets released, and in conjunction with its publication.

During each interview, make sure to

>> Talk about your book and yourself.

>> Establish yourself as an expert.

>> Convince your audience that your book offers something interesting, informative, entertaining, and/or newsworthy.

REMEMBER

What you say during an interview and how you say it are critical for achieving your objective — to tell people about your book and peak their interest enough so that they want to purchase a copy and read it. No matter what questions the media figure asks you during an interview, communicate your PR message accurately, effectively, and hopefully repeatedly.

TIP

If you've never done any type of PR work, seriously consider hiring a professional publicist or PR firm to help you develop and launch a comprehensive PR campaign for your book. In the section "Leave It to the Pros: Working with a Publicist," later in this chapter, you can discover how to hire a publicist (if you have the budget) and how this person can really help you define your marketing message, reach out to media, get your book reviewed in the media, and potentially get you booked to be interviewed by the media.

Anticipating and preparing for basic questions

After you do a handful of interviews, you may notice that the same basic questions keep popping up. Use this knowledge to your advantage; it allows you to figure out the best way to answer each of those questions. That said, anytime you have to answer the same question repeatedly, always make it sound like you're answering it for the first time, that the question is insightful, and that you're excited to answer it. To prepare for interview questions and the interview itself, follow these three steps:

1. **Create a list of 10 to 15 sample questions that you anticipate the interviewer will ask you.**

   An easy way to anticipate questions you may be asked: Provide the questions! In Chapter 18, I note that as part of your press materials, consider including 5 to 10 sample questions that you want to answer for an interviewer. The interviewer may very well ask you some of those questions because they're often too busy to come up with their own insightful questions, especially if you already provided them.

2. **Develop a short sound bite to answer each question.**

   A *sound bite* is a short sentence or phrase that delivers a powerful message — in this case, about your book. Some people refer to this as an elevator pitch (described in the next section).

   While you prepare answers to interview questions, keep your responses short. Don't babble or go off on tangents. Answer each question, providing the requested information, in less than 15 to 20 seconds.

3. **Practice answering each question, using your sound bite, and portraying yourself as a polished interviewee.**

   Your responses need to come off as natural, engaging, positive, and informative. Answer the question, get your key point across, and wait for the next question.

Listing sample questions

The questions asked during each interview may vary greatly, but most media folks start off by asking basic questions about you and your book. You can easily anticipate these questions because they typically involve answering who, what, when, where, why, and how.

TIP

As an author, create what's called an *elevator pitch* for your book. In other words, in the time it takes you to ride in an elevator with someone else (about 15 seconds), concisely describe your book, explain what it offers, and get the person you're speaking with excited about it.

Here are a few sample interview questions that you should prepare and then rehearse answers for:

>> Tell me about your book. What's it about?

>> What inspired you to write your book?

>> What initially got you interested in this topic?

>> Why should someone read your book?

>> When is your book being released, and how can someone obtain a copy?

>> What was the most interesting or unusual thing that you found out when researching your book?

>> How much research went into writing your book? What type of research did you do?

>> What sets your book apart from others?

>> Tell me three things that someone can discover by reading your book.

While you answer these and other questions, provide information directly from your book as a preview of what readers can expect. This type of answer helps demonstrate that your book has valuable, relevant, and interesting content. For example, you could respond to a question by saying, "That's a great question [*Interviewer's Name*]. In chapter [*Chapter Number*] of [*Book Title*], I discuss [*Relevant Topic*]." Obviously, if you wrote a novel or work of fiction, never reveal the ending!

In general, during a short, five-minute interview, the interviewer may ask you just two to three questions. During a 15-minute interview, you might get up to five questions. And during a 30-minute interview — say, for a podcast or radio show — the interviewer might fit in 10 to 15 questions.

Developing sound bites

Most television and radio interviews last only three to five minutes. And you need to convey a lot of information without speaking too quickly. For every question, provide a succinct answer that lasts between 15 and 20 seconds (that's fewer than 50 words), what the media industry calls a *sound bite*. Make sure that each sound bite contains useful information or specific details about your book that includes (or refers to) your marketing message or supports your credibility. By anticipating questions that the interviewer may ask you (see the preceding section) and knowing your subject matter well, you can compose answers ahead of time that communicate the appropriate information in a very concise way.

Figuring out how to speak in sound bites ensures that you can answer the maximum number of interview questions in the time allotted, giving you greater opportunity to promote yourself and your book. Also, if you participate in pretaped interviews, speaking in sound bites makes editing an interview easier. The person editing your interview doesn't have to cut your answers short, and you don't need to worry about your answers being taken out of context.

Knowing how to conduct yourself during each interview

Here are a few tips for polishing your interview skills and answering the questions that the interviewer asks you:

- >> **Convey a sense of friendly authority when you speak.** Use complete sentences. Avoid using slang, or filler words such as *umm* or *yeah*. Answer questions confidently and use humor when appropriate.

- >> **Repeat the gist of the question that the interviewer just asked you, and then provide your answer in the form of a sound bite.** For example, say that the interviewer asks you, "So, what made you write your book?" You might respond, "What inspired me to write my book was [*Reason for Writing*]." Or maybe the interviewer asks you, "What's your book about?" You can respond, "[*Book Title*] is about [*Subject of Book*]."

- >> **Answer all questions like it's the first time you heard them.** Even if you're asked the same question 1,000 times, never respond to a reporter by saying something such as, "I get asked that question constantly," "People always ask me that," or "You already asked me that." Instead, always appear to consider the question carefully and then answer enthusiastically.

- >> **Be prepared to answer uninformed questions.** Often, when someone interviews you, they probably haven't read your book. In other words, the interviewer knows little or nothing about the book's topic or you as an author — besides what you included within your press materials or information that the interviewer found by doing a quick Google search. If the interviewer asks you what you believe is a stupid question, play along. Never make the interviewer look stupid or feel awkward because they clearly did not prepare for the interview by coming up with insightful questions. Just make sure you get your marketing message across to the audience.

- >> **Don't alienate your audience.** For example, avoid offering a strong opinion about a controversial topic or making any kind of insulting or biased comment that could easily alienate your audience.

Being prepared to participate in on-camera interviews

Because so many interviews are now being done live and on-camera or during a video call or virtual meeting (with video), be sure to practice doing on-camera interviews so that you become comfortable speaking on camera. For example, practice being on camera using a free video-conferencing service such as Zoom or Google Meet. Be sure to experiment with your settings (that is, investigate different camera and sound settings) to prepare for interviews from a technical standpoint.

Make sure you have a good quality microphone for your computer, and perhaps an after-market webcam to upgrade your laptop's built-in camera — if you're not satisfied with its quality. (You could also use the camera built into your smartphone or tablet. Some of the latest digital cameras can serve as webcams, too.)

Focusing on your PR message

You may find participating in interviews fun; however, you need to focus on the reason you're doing the interview — to promote your book. People are more apt to purchase your book after listening to an interview with you (or spending several minutes reading about you and your book) than they are if they see a paid ad. Yes, paid advertising works, too — but PR offers a most cost-effective marketing tool.

No matter what questions the interviewer asks you, you have to convey your PR message at least two to three times during each interview, even if that interview lasts less than three minutes. Your PR message essentially describes your book and tells people why they should read it. Create your PR message as a one- or two-sentence summary of the unique content that your book offers or how the reader can benefit from reading it. In other words, your PR message is your elevator pitch (which I talk about in the section "Listing sample questions," earlier in this chapter). Chapter 18 gives you more details on creating a PR message.

Mentioning your book title multiple times

During an interview, try to mention the title of your book at least three times and mention where people can find the book at least twice. Maybe you promote your book's website address (see Chapter 17 for more about creating a website for your book) or mention that the book is currently available through online booksellers, such as Amazon or Barnes & Noble (see Chapter 14 for more about these sales channels). Typically, when a talk show or podcast host introduces you, they mention your name and your book title at least once. After that, however, you have to work your book title into the conversation additional times (without being annoying about it).

TIP

One easy way to mention your book's title is simply to begin your answers with it. Try using one of these statements:

>> "In my book, [*Book Title*], I wrote about [*Subject*]."

>> "That's a great question. In Chapter [*Chapter Number*] of my book [*Book Title*], I discussed that exact topic."

>> "To answer that question, let me tell you a story that I included in my book, [*Book Title*]."

Avoiding common interview mistakes

During any interview, you want to promote your book and to come across as an intelligent and well-spoken expert on a topic. You also want both the interviewer and the audience (your potential readers) to respect and like you. To ensure that you get the best possible response from your interviews, avoid making these common mistakes:

>> **Allowing the interviewer to provoke you into discussing a controversial topic:** Especially if you're a guest on a morning radio show hosted by shock jocks, you may come across an interviewer who entertains their audience by angering guests or trying to confuse them with inappropriate questions. This is showbiz. Go along with the antics, but stay focused on getting your message out to the public. You always have the option of not answering a question or changing the topic during an interview. Don't get agitated or lash out at the interviewer.

>> **Coming across as uncomfortable or aggressive:** If you demonstrate nervousness and lack of preparation, or seem offensive or confrontational, the impression you make will not be professional. The best way to avoid making a negative impression is to prepare and rehearse (see the section "Anticipating and preparing for basic questions," earlier in this chapter). Take deep breaths and speak in a normal tone.

>> **Cutting off the interviewer in mid-sentence while they ask a question because you can anticipate what they're going to ask you:** Interviewers may ask you the same questions over and over again. Even if you've heard that same question a hundred times in other interviews, that particular interviewer is asking it for the first time, and the audience is (probably) hearing it for the first time. Allow the interviewer to finish, and then respond. Otherwise, you come off as arrogant.

>> **Mumbling your responses to questions or not speaking in full sentences:** Never respond to a question by using body language (nodding your head or shrugging, for example) or with an unclear, under-the-breath answer. Also,

avoid one-word answers. You need to respond to a question with more than a simple yes or no. Speak with authority and share the knowledge that you possess.

>> **Promoting your book too much, without providing the reader or listener with information about the topic being discussed:** Although you want to work in mentions of your book at least two or three times during an interview (see the preceding section), you also want to convey information about the topic being discussed. Don't keep replying, "You have to read my book for the answer to that question." Answer the interviewer's question, and then add a phrase such as, "I go into a lot more detail on that topic in my book."

>> **Speaking too quickly when answering questions:** Pace yourself and breathe. You want to be sure that the audience can catch and understand what you're saying.

>> **Taking too long to respond to questions or babbling too much about nothing:** Make proper use of your sound bites when you answer each and every question. Stay away from irrelevant stories.

>> **Insulting or belittling the interviewer:** Even if the interviewer asks a stupid question, act like it's a brilliant question and you're excited to answer it. Remember, you're an expert on a topic. The interviewer may know nothing about the topic, but they're giving you a chance to promote yourself and your book. Use this opportunity to your advantage by educating the interviewer and the audience.

TIP

No matter what type of interview you participate in, make sure that the interviewer introduces or credits you appropriately. Develop a one-sentence introduction that the media can use to introduce you. This credit should focus on you as the author and establish your credentials as an expert in your field.

PUBLICITY BOOT CAMP: CONSIDERING PROFESSIONAL MEDIA TRAINING

If you do a lot of interviews, one of the best ways to quickly become media savvy is to undergo intensive media training. Although you can read about how to develop the skills you need, you benefit much more from working with a media training expert. This training involves one-on-one sessions with a skilled PR professional or experienced broadcaster who teaches you everything that you need to know about how to be interviewed, how to interact with the media, and how to fine-tune your PR message. Most media training sessions last one or two full days. To find media training opportunities in your area, type the phrase "media training" into your favorite Internet search engine.

Dress It Up: Looking Good When You Promote Your Book

A media outlet invites you to discuss your book because you write about a topic of interest to a particular audience. Now, in addition to sounding like an expert, you need to look like one, too. How you look adds or detracts from your credibility. The following sections focus on what to wear and how to control your body language.

Presenting your best image

When you participate in interviews, you want to look your best. Even when interviewing on the radio or for a podcast, when the audience doesn't see you, looking professional helps boost your credibility and your confidence. Here are a couple of quick tips to help you look your best:

>> **Watch or listen to the program or podcast that you're going to appear on for several days prior to your appearance.** Pay careful attention to what the hosts and other guests wear if it's an on-camera interview and dress accordingly.

>> **Don't wait until the last minute to get ready for an interview.** For all on-camera interviews, try on your complete outfit (accessories and hairstyle included) the day before the interview. On the day of the interview, get ready several hours early in case you need to make last-minute adjustments. Also, if you plan to do a bunch of on-camera interviews on the same day, change up your outfits for each of them.

Choosing your outfit

Feeling stumped about what to wear? Try the following tips:

>> **Choose a stylish outfit.** Keep in mind the image that you want to convey. For example, dress more formally for a business or news-oriented show and casually for an upbeat morning show. Overall, try to dress along the same lines as the host(s).

>> **Make sure that your attire fits you perfectly.** Wear a wrinkle-free outfit that looks good on *you* — not just the mannequin in the store.

>> **Pay attention to colors and patterns.** Never wear busy patterns or solid white on television.

>> **Display tasteful style, not trendy garb.** You want to look good, not make a fashion statement like celebrities waltzing down the red carpet at an awards show.

TIP

If you can't decide on an outfit, read a few current issues of fashion magazines and visit a store that offers a personal shopping service to help you choose what you wear. You can also hire a personal stylist to go shopping with you — if you absolutely need that help. But keep your budget in mind!

Coordinating your accessories

When putting yourself together as a complete package, you may want to consider extra accessories, such as designer shoes, hats, scarves, jewelry, and so on. Here are a few things to consider when dressing up an outfit:

>> **Shoes:** Wear clean (and new-looking) shoes and coordinate them with your outfit and accessories, especially your belt (if you wear one). Don't wear shoes that hurt your feet or that you have trouble walking in just because they look good. Unless you're doing a comedy routine, you don't want to trip on live television or while on camera.

>> **Add-ons:** The accessories that you wear should all complement your outfit. They should never pull attention away from what you're saying by being too distracting. Make sure to wear tasteful accessories that aren't visually overbearing (like a hat might be) or that cause a glare or reflection (eyeglasses or sparkly jewelry, for example).

Fine-tuning your personal grooming, hairstyle, and makeup

First impressions are important. Shower before your interview and apply any necessary products to control oiliness or dryness on your face and neck. Don't wear heavy perfumes or colognes that may knock out the person next to you. Also, have clean fingernails, and go to the interview either clean shaven or with well-groomed facial hair (if you have it).

TIP

If you have a hairstylist, make sure that they stay consistent with the image that you want to convey. For example, if you're trying to convey the image of a business professional, your hairstyle should not make you look like a rockstar or hippie. Some TV shows have a hairstylist on staff who can style your hair right before your appearance. If you find yourself in a pinch, use them; however, rely on your own stylist to work on your hair prior to the interview. But if you don't have a personal stylist (and most people don't), plan on arriving at the studio ready to go.

Controlling your body language

Most people aren't aware of their own body language, mainly because in everyday life, they don't watch themselves speak or interact with other people. But always be aware of and control your body language — especially when on camera. Figuring out how to look comfortable during an interview takes practice. If you have nervous habits, such as tapping your foot, twirling your hair, blinking too much, or waving your arms around wildly when you speak, you need to eliminate these habits.

TIP

To determine how to control your body language without professional assistance, record yourself doing practice interviews and then seek out advice from people close to you who can help you identify potential problems with mannerisms or stance. You can also figure out how to control your body language (for a fee) by undergoing professional media training (see the sidebar "Publicity boot camp: Considering professional media training," in this chapter).

Sit up straight, make eye contact with the person or people you're speaking to, and showcase your personality — without being over-the-top or over-emphasizing your gestures. For example, speak in a calm and clear voice that's not overly emotional. It's perfectly normal to be nervous before and during an interview. Try the following tips to help you relax:

>> **Take deep breaths to calm yourself down.** You can easily learn how to do quick breathing exercises or meditations, for example, by downloading and using the Calm app on your smartphone.

>> **Prepare for each interview.** Go into your interviews feeling confident and as prepared as possible, knowing that you look your best and have practiced for the interview. (I find that the more prepared I am for an interview or author appearance, the more confident and less nervous I feel.)

>> **Focus on the activity and not the surroundings.** If you're doing an on-camera interview, don't pay attention to the cameras. Usually, the host or director will tell you which camera to face if they want you looking in a specific direction. Otherwise, focus on the host and forget that the cameras are there.

Book It: Generating Reviews

Book reviews are a great publicity tool (assuming that your book generates favorable reviews). When you send out review copies of your book, include all your media materials and a pitch letter (see Chapter 18 for more about these items and about initial contact with the media). An editor, reporter, journalist, or content creator needs to have all of your information in one place. Even if you already sent media materials and are following up with a review copy of the book, send another copy of those materials with your book.

When you receive positive reviews, reprint copies of them and include them within your book's media materials. You also can use excerpts from positive reviews in your book's advertising (see Chapter 20 for more about book ads) and on your website (see Chapter 17 for more about setting up a website to promote and sell your book).

Show It Off: Coordinating Author Appearances and Book Signings

In addition to generating publicity in the media and online via interviews and reviews, you can also let potential readers know your book exists by participating in author appearances and book signings. These fun events allow you, the author, to meet and interact with people interested in the topic of your book. These events provide great networking and book sales opportunities. Unless you can drive hundreds of people to your event, you may not make a ton of money signing books at a bookstore, but you can use this event to generate local media publicity. That valuable publicity allows you to reach more potential readers than you do at the actual event.

Planning and promoting an event

A few weeks before your book's release date, contact a few bookstores in major markets and speak with the store manager about doing a book signing, hosting a discussion, or making an author appearance. Most bookstore managers welcome the opportunity to have authors visit their store because these events drive traffic into the store.

TIP

You can always more easily start booking appearances and author signings in your local area, so contact the managers of local bookstores first. Depending on how potential readers respond to your appearance, you can always plan a more extensive book tour later (I cover book tours in the section "Taking your act on the road," later in this chapter).

When planning a book signing, have an ample number of copies of your books at the location, based on the anticipated turnout. Because your book is self-published, you have to work with the bookstore to ensure that you have enough books on hand for your event and that you and the bookstore properly promote your event in advance.

After you receive a commitment from one or more bookstores to do an in-person event, contact local media — particularly newspapers, regional magazines, locally produced podcasts, and radio stations — to get them to help you promote the event in their calendar or event listings. (You can use some of the press materials that I describe in Chapter 18.)

Setting up an event for smooth sailing

Determine exactly what to expect from the event in advance so that the event itself goes smoothly. Consider the following:

- **Set the stage.** Before the event, talk with the store manager to discuss what you plan to do and what the store expects of you. Will you have a podium to speak from? Will you sit behind a table to sign books?

- **Bring props.** Find out what you need to bring (aside from markers or pens to sign books). Can you distribute promotional materials, such as postcards or bookmarks?

- **Handle the money.** Decide whether you want to sell your own books or have someone at the event location to handle the money while you interact with readers.

- **Be personable.** During the actual appearance, make yourself approachable — smile and talk to the people who come to see you. Try to strike up conversations, answer questions, and come across as a charming and caring individual.

- **Check your spelling.** If you plan to sign autographs, make sure that you spell each person's name correctly. Always ask someone how they spell their name, even if it's a popular name. For example, "Mark" or "Amy" might spell their names "Marc" or "Aimee." There are many names that have multiple spellings, so it's always a good idea to ask first.

- **Make it personal.** When you sign books, try to incorporate a short message (one sentence maximum) in addition to your signature (if you have time). You can write, "Enjoy the book," "Thanks for your support," or "It was a pleasure meeting you." Be creative and, when possible, write something more personal than just "Best wishes."

Taking your act on the road

Depending on your budget (see Chapter 7 for more about money matters), you may decide to embark on a multiple-city book tour, which combines booking signings, author appearances, and interviews with local media in each city that you visit. Such a tour requires time commitment, so make sure that the traveling fits into your schedule.

TIP

To get the most out of your investment in a book tour (because you have to pay for your travel expenses to get from city to city), see whether you can book some paid appearances or lectures at schools, universities, or various other types of organizations to help reduce the out-of-pocket expenses. See Chapter 21 for more about becoming a paid public speaker.

Leave It to the Pros: Working with a Publicist

Based on everything in this chapter and in Chapter 18 about crafting press materials, contacting the media, pitching stories, and participating in interviews, you may decide to leave this type of work to the proven professionals. Freelance publicists or PR firms can work with you to develop, launch, and manage your book's PR campaign.

Reaping the benefits of a publicist

Instead of investing your own valuable time doing all the busy work associated with developing, launching, and managing a successful PR campaign (and yes, it requires a significant time and financial investment), consider hiring a publicist or PR firm to get the job done correctly. Publicists have their own particular skillset that takes training. These professionals can

>> Create your press materials or write just your press release and author bio.

>> Use the press materials that you create to pitch stories to the media and handle all media contact on your behalf, including sending out review copies of your book.

>> Help you book interviews. Most PR professionals already have well-established media contacts and therefore have a much easier time getting you booked than you would yourself.

>> Help you define and establish your image as a published author and expert in your field.

>> Provide you with intensive media training.

>> Schedule paid and unpaid appearances, lectures, or workshops on your behalf.

>> Assist you in planning a multiple-city book tour.

Finding a publicist

Many PR firms and freelance publicists specialize only in promoting authors. Others specialize in promoting experts or companies that work in specific industries, or they cater to only certain types of media.

TIP

You can find a publicist in many ways:

>> **Check out publishing industry magazines,** such as *Publishers Weekly* (www.publishersweekly.com) or Writer's Digest (www.writersdigest.com), and look for ads from PR firms.

>> **Contact a professional trade association,** such as the Public Relations Society of America (www.prsa.org) and ask for a referral.

>> **Seek out a referral from another author or company you know** for a PR firm that they had a positive experience with.

>> **Visit Upwork** (www.upwork.com) and solicit bids from freelance publicists based on what services you require.

>> **Try out PR companies that work for small publishers,** such as PR for Writers (www.prforwriters.com) and Mindstir Media (www.mindstirmedia.com). These types of firms cater to the public relations needs of independent writers and small publishing companies. To find other resources by using your favorite Internet search engine, enter the search phrase "How to find a book publicist."

>> **Contact a local college or university** that has students looking to break into public relations as their chosen career field. Colleges or universities may offer students credit for real-world work experience by giving you a paid or unpaid intern. To find interns, contact a school's career office, internship office, or the head of the marketing/communications department.

Paying the price for a publicist

Depending on the services that you want a publicist to handle and whether you hire an established PR firm or a freelance PR specialist, the cost varies greatly. Keep in mind that, in addition to paying for the publicist's time and expertise, you also have to cover all of their expenses (including phone calls, mailing costs, printing costs, travel, and so on).

For a publicist to truly do a thorough job with your campaign, they need between one and three months because of the *lead times* (time intervals needed to prepare for a publication, broadcast, or event) of various media outlets and the time that the publicist needs to properly contact each media outlet. So budget and plan accordingly. A three-month contract with an experienced book publicist could easily cost between $7,500 and $20,000.

WARNING

Many online-based services claim that they can distribute your press release to thousands of targeted media outlets for a flat fee of between $100 and $500. This approach seldom, if ever, works. Media professionals typically don't open and read unsolicited e-mails (that contain your press release) from these services. Although your press release might show up in Internet search results if someone types in an appropriate keyword, this random web-search find probably doesn't translate into publicity for your book or book sales.

TIP

For more tips on how to generate free publicity for your book, head to www.ingramspark.com and enter "book publicity" into the search field. In the pop-up window that appears, click the blog post title "15 Tips for Getting Book Publicity" written by Dan Smith, CEO and Founder of Smith Publicity.

Chapter **20**

Marketing Your Book with Paid Advertising and Promotional Tools

n Chapter 19, you can discover how to tap the power of the media to generate free publicity for your book and yourself. You can approach print, electronic, and online media with publicity materials, such as a press release. You want to get those outlets to review your book, feature it in editorial coverage, or interview you as an expert on the book's topic.

Free publicity is wonderful. It can help generate sales of your book. However, using PR, you seldom have total control over what people write or say about your book (or you as an author), and you never know for sure when the coverage will be published or broadcast. With paid advertising, however, you have 100 percent control over your advertising message. Plus, you decide exactly when and where people see and hear your targeted advertisements.

This chapter is all about how to utilize paid advertising to help sell your book. I cover the pros and cons of paid advertising, help you decide where to advertise, and give tips on planning a successful advertising campaign. I also focus on how to use promotional materials, such as printed bookmarks or postcards, to boost awareness of your book.

Checking Out the Pros and Cons of Paid Advertising

When you use paid advertising, you create an ad (or ads), choose specific media outlets that you want to feature your ad, and then decide exactly when you want your ads to appear. If you make the right decisions when planning your ad campaigns, you can reach the targeted audience for your book in an affordable way.

WARNING

Do your research in advance. If you don't understand exactly how each advertising opportunity works, you can wind up paying for ads that appear in the wrong places or incorporate a message that doesn't resonate with your target audience. In these situations, the ads don't generate the desired results: You don't sell books, and you wind up throwing away money.

The benefits of paid advertising

A well-designed ad that appears in the right media outlet(s) has the potential to be seen or heard. And then, the consumer hearing or viewing the ad can immediately act by (hopefully) calling a toll-free number or visiting a website (or their favorite online bookstore) to order your book. Some benefits of paid advertising include the following items (check out explanation and how-to information for these in the section "Planning a Successful Ad Campaign," later in the chapter):

>> **Control:** You have 100 percent control over the content and look (and/or sound) of your advertising message.

>> **Timing:** You decide how often the ad appears and when; determining the best frequency matters.

>> **Flexible budgeting:** Depending on your advertising methods, you can start with a very small budget and expand that budget when you see success. For example, you can start a search engine or social media ad campaign for as little as $50 to $100.

>> **Pinpointing the audience:** You can target your book's specific audience when you choose the best places to advertise.

>> **Quick startup and real-time tracking:** Online ads, for example, can often start appearing within hours, and you can track results in real time.

>> **Easy modification:** You can review an ad's results and then tweak the ad's message and frequency, as well as when and where it appears, to help you achieve the desired results — selling lots of books, of course!

First, identify your exact target audience (which I talk about in Chapter 3), and then figure out how to best reach that audience. Advertise in places where those people are mostly likely to see (or hear) your ad. To avoid taking on too much financial risk, the best place to advertise your book is online — on services and webpages that your target audience frequents the most.

The drawbacks of paid advertising

Unless you're a multi-million-dollar corporation and have a huge advertising budget and the goal of reaching mass-market consumers, paid advertising has a few drawbacks that you want to consider.

Your ad may get lost in the crowd or become annoying

An ad can easily get lost in the bombardment of advertising that people are constantly exposed to. Advertisers have figured out every possible way to reach an audience, using TV, radio, print, the Internet, billboards, clothing — even placemats in diners or the walls in restaurant and airport bathrooms. Consumers are exposed to ads literally everywhere, all the time — and, as a result, have become accustomed to ignoring them. When you become the advertiser, rather than the consumer, you must find innovative ways to communicate your message so that people pay attention. For paid advertising to work, you need to

>> **Create a highly effective ad, carefully targeting your audience.** Reach your target audience when and where they're in the frame of mind to buy something, or specifically looking for a book that covers a topic they're interested in.

>> **Have the budget to ensure that your audience sees (or hears) your ad repeatedly.** Consumers typically need to be exposed to an ad multiple times before they're motivated to purchase something.

The *rule of seven* is an advertising principle developed in the 1930s; it states that someone needs to be exposed to an ad at least seven or eight times before they take action to buy a product or follow through on the ad's call to action. When it comes to TV advertising, research shows that a consumer needs to see an ad, at a minimum, three times for its message to stick with them.

REMEMBER

And the ad(s) need to do more than pay for themselves. If you spend $100 on an online ad campaign on Instagram or Twitter, you need to generate enough book sales to pay for the ads, cover the cost to print and ship your books (if you're selling printed books), pay your other expenses, and have at least some profits left over to put in your pocket.

>> **Choose the best possible media outlets to feature your advertisement.** Then select the best times for people to see your ad(s) at an appropriate frequency. Again, this means you need to target your audience and then do research to determine that audience's core media consumption habits to help you decide where (and when) to run your ads.

WARNING

On the flip side of the *rule of seven*, you never want to inundate people with an aggressive ad campaign that uses high frequency, with messaging that the consumer may deem irrelevant to them. People often unsubscribe from a company's e-mail list because of this overdone advertising — they feel like the company spams their inbox with too many sales-oriented messages too often.

Spending precious time to develop an advertising skillset

Just like writing is a skillset that people spend years trying to master, so is advertising. An advertising expert has invested a significant amount of time in developing advertising campaigns, understands how to create ads, and knows where consumers need to see or hear those ads to generate results (in your case, sell books). These people understand how to

>> **Plan multi-faceted ad campaigns that stay within a reasonable, defined budget.** When you choose to advertise on social media or use search engine advertising, for example, you need to develop a thorough understanding of how each advertising opportunity works and what it costs to execute a proper campaign that achieves positive results. After you determine where you want to advertise, access the free tutorials that each platform offers to perspective advertisers. Or you can perform a Google or YouTube search for "How to advertise on Instagram" or "How to advertise on Facebook," for example.

>> **Reach the greatest number of people within a target audience.** Advertising experts study and understand the habits of consumers and know how to utilize the various advertising opportunities to reach a campaign's goals.

> » **Create and sustain an ad campaign, and understand the results it achieves.** Recognize that if you make even one mistake, you could waste the money you invest in advertising.

Requiring the talent of an advertising expert

If you don't want to risk potentially losing a lot of money by making mistakes with your ad campaigns, consider hiring a freelance advertising specialist who has experience developing ads and campaigns for the audience that you want to reach, using the advertising opportunities that you (and they) deem most appropriate.

WARNING

When you approach a sales representative for a particular media outlet, social media platform, or search engine to inquire about advertising, that person will offer to work with you to create the "best campaign possible." However, their job involves getting advertisers to spend the most money possible, even if those expenditures aren't in the advertiser's best interest. For this reason, work with independent advertising experts who understand your audience, believe in your book, and have your best interests in mind when making ad buys and planning campaigns.

Advertising can be expensive, but it doesn't have to be

National or even regional mass media advertising (with no niche audience) is costly. Leave this type of advertising to major brands, such as Coca-Cola, Nike, Ford, Walmart, or Southwest Airlines (you get the idea). So, if mass media advertising doesn't make sense for your campaign, how do you get your name out there?

Many authors and publishers find that paid advertising to reach a mass market audience when promoting a book to the public doesn't give them enough of a return on their limited advertising and marketing dollars spent. Instead, go with niche advertising (in conjunction with a public relations campaign and other grassroots marketing efforts). With *niche advertising,* you find specific print, digital, and electronic media outlets that cater to a small but targeted audience — the same audience that your book targets. Niche media outlets focus on a narrow topic. If you can find a niche outlet that relates to the topic of your book, advertising with that media outlet virtually guarantees that you reach the perfect audience.

TIP

Although you can advertise on television or radio, in newspapers or magazines, on billboards or the sides of buses, if you're trying to reach a niche audience, quickly and in the most cost-effective way possible, *focus on online advertising.* Specifically, consider paid advertising on social media and search engine advertising (on Google, Yahoo!, and some of the other most popular search engines.) Advertising on podcasts, for example, can also help you reach an extremely targeted audience for much less of an investment than using advertising in other forms of media.

Best of all, because a niche media outlet's audience is much smaller than, say, a network television show, or a national magazine or major daily newspaper, instead of paying thousands (or even millions) of dollars for a single ad placement, you can often run an entire ad campaign for a few hundred dollars and reach people you know will be interested in purchasing and reading your book.

Deciding Where to Advertise to Reach Your Target Audience

Before launching an advertising campaign for your book, determine exactly who your book's target audience is (refer to Chapter 3). Next, figure out the best advertising vehicles that you can use to reach that audience. To decide where to advertise, you need to understand the daily habits of your audience, know what media they're exposed to, and then determine how you can best spend your advertising dollars to reach those people by using the appropriate forms of media.

REMEMBER

No one has come up with an all-in-one solution for creating an advertising campaign, or even a single effective ad. Every situation is different, based on the type of book that you want to sell, the audience that you want to reach, your budget, the geographic area(s) that you plan to target, and your timeframe. If you choose to use paid advertising, focus on what you're trying to accomplish (to sell the book directly or drive people to your book's Amazon page, for example), and then research the most effective ways to achieve those objectives.

TIP

Kick off your research by finding an already successful book or product similar to your book (and that appeals to the same target audience), and determine exactly what advertising efforts helped to make it successful. Discover what worked in the past — don't try to reinvent the wheel.

Much of this chapter focuses on online-based advertising opportunities to reach a targeted demographic. Based on your budget and your intended audience, you may determine that other media, such as certain print publications, can also benefit your advertising campaign. But most forms of mainstream media advertising are considerably more expensive than online advertising opportunities, especially when you consider the need for your audience to see your ad(s) multiple times.

Devising an Online Ad Campaign

Literally billions of people around the world spend a lot of time each day on their favorite social media platforms. When each of those people creates an account with any social media service, the service encourages them to create a profile that reveals information about them. Advertisers use this information to target the specific demographics that they want to reach. In addition, the social media service tracks everything that account holders do while they're using the platform. This tracking allows the service to get know each person's interests and buying habits, for example. The social media platforms also use this information to help advertisers effectively target their ads.

Identifying ad types and opportunities

So, whether you opt to create an ad campaign on Facebook, Instagram, Twitter, TikTok, or any other social media service, as an advertiser, you can tell that social media service the exact niche audience you want to reach and when. Each service also offers a handful of ad formats that you can use. For example, you can create

>> A text-based ad

>> An ad that includes a photo (or graphic) with text

>> A video-based ad

>> An ad that includes a combination of text, audio, animations, and other multimedia components

TIP

Any displayed ad should include a Buy button that someone can click or tap on to place their order. When creating an audio-based ad, make sure it includes a clearly stated call to action.

REMEMBER

You can also use an ad to drive traffic to your e-commerce website or the listing for your book (on Amazon or Barnes & Noble's website, for example). You have plenty of options, but you don't have to spend a lot of money. And you can create and launch a campaign in hours — and potentially start generating orders for your book very quickly.

Here are some links to follow if you're interested in advertising on any of the top 10 most popular social media platforms (as of mid-2023):

>> **Facebook:** www.facebook.com/business/ads

>> **Instagram:** https://business.instagram.com/advertising

- » **LinkedIn:** https://business.linkedin.com/marketing-solutions

- » **Pinterest:** https://business.pinterest.com/advertise

- » **Reddit:** www.redditforbusiness.com/advertise

- » **Snapchat:** https://forbusiness.snapchat.com/advertising

- » **TikTok:** www.tiktok.com/business

- » **Twitter:** https://business.twitter.com/en/advertising.html

- » **WhatsApp:** https://business.whatsapp.com/products/ads-that-click-to-whatsapp

- » **YouTube:** www.youtube.com/ads

Keep in mind, advertising on social media is entirely different than setting up a free account for yourself, your publishing company, or your book that you then use to interact with (potential) readers in an informal way. Refer to Chapter 17 for details on how to use social media to promote yourself (as an author) or your book on social media for free.

Looking beyond social media platforms

Beyond advertising on the various social media platforms, you can also find countless opportunities to run ads in popular blogs, on podcasts that cater to a niche audience, or even on music streaming services, such as Spotify (http://ads.spotify.com).

If you want to use audio-based ads to advertise on podcasts that cater to your book's target audience, you can directly approach the producer or ad sales representative for each individual podcast. Or you can work with an agency, such as

- » **AdvertiseCast:** www.advertisecast.com/podcast-advertising

- » **AudioGo:** www.audiogo.com

- » **SXM Media:** www.sxmmedia.com/advertise

Considering shoppable posts on social media

In mid-2023, while I write this second edition of *Self-Publishing For Dummies,* one of the biggest developments in social media advertising is an ad format called *shoppable ads.* These ads appear on the various social media platforms and include a Buy button that allows people to purchase a featured product directly from that ad, without ever leaving the social media platform. For the consumer, these ads make the purchasing process very fast and easy, and they can pay for purchases by using a major credit card, debit card, or payment service (such as Apple Pay, PayPal, or Google Pay).

TIP

When contacting any of the social media platforms about advertising opportunities, explore the shoppable ads and shoppable content options that each platform offers and determine whether this type of advertising might work better for you than would traditional online ads when it comes to selling your book. In the two previous sections, I list links where you can learn more about advertising on social media and on podcasts.

The sales concept

The concept of shoppable ads and the formats they take are evolving quickly. Using this method offers an extremely effective and relatively low-cost way to advertise to a very niche audience and to quickly convert ad viewers into paying customers. According to the SproutSocial article "Shoppable content: The new way of buying online (and 3 brands doing it right)" (https://sproutsocial.com/insights/shoppable-content):

> "Shoppable content is a digital asset, such as a social media post, image, video or ad, that consumers can click through to make a purchase. For example, Instagram Product Tags let you highlight items from your catalog directly in your images and videos, so people can easily tap and learn more. There are instances where the customer must complete their checkout process on the brand's website, but some shoppable content enables transactions all in one place. Shoppable content on platforms like Facebook, Instagram or TikTok lets users buy without leaving the app."

The sales approach

REMEMBER

As of mid-2023, shoppable content can act as an extremely effective advertising and sales tool for reaching millennials and Gen Z consumers, but this audience is quickly expanding to people of all ages and from all walks of life. This type of advertising allows customers to easily buy what they want, when they want it, with no extended sales funnel. In fact, the best shoppable ads appear more like content posts (and use a soft-sell approach), as opposed to traditional ads that use a hard-sell approach.

> » A *soft-sell approach* takes on a more conversational style, where you provide information that you perceive as valuable to get someone's attention. And then you work in a sentence such as, "In the book [*BookTitle*] that's available

from Amazon [*Amazon link or your own website address*], you can learn more about [*topic*]."

>> A *hard-sell approach* is more of a traditional advertisement in which you grab attention and then tell readers something like, "Click here right now to purchase a copy of [*BookTitle*] and receive free shipping with your order."

Because shoppable content appears on social media, you can't take a traditional advertising approach. Instead, create compelling content that caters to the strength of the social media platform that you choose, tell stories, and engage with your audience in an appealing way. Shoppable ads and shoppable content give you, the advertiser, creative control in a way that helps you communicate with your audience on a platform they're already active on.

Engaging search engine marketing (SEM) opportunities

Various search engines offer a low-cost and highly targeted advertising option. Anytime someone enters a search term into Google, Yahoo!, Bing, or just about any other search engine, in addition to seeing search results (websites) that meet their search criteria, they also get ads that appear prominently on every search results page.

Search engine marketing (SEM) — also referred to as search engine advertising, pay-per-click advertising, content marketing, or keyword advertising — is a marketing strategy used to increase a website's visibility in search results pages. You can use SEM to help you sell books because you can start with a very limited ad budget based around specific keywords or search terms. Then, over time, you can expand your budget and the search terms that your ads match. In many cases, search engine advertising relies on a pay-per-click model, rather than the advertiser paying for a pre-determined number of ad views.

If you opt to sell your eBook through Amazon, you're able to pay for targeted ads that appear on peoples' Kindle e-readers. When Kindle users see the ad, they can click on a link and immediately purchase and download your book directly to their Kindle device. To learn more about this paid advertising opportunity, visit https://kdp.amazon.com/en_US/help/topic/G201499010.

According to the Semrush article "What Is SEM (Search Engine Marketing)?" (www.semrush.com/blog/search-engine-marketing):

"While SEM broadly covers more than just paid marketing, it's often referred to as pay-per-click (PPC) marketing. This is a business model where marketers pay each time someone clicks their ad."

REMEMBER

Each search engine that offers search engine marketing (advertising) opportunities does so in a slightly different way. A novice may find the process of creating, running, and then analyzing the results of an ad campaign confusing, so do your research and understand exactly how each opportunity works before creating and launching ad campaigns. Carefully consider and craft the keywords that you target, your ad's headline, and the short ad message. Then, determine exactly how and when you can most effectively spend your ad money.

To find out about advertising opportunities on the most popular search engines, visit these websites:

>> **Google:** From https://ads.google.com, choose Campaigns & Tools ⇨ Search to access discussion of Google's search engine ad options.

>> **Microsoft Bing:** Go to www.microsoft.com and enter "search engine marketing" in the Search text box. Click the link that appears for the article "The complete guide to search engine marketing — Microsoft Advertising."

>> **Yahoo!:** Access Yahoo!'s "Native advertising" information at https://gemini.yahoo.com/advertiser.

Planning a Successful Ad Campaign

Developing a successful advertising campaign has multiple steps that you must follow. You can't just throw something together haphazardly — especially because you're forking out your hard-earned money for this service. Look at the money that you spend on advertising as an investment in the future sales of your book (or books). If the advertising works, you sell a lot of copies of your book and make money. If the advertising campaign fails, you waste the money that you spend.

Why ad campaigns sometimes fail

Unfortunately, an ad campaign can fail for many reasons. The most common reasons are

>> **Poor ad design and focus:** You put out a poorly written or designed ad, and it doesn't properly address the needs and wants of its audience or doesn't capture their attention. Perhaps rewrite or redesign that ad so that it better describes your book and better targets the right audience.

>> **Wrong messaging:** The message that you convey with your ad appears unprofessional, lacks credibility, or doesn't resonate with the audience.

Consider creating ad copy that's more honest and authentic — and doesn't create expectations that are unrealistic.

>> **Mismatched platform:** You have a good ad, but the media outlet that you advertise through doesn't attract the audience that you want to reach. Do some additional research to determine what media outlets your target audience relies on.

>> **Unfortunate positioning:** You choose poor timing or placement of your ad. For example, you try to sell a Christmas-related book in July, or your ad appears directly next to a competing book that's better targeted to the audience and less expensive.

>> **Lack of reiteration:** Your ad doesn't have enough repetition to properly capture the attention of your intended audience. Remember that your ad needs to be seen multiple times by the same person before they'll respond to it.

>> **Unsellable product:** You just can't find a market for or interest in your book. Yikes! In this case, you may need to make some changes to your actual book's content to broaden its focus and appeal, make its design more palatable to the intended audience, or determine a more appropriate target audience.

Creating your ads

Assuming that the book you wrote and published has a viable market and you understand exactly who your potential readers are (see Chapter 3), you need to create an ad that captures those readers' attention. Whichever advertising medium you ultimately use, the advertising message that you convey must quickly and powerfully answer the W (plus H) questions: who, what, where, when, why, and how. At the same time, focus the message on the potential reader's wants and needs.

Answering the right questions

Your ad needs to appeal to your target audience, the ad must also quickly answer a number of questions. Here are some questions whose answers clarify who you are, what you're selling, and why people should care:

>> **Regarding the seller:**

- *Why should the reader trust you as an author? What makes you an expert?* List a few of your key credentials to impress potential readers. This can help add to the book's perceived value.

- *Who else thinks your book is incredible?* Many successful book ads utilize excerpts from positive reviews or quotes from celebrities, or list awards the book has won.

>> **Regarding the product:**

- *What are you offering?* You have a book to sell. People need to know that.

- *What's the book about?* In one sentence or less, clearly and succinctly summarize what your book is all about.

- *What's unique about your book?* Focus on why someone should read your book, as opposed to another book on the same topic.

- *Where can they obtain a copy of your book?* Is the book "Available now from bookstores everywhere!" or "Available exclusively at www.[WebsiteURL].com"? Don't make potential readers search for your book. Tell them exactly where they can purchase it right away.

- *How much does the book cost?* List the cover price of the book. If you create a perceived value for the book's content in your ad, potential readers should think the book's actual cost is a bargain.

>> **Regarding the consumer:**

- *Who will be interested in reading it and why?* Focus on what your book's target audience wants to know about your book.

- *What content does the book offer to its readers?* Does your book offer exclusive or valuable content? If so, your ad needs to bring this fact to the attention of potential readers.

- *How can readers benefit from reading your book? What can they learn?* Focus on the value or knowledge that the reader can obtain. List a few specific examples of topics covered in the book. Give readers a taste of what they can expect.

- *How can your book help the reader?* Be specific and address issues or topics that relate directly to your intended audience. For example, focus on how the book can help your readers overcome a problem.

- *Why should someone buy your book right now?* Create a sense of urgency. Provide one or more reasons why the reader should obtain the information in your book right away.

REMEMBER

In all your ads, include basic details, such as the book's publisher, author (that's you!), ISBN, and a website where the reader can purchase the book.

Calling the consumer to action

The most powerful ads create a sense of urgency. You want the person who sees or hears your ad to believe that they must get their hands on your book immediately. Creating a sense of urgency helps encourage the potential reader to take immediate action, such as visiting a bookstore, calling a toll-free number, or going to a specific website to purchase your book. Every ad should include a call to action that tells the reader exactly what they need to do next.

You can create a sense of urgency by featuring a special offer, such as, "Order online before [*Insert Date*] and receive 20 percent off the cover price!" People love to save money and receive special offers.

Pulling together text, graphics, and video

After you determine what information needs to go in the ad (see the preceding section), figure out the best way to communicate that information, using powerful and attention-getting language. To write effective advertising copy, you need training and practice, even if you're an experienced writer or author. Keep in mind, you have only a few seconds to make a positive impression. Composing effective ad copy requires a different skill set and an understanding of advertising that most authors do not inherently possess. You can, however, learn these skills by taking an advertising and marketing copyrighting course online, for example. Or to save time and money, hire someone who is already an expert at writing this type of copy.

Whenever you advertise in any type of media that allows for visuals, prominently display your book's cover. The cover of your book should sell itself. (See Chapter 10 for details on putting together an attractive book cover.) Also, you can create a video trailer for your book as a powerful sales tool that appears on your book's webpage and that you distribute via social media and make available on YouTube. See Chapter 17 for more info on this topic.

Take a look at ads for other books. Examine the format, the wording, and the approaches that the various ads take. Determine which approach most likely works with your book and try to use those same advertising techniques — assuming they apply to your book and your potential audience.

Timing your campaign

Timing is a critical component for any ad campaign. If your ads start running too early, before you publish the book and have it readily available, people can't find the book right away and might forget about it. Ideally, you want ads for your book to run at the same time that the book is available so that the reader can get their hands on a copy quickly — when they order a copy online, they can expect to receive it quickly, or they can go to the bookstore and purchase a copy right away.

Proper timing of your paid advertising campaign means coordinating the ads to run around the same time as the free publicity that you generate, as well as in conjunction with any other marketing and promotional activities that you plan. Ideally, expose readers to as many impressions of your book as possible without overdoing it (see the section "Your ad may get lost in the crowd or become annoying," earlier in the chapter).

TIP

Depending on where and how you plan to sell books, you may want to promote and accept pre-orders for your book (where people purchase the book before it's published and available; see Chapter 8). For example, if you plan to have your own books printed (using a short run or offset printer; see Chapter 12), and then sell it through an online sales platform, such as Amazon or Barnes & Noble's website (www.bn.com), you absolutely must generate pre-orders for your book because these services measure printed book pre-orders to determine how many initial copies of the book it should have on hand to sell.

Tracking the results of your ads

You need to know whether the ads that you run effectively generate the desired response rates. Therefore, carefully track what ads you have running, where you have them running, and what response you get from them. This tracking system helps you fine-tune your advertising on an ongoing basis, improve the message, and focus more heavily on the aspects of the paid advertising campaign that are effectively selling books. Almost all online-based advertising opportunities offer free analytics that enable you to track an ad's performance in real-time. You can also use a wide range of free tools, such as Google Analytics (https://marketing platform.google.com/about/analytics), to help you track traffic and sales related to your e-commerce website, for example.

Effectively Using Promotional Materials

In addition to paid advertising, you can use a wide range of promotional materials to help spread the word about your new book. If you have an easy and inexpensive way to distribute these materials, you can experience even greater sales success.

Distributing bookmarks

Full-color, 2-x-6-inch bookmarks are an ideal and extremely inexpensive way to promote your book. You can give away these promotional items at bookstores, libraries, author appearances, or anywhere that you can obtain permission to distribute them to large numbers of people. For under $250, you can have several thousand promotional bookmarks printed. Design the bookmarks yourself by using a graphics software program or have the printing company that you use handle the graphic design work on your behalf (which often costs extra). You can also hire a freelance graphic designer to do this for a small investment. (Use a service such as Upwork, www.upwork.com, to quickly find a freelance graphic designer.)

Formatting the bookmark

The front design of your bookmark can include the following:

>> The cover artwork for your book

>> The book's title and subtitle (using the largest font and type size possible)

>> The book's publisher, author, ISBN, and cover price

>> The book or author's website, along with text stating exactly where someone can purchase the book (you may choose to place purchase info on the back)

Figure 20-1 shows a sample layout for the front of a full-color promotional bookmark. Of course, you can choose the typeface(s), point sizes, type styles, and color scheme used. Also, make sure that a full-color version of your book's cover artwork appears on the bookmark.

FIGURE 20-1: A sample bookmark (front) template.

On the back of your promotional bookmark, you can include a very short author biography (maybe one or two sentences), a thumbnail photo of the author, and/or a bulleted list that describes in more detail the topic(s) your book covers. You can also display social media links for yourself (the author) or your book. Remember, you need to ensure the font size you use on both sides of the bookmark are easily readable.

Finding a bookmark printer

Whether you print full-color bookmarks or postcards (see the section "Promoting with postcards," later in this chapter, for more about postcards), find a competitively priced printer that offers professional offset printing. Use these specifications to ensure that the promotional items look highly professional:

>> Ultra-bright, 130-pound paper

>> 16-point coating (and/or glossy spot UV coating)

>> High-resolution, photo-quality, 200-line screen printing (at 2400 dpi)

TIP

Just a few of the many companies that can print full-color promotional bookmarks or postcards include

>> **48HourPrint:** On the top menu at www.48hourprint.com, choose Shop by Products ➪ Promotional Products ➪ Bookmarks.

>> **PrintRunner:** Go to www.printrunner.com and from the top menu, choose Promotional Products ➪ Bookmarks.

>> **UPrinting:** From www.uprinting.com, choose View All Products ➪ Promotional Products ➪ Bookmarks from the top menu.

>> **VistaPrint:** Open www.vistaprint.com, choose Home & Gifts from the top menu, and then under the Best Sellers section of the pop-up menu that appears, select Bookmarks.

Promoting with postcards

Like bookmarks, full-color postcards provide an excellent way to promote your book at bookstores, libraries, author appearances, and other events. You can also use them for a targeted direct mail campaign. You can have 3-x-5-, 4-x-6-, or 5-x-7-inch postcards printed inexpensively, when compared to other forms of advertising. The cost is less than $100 for at least 1,000 full-color postcards. Prices vary based on the quantity that you publish and the printing company that you use.

Make the content of a promotional postcard virtually identical to what you include on a bookmark, and you have more space to get your message across. Instead of cluttering the postcard with too much information beyond what I list in the section "Formatting the bookmark," earlier in this chapter, use large font sizes and graphics to take up the space.

Exploiting excerpts from your book

Get people interested in reading your book by offering them a free sample of it. You can create a free, downloadable PDF file and make it available on your website (see Chapter 17) and from online booksellers, such as Amazon and Barnes & Noble (see Chapter 14). You can also have excerpts printed as booklets or mini-books, and then distribute those excerpts at author appearances, trade shows, or anyplace else where you can distribute printed materials to the masses.

Particularly for fiction, excerpts can draw the reader into the story and then encourage them to actually purchase and read the entire book. For nonfiction, offering an excerpt can help clarify the approach your book takes in covering its subject matter. However, a well-written and designed piece of promotional material or ad potentially sells the book just as well to someone who's interested in the topic.

Attracting attention with book displays

As a publisher looking to make a positive and professional impression on booksellers and retail stores that may want to sell your book, offer a free cardboard floor or countertop display when they purchase a specific number of books. Plus, if you plan to promote your book at appearances or trade shows, a customized retail display helps enhance your professional image.

TIP

If you plan to do a bunch of in-person appearances, or sell/promote books at tradeshows, consider investing in an affordable and portable trade show display. Check out what's available for between $500 and $1,000 from companies by searching their sites for "trade show display":

>> **Affordable Exhibit Displays:** www.affordabledisplays.com

>> **Displays2Go:** www.displays2go.com

>> **Pop Up Stand:** www.postupstand.com

>> **VistaPrint:** www.vistaprint.com

Chapter **21**

Expanding Your Income with Spin-Off Merchandise and Services

C ongratulations! You published your book and became an author. But, as you may have discovered, you have a somewhat limited profit potential from selling just your stand-alone book, mainly because of its relatively low cover price. For most self-published authors, simply publishing and selling a single book doesn't provide an effective get-rich-quick scheme, nor does it allow them to earn a full-time living.

By positioning yourself as an expert in your field, however, you can take jobs as a lecturer, instructor, or consultant — and potentially earn several hundred dollars per hour (or more). You can also create spin-off products, such as audiobooks or instructional videos, that come with much higher price tags than the one you put on the cover price of your book. You can then bundle your book with these spin-off products to help further boost your credibility and earning potential.

In this chapter, you can discover ways to use your newfound credibility as a published author — not just to sell books, but to create higher-priced spin-off products and services that can boost your revenue by allowing you to repackage and expand on the content in your book.

Considering a Few Important Points before You Create Spin-Offs

Creating spin-off products in conjunction with your book can help you generate more revenue over the long term, but initially, doing so will require a significant time and financial investment to develop the products, and then properly market and distribute them. You also need to make sure that you choose the right products and services that will appeal to your target audience.

TIP

Most of the time, nonfiction books lend themselves better to spin-off products. Also, authors of nonfiction books are often in higher demand as speakers, freelancers, and consultants. However, fiction authors can create and sell merchandise based on their book's characters or storyline, and potentially license the rights for their novel to be adapted into a movie, TV series, graphic novel series, video game, or even a mobile app.

Recognizing the investment you need to make

You invested the time and money to self-publish your book and properly market and promote it. Unless you sell or license the subsidiary rights for your book to another company, you face an additional investment for developing and selling your own spin-off products. You want to target the audience that you already have for your book (your readers; see Chapter 3) and sell related products and services to those readers — *and* to new customers.

REMEMBER

The actual financial and time investment that you need to make depends on the type of products and services that you want to produce. You need to do more than simply publish your book to make the publishing venture profitable. You need to properly market, distribute, and sell the book. The same holds true for any spin-off products that you create. Before investing the money to produce any type of product, be sure (or as sure as possible) that you can market it to your intended audience and generate enough sales not only to recoup your investment, but also to earn an ongoing profit.

Another option for expanding your book's reach involves working with an agent who can help you license your book or its content to companies that can develop and sell products based on your book. An agent can also potentially connect you with producers or production companies interested in transforming your book into a TV show, movie, documentary, graphic novel series, audiobook, video game, or mobile app, for example. One way to find an agent is to utilize the listing offered by the Writer's Guild of America West (`https://apps.wga.org/agency/agencylist.aspx`). You can research each agency online and then directly contact those that are of interest.

Unless you have a massive budget and the vast resources that you need to market your products, start off small and build your product line as demand dictates and new opportunities arise.

Envisioning the right products and services

If you possess an expertise that others can benefit from, people likely are willing to pay for that information in whatever form you make it available — a book, an audiobook, a live seminar, an online course, or an in-person workshop. Because you wrote a full-length book, you clearly have information to share with others. Now that you have a published book, use your business savvy, marketing skills, and creativity to develop new ways to repackage and sell the content that contains your knowledge and experience.

While you develop and produce spin-off products related to your book and its content, be realistic. Focus on your own strengths and showcase them in whatever spin-off products you choose to develop and market.

If you have no on-camera experience and lack the personality, looks, and the voice to star in your own video course, don't waste your time and money developing a product that ultimately looks unprofessional and could damage your credibility. Furthermore, if you feel extremely uncomfortable speaking in front of crowds, don't pursue public speaking opportunities until you gain the required skills and confidence.

Using Multimedia to Repackage Your Content

Adapting the information that you offer in your book into other formats allows you to use video, audio, and multimedia to create products that expand the value of your book. When you wrote your book, you could use only the written word and potentially a few photographs or illustrations. Tap your creativity and come up with a handful of ways to repackage or rework your book's material. Here are some ideas:

>> **Give readers insight into your research.** If your book featured interviews with experts, the audio or video adaptation of your book can feature those same people, which allows your audience to hear or see the interviews. This presentation might take on a standard question-and-answer format or use a more video-based documentary style.

>> **Offer new and expanded content.** Provide additional or expanded examples, new statistics, updated information, or other content not originally included in your book. Offering these add-ons helps create a perceived value for the new product(s) that you create, especially among people who have already read your book and want more.

To find innovative ways to repackage the content from your book and create new types of products, tap into your creativity. The types of spin-off products that work for your book depend a lot on the type of book that you wrote and its intended audience. Although you can potentially develop a novel into an audiobook or even a video game, nonfiction works can transform into instructional videos, audiobooks, or interactive multimedia applications.

REMEMBER

When deciding how to cater to your potential audience and repackage the material in your book, consider the habits of your target audience and how you can utilize the latest technologies to best communicate with those people. See Chapter 3 for information about determining your target audience.

Opting for audiobooks

You can produce almost any type of book as an audiobook. However, before investing the time and money into creating this type of product, determine whether the type of book you wrote would appeal to your intended audience in audio form.

Ask yourself these questions: Would someone potentially learn more or be better entertained by listening to your book, as opposed to reading it? If so, do you think that they would pay extra for an audiobook? If you can answer yes to those questions, you can

>> **Record yourself reading the book.** Rent a recording studio and hire an audio engineer to record you reading your own book. Then, make your audiobook available for sale and download through Amazon, Audible, Apple Books, and other digital audiobook services.

>> **Hire a professional voiceover actor to read your book to your audiobook audience.** Online services, such as AirGigs.com, Voice123.com, Voices.com, or VoiceJuice.com, allow you to listen to demos of professional voiceover actors and then hire the one you like the sound of. In many cases, these actors have their own recording studios (or access to a studio) and work remotely.

>> **Ask AI to record your book.** Thanks to advancements in technology, a specialized AI-based application that has the text-based manuscript of your book can provide a computer-generated voice that sounds (almost) human to read the audiobook adaptation. This option can work for some types of audiobooks (for example, when you don't need a human voice that conveys emotion and natural speech inflections).

TIP

As of this writing (mid-2023), these AI apps are not yet suitable for many works of fiction and some other types of audiobook productions. They generate monotone, emotionless voices that can be difficult for someone to enjoy listening to for extended periods. As this technology evolves, that situation will no doubt change. Revoicer (`https://revoicer.com`) is an example of a text-to-speech generator that's evolving. It offers virtual voices which have some level of emotion and inflection reflected in the AI-generated voice that reads the text.

>> **Engage an audiobook production service.** If you don't want to handle the production, editing, sales, and distribution of your own audiobook, you can approach an audiobook production service. With this option, the company produces original audiobook content, and licenses the rights to market and distribute the audiobook on your behalf. Within the Search field of any search engine (such as Google), enter the search phrase, "Audiobook production service" to find a production company to work with. One example is the Audiobook Network (`https://inquiry.audiobooknetwork.com`).

TIP

If you have your heart set on recording, producing, and selling your own audiobook, the place to start is with Audible's ACX service (`www.acx.com`) which offers the tools and resources needed for self-published authors to become self-published audiobook producers, with distribution through Audible and Amazon. According to the ACX website

> "ACX is a marketplace where authors, literary agents, publishers, and other Rights Holders can connect with narrators, engineers, recording studios, and other Producers capable of producing a finished audiobook. The result: More audiobooks will be made. ACX puts you in the driver's seat. If you're a Rights Holder, you choose how you produce your audiobook — whether on your own or by engaging a Producer on ACX — and you choose among two royalty models."

Producing pre-recorded, video-based classes

Instructional and how-to books often lend themselves perfectly to instructional videos and online-based courses. You can also easily adapt other types of nonfiction, perhaps using more of a documentary style of filming. Of course, if you have a work of fiction, adapting your book into a direct-to-video movie is always an option, but team up with a TV or movie production company to do that.

Countless online services sell and distribute online-based courses. Each service offers a different royalty-splitting opportunity. If producing online-based video courses seems like a viable opportunity for your book's content, here are some services worth contacting:

>> **Coursera:** www.coursera.org

>> **edX:** www.edx.org

>> **LearnWorlds:** www.learnworlds.com

>> **LinkedIn Learning:** www.linkedin.com/learning

>> **MasterClass:** www.masterclass.com

>> **Skillshare:** www.skillshare.com

>> **TrainerCentral:** www.trainercentral.com

>> **Udemy:** www.udemy.com

Generating Revenue with a Wide Range of Services

Depending on your area(s) of expertise, you can generate additional revenue by making yourself available as a public speaker and offering seminars and/or workshops. You can also enter the ranks of the media and become a consultant, paid spokesperson for a company, or a freelance expert.

Based on your areas of expertise and comfort level with public speaking, come up with a series of topics that you can teach and/or lecture about, and then develop one-, two-, and three-hour versions of that lecture that you can present in person or via a live video meeting to special interest groups, professional associations, companies, and/or educational institutions. Although you can use these speaking and teaching engagements as an opportunity to sell books, you need to leverage your credibility as an author and topic expert to market yourself as a speaker or instructor.

Speaking publicly

As a published author and expert in your field, take advantage of the wide range of public speaking opportunities available to you. Many of these opportunities pay speakers and instructors either a fee or honorarium. (An *honorarium* is a payment given to a professional person for services that don't legally or traditionally require fees.) Some occasions provide promotional opportunities or the ability to sell books directly to program participants.

Public speaking also offers the opportunity to further establish yourself as an industry leader or expert in your field. The following sections focus on ways to use your public speaking skills to generate revenue and sell your book.

Here are some tips to help you get set for teaching and speaking engagements:

>> **Figure out what you have to say and who wants to hear you speak.** For example, if you're a fiction author, you can offer readings from your book or attend a gathering to discuss the book's topic. You might also get an opportunity to appear at various special interest conventions centered around book genres: science fiction, comic books, romance novels, horror, and so on. On the other hand, if you're a nonfiction author, you can offer how-to instruction relating to your area of expertise.

>> **Schedule free speaking engagements.** Author appearances and lectures at local bookstores, volunteering to speak at gatherings hosted by nonprofit organizations, or speaking at public libraries or in schools within your community can give you practice speaking in front of crowds and at the same time promote and/or directly sell your book.

>> **Join a public speaking organization.** Joining groups such as Toastmasters (www. toastmasters.org) or the National Speakers Association (www.nsaspeaker.org) can help you establish yourself as a professional public speaker.

Teaching through adult education programs

Throughout the country, community colleges, public school systems, and other organizations sponsor organized adult education and continuing education programs. These programs hire experts, authors, and industry leaders to teach a wide range of classes, workshops, and seminars. Consider these opportunities:

>> Students register and pay for your class, which can be a one-time seminar or a class that spans three to eight weeks (based on your topic). In addition to teaching the class, you can sell your book to students.

>> You can also benefit from the exposure that you receive by being promoted as an instructor in the course catalog, promotional mailings, on the group's website, and in advertising done by the adult education program.

>> Some authors even create one course or workshop curriculum based on their book, and then they work as an instructor for multiple adult education programs in various regions. This scenario ensures an ongoing income stream and book-sales opportunities.

TIP

If you choose to sell your book in-person at classes that you teach or lectures that you give, be prepared to accept credit, debit cards, PayPal, Apple Pay, and Google Pay as payment for your book. You can easily accept a variety of payments through services such as PayPal (www.paypal.com) or Square (www.squareup.com).

To become an instructor for an adult education or continuing education program, contact the school or adult education program organizer directly and inquire about the process for proposing a new course or workshop. You typically need a written proposal and an in-person meeting to pitch new course ideas. Become familiar with the types of courses already offered through the program, and then propose new ideas based around your book that can interest and benefit students.

The Learning Annex is a well-established adult-education program offered around the country. Each year, it hires and pays hundreds of experts and authors to teach more than 8,000 classes and seminars on a wide range of topics. Contact the organization at www.learningannex.com/sell_your_expertise.

Hosting your own seminars

Hosting a seminar can provide you with a great way to increase your revenue. But you may find getting enough people to attend your seminars to make such an event financially worthwhile a bit challenging, so start off small — with relatively low expectations. For your first few seminars or webinars, plan on attracting a dozen or so paying attendees. Based on your success, you can expand your efforts accordingly.

REMEMBER

Another option for delivering seminar content is to host a virtual webinar via a video conferencing service, such as Zoom (https://explore.zoom.us/en/products/webinars) or GoTo Webinar (www.goto.com/webinar). While this option is easier and less costly to organize and host, many people in this post-COVID-19 world have *Zoom fatigue* or *virtual meeting fatigue*. In this case, they may be reluctant to pay for and participate in a long virtual webinar experience.

If you want to host your own in-person seminars, consider the following steps before getting started:

1. **Develop a half-day or full-day seminar curriculum.**

   If you have experience with public speaking, you can probably easily put together a seminar based on content from your book.

2. **Rent a conference room at a hotel or small theater.**

   The venue should provide the audio/video equipment that you need and ample space for participants to sit comfortably for the duration of the seminar. For example, you can rent movie theaters or hotel conference rooms around the U.S. for this purpose, and they probably already have the audio/visual equipment in place to host lectures or seminars.

3. **Set a price for your seminar.**

   Charge between $25 to $500 a person, depending on the topic, the length of the seminar, and your target audience.

4. **Invite participants to attend the seminar.**

   To find people to invite to your seminar, you can use social media, email, or online advertising, or you can contact your existing readers and followers to promote the event.

While you start figuring out how to price and coordinate your events, consider hiring someone who has event or seminar planning experience to help you plan and market your seminars properly. Alternatively, you can offer the course as a live, online-based webinar through a service such as

>> **GoTo Webinar:** www.goto.com/webinar

>> **Zoho:** www.zoho.com/webinar

>> **Zoom:** https://explore.zoom.us/products/webinars

Lecturing at colleges and universities

Many colleges and universities (as well as organizations and clubs affiliated with schools) have budgets to bring in guest speakers and lecturers. If you're an expert on a topic that college or graduate-level students want to know more about, consider contacting schools and making yourself available as a guest lecturer. If you're a fiction author, perhaps you can speak about the creative writing process to English or literature majors, for example.

If you can make a large time commitment, you can become a visiting faculty member at a college or university and teach one or two classes. To become a faculty member, however, you have to commit to teaching for at least one full semester and holding classes one or more times per week.

Speaking at trade shows and conferences

Industry trade shows and conferences always utilize guest speakers and lecturers. And the trade show or conference often pays for these gigs. Even if speakers don't get paid, these gatherings provide an excellent opportunity to

>> Further position yourself as an expert in your field.

>> Sell books to your target audience.

>> Promote yourself as a speaker/trainer that companies can hire.

>> Publicize yourself as a consultant or freelancer within your industry (see the section "Becoming a consultant or freelancer," later in this chapter).

To access a directory of trade shows, exhibitions, conferences, and business events, visit any of these websites:

>> **10Times Trade Show List (Sorted by Industry):** www.10times.com/tradeshows/by-industry

>> **Events in America:** www.eventsinamerica.com

>> **EventsEye:** www.eventseye.com

>> **Orbus USA Trade Show List:** www.orbus.com/usa-tradeshow-list

>> **The Trade Show Calendar:** www.thetradeshowcalendar.com

>> **Trade Show Advisor:** www.trade-show-advisor.com

The Events in America website (www.eventsinamerica.com) includes a directory for keynote speakers, panel speakers, seminar leaders, workshop facilitators, trainers, and industry speakers, which you can access by choosing the Speakers option in the top menu. Click the Create Profile button to create an online profile for yourself as an available speaker or click the Call for Speakers button to discover potential speaking opportunities.

Working with a speaker's bureau

A *speaker's bureau* is an organization that matches speakers with venues and organizations looking for people to host lectures, seminars, or workshops. The agency promotes you as a public speaker, schedules speaking gigs on your behalf, and then takes a commission based on the revenue that you generate from the appearances.

To sign up as a client with a speaker's bureau, most agencies request that you first submit a video or recording of yourself speaking, along with a copy of your book and related promotional materials. You can find reputable speaker's bureaus, such as the National Speakers Bureau (www.nationalspeakers.com), by visiting the Speakerflow website at www.speakerflow.com/30-plus-speakers-bureaus-to-consider-as-you-grow.

Entering the ranks of the media

As an expert in your field, you can share your knowledge and attract attention by taking advantage of social media or the tremendous growth in the popularity of podcasts.

Becoming a micro-influencer around your book's topic

In addition to using social media as a tool to promote and sell your book (see Chapter 17), by developing a loyal following of at least 10,000 followers or subscribers, you can become a micro-influencer, and then get paid by companies to promote their products or services to your niche audience. For example

>> **Influencer Marketing Hub** (www.influencermarketinghub.com) is one of many online resources that you can access to find out more about becoming a successful and revenue-generating micro-influencer.

>> **SocialLadder** (www.socialladderapp.com) or a service like it can help you build and generate ongoing revenue from your social media following.

After you build up your social media following to at least 10,000 followers, you can work with a social media marketing agency to help match you up with companies and organizations willing to pay you to promote their products and services. You can find a listing of these agencies by going to www.influencermarketinghub.com and choosing Agencies ⏷ Influencer Marketing from the top menu.

TIP

For step-by-step instructions on how to become a social media micro-influencer, in the Search field of your favorite search engine, type "How to become a micro-influencer" to find strategies for getting started. Or you can start by reading these articles:

>> **Indeed's How To Become a Micro-Influencer (Plus Salary and Duties):**
www.indeed.com/career-advice/finding-a-job/how-to-become-micro-influencer

>> **LinkedIn's How to Become a Micro-Influencer in 9 Steps (or Less):** `www.linkedin.com/pulse/how-become-micro-influencer-9-steps-less-adam-houlahan`

>> **CreativeLive's How to Become a Micro-Influencer:** `www.creativelive.com/blog/how-to-become-a-micro-influencer`

Starting a podcast that gets sponsored

You can create, produce, host, and distribute an audio podcast relatively easily and at a fairly low cost. And after you establish a loyal audience for your podcast, you can attract paying advertisers so that you can earn revenue from your efforts, while also using the podcast as a tool for selling books. Keep in mind, however, that although podcasting is the fastest growing form of media in the world, as a podcaster, building a large enough audience (at least 10,000 regular listeners) to attract paying advertisers takes a lot of time and requires a lot of grassroots marketing.

TIP

For step-by-step instructions on how to create and produce a successful (and potentially profitable) podcast, read my book, *Start Your Own Podcast Business*, published by Entrepreneur Books (on Amazon).

Becoming a consultant or freelancer

If a company can benefit from your expertise, consider offering yourself as a consultant, freelancer, or contractor, and charging by the hour or the day for your services. Consultants who have specific areas of expertise can earn $50 to $500 per hour to share their knowledge and help companies solve problems, increase sales, train employees, create content, or overcome challenges. The fee a consultant can charge depends a lot on their level of expertise, the value they bring to the client, the industry, and the geographic region. For example, a company will pay more for a consultant with a specialized degree or license and/or a unique skillset, as opposed to someone with more generalized skills.

WARNING

Don't quit your day job to become a consultant. Building up a successful consulting business can take months or even years. Sure, as a published author and recognized expert in your field, you enhance your reputation, but establishing a large-enough client base to support yourself financially takes time and hard work. Consider starting off working as a part-time consultant and building up your clientele before giving up your steady paycheck and job-related benefits.

6

The Part of Tens

Discover ten common pitfalls to avoid while you embark on your self-publishing project.

Find out how to dodge ten e-book publishing blunders.

Take note of ten ways to improve your writing skills and establish yourself as a credible, well-respected author and subject-matter expert.

IN THIS CHAPTER

» Ignoring or misidentifying your audience

» Steering clear of research, writing, and editing problems

» Making sure you don't waste money and resources

» Dodging a loss of focus on cover creation and book printing

» Putting sufficient effort (no slacking) into publicity and marketing

Chapter **22**

Ten Self-Publishing Mistakes to Avoid

I f you plan to self-publish a first book, you can easily make a handful of mistakes that can mean the difference between a successful publishing venture and a total bomb. Carefully plan all aspects of getting your book on the market, and then apply your own common sense to help guarantee your success. This chapter focuses on ten mistakes that inexperienced self-publishers often make and offers advice on how to avoid making these costly missteps.

Not Targeting Your Audience Appropriately

In addition to ensuring that the content within your book is appropriate for your intended readers, craft the language and vocabulary to appeal to your readers. You want readers to find your book easy to read and understandable. You don't want a fun, upbeat book about how to create a scrapbook or plan a family vacation to read like a history textbook or scientific research paper. Know your audience and write specifically for those people (keeping their level of education and literacy in mind). Look to Chapter 3 for good advice on targeting your audience.

WARNING

At the time I'm writing this book, AI-based writing tools, such as ChatGPT (along with tools being added to web browsers and popular word processors by Microsoft, Google, and other companies) are becoming widely available. These tools can, theoretically, write a full-length book manuscript on an author's behalf. However, in Chapter 5, I strongly advise against using these tools to do your writing for you. Not only can most people tell when a computer (rather than a human) wrote something, but the AI-based tools don't properly consider issues such as plagiarism or copyright infringement, and they don't know how to target a writing style and voice that appeals to the book's intended audience.

Producing a Book That's Inaccurate Disorganized, and Poorly Written

Just because you decide to write a book doesn't automatically mean that you're a talented writer. Many authors spend years fine-tuning their craft. If you feel that you don't have the skills to create a well-written, well-researched, well-organized, and full-length manuscript, seriously consider hiring a professional writer or a ghostwriter to act as co-author, and/or find yourself a good editor (see Chapter 6) to work with you.

You can also avoid ending up with a book that's lacking in quality by focusing on these aspects of the creation process:

>> **Solid content:** Providing inaccurate, incomplete, outdated, or misleading information to your reader damages your credibility and takes away value from your book. Avoid this mistake by doing proper research. Even if you're writing fiction, you want your plots and characters to be realistic, within the realm of possibility, or at least somewhat believable.

>> **Logical flow:** Proper organization makes your book easier to read. The content should flow in a logical order so that the reader can easily understand it. The trick to developing a well-organized book involves developing an extremely detailed outline before you start writing (see Chapter 5 for more details about how to organize and structure the content of your book).

TIP

>> **Professional tools:** Every writer, no matter their skill or experience level, should utilize the latest tools to help enhance their grammar, spelling, and overall writing style. These tools may come built into a word processor, or you can use them in conjunction with the documents that you create with your favorite word processor.

Two of the tools I recommend for polishing your work are Grammarly (www. grammarly.com) and ProWritingAid (www.prowritingaid.com). *Note:* These tools rely on AI to help fine-tune your original work, but they don't write the content for you.

A Lack of Attention to Detail and Editing

A well-written book contains absolutely no spelling mistakes, grammatical errors, inaccurate information, misprints, incorrect details (such as incorrect names, phone numbers, website URLs, statistics, chapter references, facts, or figures), or mislabeled figures and captions. In addition to proofreading your own work, hire a professional editor to review your manuscript before it goes to press. See Chapter 6 for more about working with an editor.

Inefficiently Using Money and Resources

You have many potential expenses related to creating, editing, laying out, printing, distributing, advertising, marketing, and promoting your own book. These upfront costs likely have to come out of your pocket. Budgeting carefully and knowing what expenses you may incur during each stage of the self-publishing process helps you best utilize the money that you have available to invest in publishing your book. See Chapter 7 for details on crafting a business plan and a budget.

WARNING

Don't take cost-cutting shortcuts. For example, even if you consider yourself a highly skilled writer, you still need to hire a professional editor to review your manuscript at least twice before it gets published. Likewise, you need to have enough money in your budget to properly advertise, market, and promote your book, or it simply won't sell.

Having Poor Cover Design and Copy

Offering a well-written book that has a poorly written and designed cover or a bad title will have a negative impact on sales. Conversely, having an amazing cover and catchy title on an otherwise average book could dramatically improve sales. Have a professional and attention-grabbing cover designed for your book, and then create a top-notch manuscript that caters to the book's target audience.

Hiring a professional graphic artist or experienced book cover designer to create your book's cover is an essential piece of the puzzle. Unless you have professional graphic design experience, hire someone who does! Chapter 10 goes into detail about book covers, including their design and the absolute importance of having a catchy title and subtitle.

Choosing the Wrong Printing Method

For many self-published authors, print-on-demand (POD) publishing offers the perfect solution. It's inexpensive, relatively quick, and allows virtually anyone who has a good book idea to get published. POD (described in Chapter 13) has many benefits, but it doesn't offer the ideal publishing solution for everyone. Other printing options, such as offset printing and e-book publishing opportunities, may make more sense for your book, based on your audience and your goals. Part 3 focuses on your printing and publishing options.

REMEMBER

Because the reading habits of people are rapidly changing, you may want to publish your book exclusively in various digital formats — which readers can obtain on popular e-readers (such as a Kindle), tablets, and computer screens. Many people these days prefer to read an e-book on their e-reader or tablet, rather than purchase and read a printed book. Get to know your audience, and then choose how you can make your book available to them, specifically.

A Lack of Comprehensive Distribution

In addition to writing an awesome book and heavily promoting it (see Part 5), the third key ingredient for success involves making sure that your target audience can find and buy it. Based on how you plan to publish your book, figure out the best and most achievable distribution methods, and then make full use of them. Part 4 focuses on various distribution methods and opportunities available to self-published authors.

TIP

When you choose which distribution method(s) to use, crunch the numbers and set your book's cover price accordingly. Services such as Amazon, Barnes & Noble, and Apple Books charge a sales commission of between 30 and 65 percent of the cover price. Meanwhile, traditional bookstores and retailers expect to purchase books at a 50 percent discount so that they can resell at a profit. In other words, they buy the books at wholesale pricing and sell them at retail pricing.

Wasting the Potential of Online Distribution

Online sales, whether through your own website or any of the well-established online booksellers (such as Amazon and Barnes & Noble), are extremely cost effective and powerful distribution channels that self-publishers just can't ignore. These days, more and more people are Internet savvy and find ordering books online convenient — especially because retail bookstores are becoming scarce.

As you can discover in Chapter 14, however, simply getting your book listed with an online bookseller doesn't generate sales. Ways do exist, however, to promote your book heavily online. Also, don't ignore the quickly evolving trend related to shoppable content on social media. Merchandising posts allow you to promote and sell your book directly through a popular social media platform. I cover this advertising and sales strategy in Chapter 20.

Improperly Planning a Publicity and Marketing Campaign

Although you need to write and publish a book if you want it to become a best-seller, you also need to make sure that potential readers know about your book's existence if you want to generate sales. Many self published authors do an excellent job of creating and publishing their books, but they either inadvertently forget about marketing and advertising, or don't realize the importance of these efforts.

For a book to succeed (sell a lot of copies, be profitable, and receive favorable reviews), you need a comprehensive and well-timed advertising, marketing, and public relations (PR) campaign. If you don't have the advertising, marketing, and

PR savvy to create, launch, and manage an effective, well-planned, and comprehensive campaign, hire experienced experts to help. Check out Part 5 for more on publicity and marketing.

REMEMBER

Properly advertising, promoting, and marketing a book, even if you rely on grassroots methods, costs money. Make sure that you have an adequate budget in place to handle these tasks properly — otherwise, your book sales will suffer.

Bad Timing throughout the Self-Publishing Process

While you complete the various steps in the publishing process, pay careful attention to scheduling, lead times, and deadlines. Rushing steps, cutting corners, or taking shortcuts can lead to costly mistakes and even failure. See Chapter 1 for a brief overview of timeline and steps in the self-publishing process.

TIP

Carefully consider timing as it applies to when your book actually gets published and becomes available to readers online or at retail. Do you know of a specific date, season, holiday, or time of year when interest in your book may be stronger? Choose the most appropriate release date — especially if the book somehow ties into or relates to a specific date, holiday, or season — so that you reach your audience at a time where your book's topic is already on their mind. For example, most people probably don't shop for a Christmas cookbook in July.

WARNING

You have to do some of the steps involved with self-publishing in a certain order. When I was working as a ghostwriter for another author's autobiography, that person insisted on having the graphic artist handle the layout and design of the book before the freelance copy editor got a chance to properly edit it. I advised against this approach. However, he wanted to see what the book would look like before he read it in its entirely. (Until that point, he had reviewed only one chapter at a time, and read them out of order.) As predicted, this ordering of steps caused some serious problems. Not only did the person doing the book's interior layout and design need to incorporate smaller grammatical edits into the already laid-out pages after the editor and designer did their work, but the author then wanted to add content and move a few things around. So he had to pay the freelance graphic designer a lot of extra money to make these edits and changes that the author should have made much earlier in the process. In order words, the graphic designer had to basically reformat the already laid-out pages and chapters, almost from scratch.

Chapter **23**

Ten E-Book Publishing Mistakes to Avoid

With more and more people purchasing e-books, rather than traditionally printed books, as a self-published author, don't overlook this fast-growing publishing opportunity. Although publishing and distributing e-books generally costs less than printing books, to create content that appeals to and is accessible to your target audience, you must understand the different e-book file formats and the limitations many e-readers have. Also determine whether your book's target audience comprises people who have the wherewithal to acquire and read e-books on their e-reader, tablet, or computer. This chapter focuses on 10 common mistakes that self-publishers make when designing, publishing, and distributing e-books.

In this chapter's discussion of e-book publishing mistakes, remember that you can (and probably should) sell your book through the major e-booksellers, including Amazon (www.amazon.com), Barnes & Noble's website (www.bn.com), Apple Books (www.apple.com/apple-books), Google Play Books (https://play.google.com/store/books), and Kobo (www.kobo.com).

Don't Ignore Proprietary E-Book File Formats

As you can discover in Chapter 11, *ePub* is an industry-standard file format that's compatible with all e-readers and e-reader apps. You can also offer your e-book in a PDF file format, which users can read on any e-book reader. But if you want to sell your book through major e-booksellers, you must offer your e-book in the proprietary file format for each of them.

Software applications, such as Vellum (`https://vellum.pub`) and Adobe InDesign (`www.adobe.com/products/indesign.html`), allow you to lay out and design your e-book, and then export it into every popular e-book file format. Alternatively, you can use the file conversion tool offered by each e-bookseller when you register as a publisher. Here are some considerations when deciding whether to make your e-book available through online e-booksellers:

» **Automatic copy protection:** When you sell your e-book through popular e-bookstores, the digital file that you create for that e-bookstore is automatically copy protected, which means that your readers can't copy and share your e-book without paying for the additional copies.

» **Findability:** Each e-bookseller's powerful search tools allow readers to stumble upon your book just by entering a relevant keyword or phrase that relates to its title, description, or content.

» **Bookseller commissions:** The drawback of selling through online outlets is that each of these booksellers charges a commission on each sale of your e-book.

By making your e-book available in the ePub file format, you can sell and distribute it directly from your own e-commerce website. This sales outlet allows you to potentially earn more money from each copy sold. The drawback is that you can't copy protect the ePub e-book file.

Don't Publish Your E-Book in Only the PDF Format

If you choose to distribute your e-book as a PDF file, although someone can view that file on any e-reader or e-reader app, the reader can't change the font, or make the text larger or smaller, without messing up the page design. If you offer the book in other popular file formats, when the reader changes the text font (typeface and size), the e-book automatically reflows on the screen to keep the formatting easy to read. With a PDF file, your e-book maintains a consistent layout and design, but it doesn't reflow. This limitation can make the e-book more difficult to read, especially on a smaller screen. The reader may need to zoom in on a section of a page to see it, then zoom back out to see the entire page, then zoom in again, and so on — which they may find tedious and annoying.

Avoid Design Decisions That Make Your E-Book Difficult to Read

Although you can include a lot of full-color photos, charts, graphics, or illustrations within an e-book, you face the potential problem that the reader may see all non-text content in grayscale on their e-reader's e-ink display (for example, on a Kindle Paperwhite). But readers can see the full-color content if they read your e-book by using a tablet, smartphone, or computer screen.

It comes down to knowing your audience, determining which equipment they'll probably use to read your e-book, and then formatting that content accordingly — while making it available in the proper formats. For example, if you determine that most people who will read your e-book use an Amazon Kindle, those readers don't benefit from the inclusion of any color within your e-book's content. But, if your readers use their traditional tablet, such as an Apple iPad, to read your e-book (or they read it on their computer's screen), they can see all your book's content in full color.

Never Use Typestyles That Are Difficult to Read

When you publish your e-book in the ePub file format or any of the proprietary file formats used by the popular e-booksellers, the reader can choose from a collection of fonts in which to display the text from your book. They can also adjust the size of the font to make it easier for them to read on their e-reader's display.

However, while you're formatting and designing your e-book's interior, the reader can't alter the typestyles that you use (such as **bold**, <u>underlined</u>, *italics*, ^{superscript}, _{subscript}, ~~strikethrough~~, and so on), including if you combine typestyles together (such as ***bold/italic*** or **<u>bold/underlined</u>**). Although you can use different typestyles sparingly to add emphasis to a key point, mixing up typestyles too often makes the text look cluttered and difficult to read. **This** *paragraph* <u>is an</u> *example* **<u>of that</u>**.

Don't Overuse Hyperlinks

With an e-book, the author/publisher can incorporate hyperlinks into the main body of their book's text. When a reader taps on a hyperlink, they either instantly jump to another page or section of the book, or they get redirected to a website (if the device they're using to read the e-book has Internet access). The e-book creation or formatting software/service that you use will automatically set up the table of contents of every e-book with hyperlinks, so the reader can instantly jump to a specific page or chapter. The e-reader also automatically saves digital bookmarks to keep track of where a reader stops reading so that they can pick up from that location later.

As the author, however, if you include too many hyperlinks within the body of your e-book, a reader can easily get lost by jumping around too much. Excessive linking can ruin the intended continuity of your book; what you want the reader to get when they move from one chapter to the next. In a fictional book (unless it's a choose-your-own-adventure–type story), the reader can find diverting with hyperlinks extremely confusing and therefore struggle to follow the story's plot. For a non-fiction book, easily jumping around in the text by using hyperlinks can also cause confusion, especially if a reader needs to go through content in a specific order to make sense of it.

Don't Make Finding Your e-Book Difficult

Yes, you can make your e-book available exclusively from your own e-commerce website and likely generate the highest level of profit from each copy sold. However, selling your e-book only on your website puts the burden exclusively on you to drive traffic to that website. You likely need to do a lot of extra advertising, marketing, and promotion to reach your potential readers, and then get them to visit your website to purchase and download your e-book.

TIP

If you choose to sell your e-book directly through your own e-commerce website, make sure that you make your book-specific website URL easy to remember, easy to spell, and relevant to your book. For example, register the domain www.[*YourBookTitle*].com, and have that URL forwarded to your e-book's description page on your own website.

You definitely can sell your e-book via your own website, but you likely lose potential sales if you don't also make it available from all of the popular e-bookstores.

Never Select E-Book Subject Categories or Keywords That Don't Apply

When you submit your book to any of the popular e-booksellers, as the author/publisher, you have to select from a list of subject categories and subcategories, which allow that seller to properly categorize your book. You then have to provide a series of relevant keywords or phrases that best describe your book and its content. If you want potential readers to easily find your e-book, choose the most relevant subject category and, if applicable, subcategories for your book, and then brainstorm and provide a list of relevant keywords. Failure to properly provide this information can result in the e-bookseller incorrectly categorizing your book, or your book may not show up in search results relevant to what your potential reader wants.

Beware of Limited Layout and Design Software

You have many ways to convert a text-based manuscript file into a properly formatted e-book. However, to do so, some software applications work much better than others, especially if you want to create and export your e-book in all the popular file formats at the same time. To save yourself a lot of time, use e-book layout and design software, such as Vellum (`https://vellum.pub/`) or Adobe InDesign (`www.adobe.com/products/indesign.html`), that supports all the popular e-book file formats. Otherwise, you may wind up having to format the e-book separately by using the tool offered by each specific e-bookseller — a process that takes more time and can lead to layout issues if you don't properly proofread the e-books while you view them in each separate file format.

Don't Lowball Your E-Book's Cover Price

Just because you offer your book in electronic format, rather than a printed version, don't necessarily charge less for an e-book than you would a print book. These days, for a new book title, most readers expect to pay the same price (or close to the same price) for the printed or e-book version. And although you don't have printing costs, remember that you have other costs associated with publishing your book in e-book formats — formatting the text appropriately, e-book file creation, and e-book distribution and marketing — that you need to recoup. As you can discover in Chapter 11, each of the popular e-booksellers charges a commission on each sale. And if you're operating your own e-commerce website to directly sell e-books, you incur costs associated with creating and maintaining that website, plus commissions that you need to pay to the merchant account provider for processing payments.

Don't Rely on E-Booksellers Only to Distribute Your E-Book

You get many benefits from selling your e-book through all the popular e-booksellers, despite the commission you need to pay for each copy sold. However, to make your book accessible to the widest audience possible, also consider selling it via your own e-commerce website and/or using shoppable ads on social media, for example. In other words, take advantage of all possible opportunities to distribute your e-book, and then really focus your advertising, marketing, and promotional efforts, based on how or where you see the book selling the most copies.

Index

Independent Book Publishers Association (IBPA), 115, 201, 252

independent booksellers, 33, 253–255

Independent Publishers Group (IPG), 253, 255

indexes, 86–87, 139

Indie Authors International, 36

Influencer Marketing Hub, 311, 357

Influencers.club, 312

Ingram Content Group, 252

IngramSpark, 99, 183, 198, 203, 233, 243–244, 252, 279, 328

inserts, 209, 212

Instagram, 332

Instasize, 285

International Standard Book Numbers (ISBNs), 14, 21, 84, 118–122, 166, 181

interviews, 88, 315–323

introductions, 85

Intuit QuickBooks, 110, 261, 264

inventory management software, 260–261

Issuu Digital Publishing, 99

iStockphoto, 83

iTunes Connect, 194

iUniverse, 99, 233

J

Jasper, 285

K

Keyword Tool for Instagram Hashtags, 285

Kindle. *See* Amazon

KitaBoo, 185

Kobo. *See* Rakuten Kobo

Koji, 187

KotoBee Author, 185

L

layout and design, 15, 135–154

book covers, 15, 21–22, 42, 51, 159–163, 169–170, 205–206, 223–225

color, 138

content distribution, 137

desktop publishing software, 146–150

errors in, 92–93

fonts, 137

mistakes to avoid, 364

page design, 139–146

page layout software, 63

printer-friendly files, 150–151

print-on-demand, 220–221, 223–226

purposeful design, 137

short run printing, 204–209, 221

spine, 168

task list and timeline, 21

trim size, 138

word-processing apps, 136–137

Learning Annex, 354

LearnWorlds, 352

LegalZoom, 106, 127

Libby app, 179

libraries, 179

Library of Congress Control Numbers (LCCNs), 14, 84, 125–126

LibreOffice, 62

Lightning Press, 202

Lightspeed, 187

limited liability companies (LLCs), 106

LinkedIn, 99, 336, 352, 358

literary agents, 26, 31

Livescribe Echo 2, 67

Locklizard, 182

M

Mailchimp, 302

manuscript writing, 70–71

audience, 12–13, 36, 42, 70–71

creativity and personality, 37

defined, 13

distractions, 11, 57–61

editing, 13, 91–100

ideas for manuscripts, 12

lacking knowledge of topic, 40

length of manuscripts, 12

mistakes to avoid, 362–363

outlining, 13, 61, 74–79

About the Author

Jason R. Rich (https://jasonrich.com) is the author of numerous books published by major publishing companies, as well as several self-published eBooks, including *iPhone 14 Pro Max Digital Photography: An Unofficial Mini-Guide* (which is available wherever eBooks are sold). He's also served as a ghostwriter for a handful of non-fiction books and autobiographies and is an accomplished photographer whose work regularly appears within his books and articles.

He has served as a full-time consumer electronics writer for *Forbes Vetted* and continues to regularly write about technology for *AARP the Magazine,* as well as other national magazines and popular websites.

Working with several major book publishers, some of his recently published, non-fiction books include: *The Remote Worker's Handbook, The Ultimate Guide to Shopify, The Ultimate Guide to YouTube for Business* (2nd Edition), *Start Your Own Podcast Business,* and *Start Your Own Airbnb Business: How to Make Money with Short-Term Rentals.*

Because he works remotely, several times per year, he also travels throughout the world serving as an enrichment lecturer aboard cruise ships operated by Royal Caribbean, Carnival Cruise Lines, Celebrity Cruise Lines, Norwegian Cruise Lines, and other popular cruise lines. He offers a series of one-hour lectures for passengers that cover consumer electronics, digital photography, Internet security, and social media. He uses these speaking engagements to promote his latest books.

Please follow Jason R. Rich on any of these social media platforms: Instagram (www.instagram.com/jasonrich7), Facebook (www.facebook.com/JasonRich7), Twitter: (https://twitter.com/JasonRich7), or LinkedIn (www.linkedin.com/in/jasonrich7).

Author's Acknowledgments

Over the years, I have read and relied on information from a wide range of *For Dummies* books. Way back in 2006, I wrote the original edition of *Self-Publishing For Dummies.* Since then, the publishing industry has changed dramatically, and many new technologies have been introduced that make self-publishing easier and more lucrative than ever. Thus, I am very proud to now contribute this all-new and fully revised second edition to the popular series. I hope that you, the reader, find this book helpful on your quest to become a self-published author.

Thanks to Elizabeth Stilwell at Wiley for inviting me to work on this project. Thanks also to Leah Michael, this book's project editor, for her hard work and guidance. The work of Melissa Perenson (the book's technical editor) is also very much appreciated. Throughout this book, you read about the importance of hiring an editor to review your work before it gets published. Thank you to Laura Miller, who did a marvelous job as this book's copy editor. Many people work extremely hard to make the *For Dummies* series successful. I'd like to offer my sincere gratitude to everyone involved, including the editors, illustrators, designers, proofreaders, reviewers, editorial supervisors, and the sales team. This book truly is a team effort. Thanks also to Jeff Herman, my long-time literary agent.

Publisher's Acknowledgments

Associate Acquisitions Editor: Elizabeth Stilwell

Development Editor: Leah P. Michael

Copy Editor: Laura K. Miller

Technical Editor: Melissa Perenson

Production Editor: Pradesh Kumar

Cover Image: © Billion Photos/Shutterstock